I0762880

RODDY McDOWALL

RODDY McDOWALL

AN ACTOR'S LIFE—FROM *HOW GREEN WAS MY VALLEY* TO *LASSIE* TO *PLANET OF THE APES*

SAMUEL GARZA BERNSTEIN

Citadel Press
Kensington Publishing Corp.
kensingtonbooks.com

CITADEL PRESS BOOKS are published by

Kensington Publishing Corp.
900 Third Avenue
New York, NY 10022

All Kensington titles, imprints, and distributed lines are available at special quantity discounts for bulk purchases for sales promotions, premiums, fund-raising, educational, or institutional use. Special book excerpts or customized printings can also be created to fit specific needs. For details, write or phone the office of the Kensington sales manager: Kensington Publishing Corp., 900 Third Avenue, New York, NY 10022, Attn. Sales Department. Phone 1-800-221-2647.

10 9 8 7 6 5 4 3 2 1

First Citadel Hardcover Printing: June 2026

Printed in the United States of America

ISBN: 978-0-8065-4426-7

ISBN: 978-0-8065-4428-1 (e-book)

The authorized representative in the EU for product safety and compliance
is eucomply OU, Parnu mnt 139b-14, Apt 123,
Tallinn, Berlin 11317, hello@eucompliancepartner.com.

For Ronuel, the worst kind of boy.

Even now, after all these years, I find it totally impossible to stand the sight of myself on the screen—or the sound! I suppose it's because we all lie to ourselves and as I sit in the theatre and watch that scrawny, long-necked, big-nosed, bug-eyed creature with that high-pitched voice crawling around on that giant screen—I want to cry out, "No . . . no . . . no . . . no . . . that monstrous creature—that ugly thing cannot be the beautiful me I know and love!"

—Roddy McDowall

Contents

Introduction

"I'm the same age as Shirley Temple *and* Mickey Mouse!"

When the topic of Roddy McDowall's childhood stardom pops up in interviews, as it always does throughout his adult life, Roddy gets a giggle marveling at how Shirley and Mickey share his birth year. It's a win-win. He comes across as funny and self-effacing while coyly positioning himself in the company of a pair of cultural icons.

It's wrenching but inevitable that his early fame goes sour once he has the bad taste to grow up. "Bad taste" is Roddy's own description, from a 1988 interview with *Films in Review*, when he speaks about his studio, 20th Century-Fox, wanting him to stay a kid forever, sending him scripts for roles that barely acknowledge his adolescence, never mind that he's pushing twenty. "I was running at a standstill," he tells Hedda Hopper, in 1959, for her *Los Angeles Times* column. "Like a squirrel in a cage or a horse on a treadmill."

"Roddy was kicked out of stardom as a child," says his friend and colleague Lee Grant, in a 2025 interview with me. "I love that he didn't let it stop him. He came back anyway. This joyous, wonderous man. A star." She is ninety-nine years old at the time, but she remembers everything. "Actors live precarious lives. All you've got behind you is the history of your talent. And earning a living is always precariousness."

In 1938, Roddy McDowall starts earning *his* living in low-budget British films, and his career thrives for sixty years, all the way to 1998, when he's playing Scrooge, as many as eight shows a week, for 5,600 people at each performance of *A Christmas Carol* at the Theater at Madison Square Garden in New York. His six decades in show business give Roddy ties to multiple generations, rivaling the connection possibilities of Six Degrees of Kevin Bacon, a game started in 1994 where the goal is to link any actor to Kevin Bacon within six projects or people.

Here is how Six Degrees of Roddy McDowall might go . . . In 1960, Roddy wins a Tony Award for *The Fighting Cock.* His costar is Rex Harrison, who's also his costar in the film *Midnight Lace.* Roddy's next Broadway appearance is in *Camelot,* playing Richard Burton's bastard son. In 1961, over a year into the *Camelot* run, Richard and Roddy leave the show and fly to Rome to join the cast of *Cleopatra*, also starring Rex Harrison. And Elizabeth Taylor—one of Roddy's best friends since childhood, a woman he nicknames "Bessie"—is Cleopatra. Roddy and ten-year-old Elizabeth first work together on the 1943 film *Lassie Come Home.*

One Degree of Roddy McDowall across the board. Oh, and just for the sake of Hollywood symmetry, Roddy McDowall appears in *The Big Picture* in 1989, which stars . . . Kevin Bacon.

The 1941 Best Picture Oscar winner, *How Green Was My Valley*, the story of a turn-of-the century Welsh mining family and their epic struggles, is the film that shoots him into the stratosphere of international stardom. Maureen O'Hara plays his older sister. She calls Roddy's work in that film "the finest performance by a child in movie history" in her 2004 memoir. Roddy's *Fright Night* costar in 1985, Chris Sarandon, is just as enthralled. "He had this preternatural kind of presence on screen," he tells me on Zoom. "The reality that he was able to attain . . . I can't imagine any other human being playing that role, or his role in *Lassie Come Home* either—I mean, he was wonderful in that movie and heartbreaking. It's hard to express how meaningful those films are to me."

In his early career, Roddy is incredibly popular on the Fox lot. He's always prepared, always a pleasure to work with, always mindful, and best of all, he never takes things personally, maintaining his composure no matter how tense the set gets. What no one quite realizes is that children under pressure learn to lie. My own experiences bear this out. When my husband, Ronald Shore, and I made a movie in Ireland some years ago, the narrative turned on a ten-year-old actor named Thomas Brodie Sangster. (He's still working; like Roddy, he manages a successful transition to an adult career.) He and Roddy McDowall's situations aren't unalike on this film. Thomas plays a tremendously sensitive character, and if he doesn't deliver, the whole project falls apart.

So there we are. We shoot his big emotional scene that everything hinges on, and his performance doesn't work. He just can't seem to cry, and he has to—Bernadette Peters and Rachel Ward have dialogue about him crying. He did at the audition, but today he's coming up dry. It's not the end of the world. We're under budget and can shoot the scene again another day.

When we schedule the reshoot, we're very mindful about not putting too much pressure on Thomas. We tell him the reshoot isn't because of him, that we didn't think the scene through properly. It's our responsibility that the scene doesn't work. And that's the end of it. On the day of the reshoot, we check in with him. "How are you doing? Sleep okay?" He smiles and nods. "Uh huh." Terrific. He nails the scene. We love him. He's a pleasure to work with, and he never takes anything personally.

We don't immediately understand that he's not telling the truth.

Later I find out from his mother that the night before the reshoot, Thomas can't sleep. He's on an emotional roller coaster, panicking that the reshoot is because he let everyone down. He's positive everyone is furious with him, everyone is disappointed, he's failing us all. His eyes finally close at four in the morning. He's up at six for his seven o'clock call. He's a professional. *He's also ten years old.* I learn that this isn't his only sleepless night. Many nights, he's up past midnight, unable to fall asleep, bouncing off the walls to blow off steam after a day of constant concentration and people pleasing.

As it happens, I understand a little about Roddy's situation from another angle as well, albeit in a far less prominent arena. From age eleven, I begin acting where I'm living at the time, in Austin, Texas. I do four productions in a row. I'm tangential in two of them, central to the action in the other two. We do between four and six shows a week for long runs, sometimes several months for each show. The longest performance time for any of the shows is around two hours and forty-five minutes, including intermission, for *To Kill a Mockingbird*, where I'm a last-minute replacement for the actor originally cast as Jem, Scout's older brother. (The director calls me at school. I go into the principal's office and learn I start rehearsal that evening.) Three school nights a week I finish the show at close to eleven pm. By the time a fellow cast member drops me home, it's after midnight. I'm hungry and keyed up. My mother and stepfather are fast asleep, often before I'm home, but I'm usually up until two or three in the morning. I sing in a school choral group that meets every school day at seven thirty. School is an hour away. My alarm rings at five thirty each weekday morning. I keep this schedule for months at a time. When anything goes wrong, I'm convinced it's my fault, and something amorphously terrible will happen unless I fix it. *I am eleven years old.* People comment on how remarkably mature I am. How it's great that I take everything in stride.

Roddy McDowall signs his studio contract in November 1940, in Los Angeles, six weeks after evacuating London. From the moment he signs that contract, the clock is ticking. He looks nine or ten years old, but he's actually twelve. He can never be a "cartel" as Roddy puts it, a cottage industry like Shirley Temple or Jackie Coogan or Baby Peggy—stars who carry studios on their backs from the time they can walk until adolescence brings obsolescence. He always insists they're the true "child stars." Similarly, in Roddy's thinking, Elizabeth Taylor is famous as a child but isn't a child star. Jodie Foster is someone who's a phenomenally successful actor as a child but not a child star. When Foster starts transitioning into adult roles, Roddy acts as something of a mentor, befriending her and her mother. It isn't so much that they're looking for specific guidance. It's more that there can be a comfort level that comes from spending time with someone who has walked the same path, faced some of the same obstacles, survived, and thrived.

Roddy lives a dichotomy as a Hollywood kid. He's working every day with stars he idolizes on the screen, people like Tyrone Power, Irene Dunne, and Joan Bennett. They become real people in their everyday encounters. Yet he continues to go to the movies as often as he can, sitting in the dark, worshipping them as gods and goddesses too, imagining what it would be like to be glamorous and grown-up like them. Films aren't his only outlet for fantasy. For years he works on constructing an elaborate make-believe world of heraldry, beauty, and justice. He designs blueprints and writes stories, first about a kingdom, then an entire universe. During the day he lives in the real-life world of soundstages and backlots. It isn't acting so much as *believing*, with a playing-at-toy-soldiers sense of total concentration. His talent is something that resides in him naturally, making his work stunningly real. He doesn't know exactly how he's doing it, but he instinctively translates whatever is asked of him by his directors—filmmakers like Fritz Lang and John Ford, men not known for their kindness or patience.

Onscreen, Roddy embodies a wartime little man—the kid who faces difficult, even life-threatening demands without complaint, somehow retaining his air of innocence and purity while bravely shouldering adult responsibilities. His expressive eyes reflect the weight of the world. The American moviegoing population, grappling with the uncertainties and looming horrors of World War II, see in him a projection of their own fears and of their own hopes that they will find the strength to be ennobled by their sacrifices and losses. His British accent and winsome pluckiness suggest a Dickensian waif. His grit demonstrates his willingness to emulate the masculine ideal, a quality that makes American support for the Allied war effort seem right and true.

Hollywood columnist Louella Parsons tells the story of how they meet in church on Easter Sunday when he's just starting out at Fox. She embellishes the tale over the years with additional poignant details. At the crowded Church of the Good Shepherd, Roddy is squeezed in a pew, sitting between two rather large masses, his mother and Louella, who's so taken with Roddy's sincerity and goodness that she gives him her treasured prayer book and an extra set of rosaries that she apparently carries around in her handbag all the time.

As his star rises, the demands on him grow. He must function as an adult. His father is away at sea in the British merchant marines. Roddy is the family breadwinner. He has no friends his own age. The neighborhood kids refuse to play with him. "Double jeopardy," former child actor Dickie Moore remembers Roddy telling him for Moore's 1984 memoir. "I was English and talked funny and I didn't go to school," Roddy says. "I was totally isolated, really suffocating." It isn't much of a stretch to connect his childhood loneliness to his fabled talent for friendship as an adult. Roddy's most telling quote from the book: "As a child, I was always lied to about myself and about the world."

Distinguishing truth from fiction extends to cataloguing his early career. There are bogus credits for Roddy McDowall on various sites—some reflecting his own faulty memory, others that conflate various bits of information. Roddy swears to his dying day that he appears in a film about the legendary actress Sarah Siddons, starring Ellen Pollock, an actress whose film career starts in 1928 just before Roddy is born and continues through 1983. There is no record of any such film, and Pollock, always a featured player, is not an obvious candidate for such a glamorous starring role. When friend and colleague Gavin Lambert asks Roddy about the discrepancy, in a 1989 *Interview* feature, Roddy sticks to his guns but allows that perhaps it could be that production started on the film, but it never got finished, or if finished, it was never released.

His credit for *Yellow Sands*, a brilliant 1938 comedy-drama starring Dame Marie Tempest, is another mistake. He isn't the McDowall in the party sequence, it's his sister, Virginia. I know this for a fact. In April 2025, I sit and watch the whole thing at the British Film Institute (BFI). Plus, a 1940 notice in the London actors' *Spotlight*, a publication, used for casting, that features photos and credits, Roddy and Virginia share a half-page ad. *Yellow Sands* is her credit.

BFI in London is where I watch many of Roddy's early films, on a flatbed editing contraption, where you thread separate sound and picture film through sprocket rollers. These movies aren't commercially available and aren't accessible to view online anywhere, not even on a Russian website I guiltily utilize, where you can find just about anything, copyrights be damned. At BFI, I see seven of Roddy's films over two days. Three more are seemingly unavailable anywhere. Two, *Murder Will Out* (1939) and *His Brother's Keeper* (1940), are considered lost, and BFI holds one original copy of the third, a film called *Scruffy* (1938), but they haven't yet made viewable modern copies. It may be that the original is too fragile or isn't considered an important enough title to warrant the time and cost of restoration.

Of these, Roddy is certainly in *Scruffy*, as a waif befriended by two orphans on the lam with their dog. *His Brother's Keeper* is the story of a pair of brothers with a circus act and a gold-digging blues singer who comes between them. Roddy isn't credited in any materials related to the film, but the title is listed on Roddy's 1940–1941 *Spotlight* page, so it's safe to assume he's in it, however small the role. *Murder Will Out*, a caper film involving priceless jade, doesn't appear in *Spotlight*, and there's no reference to it anywhere in his archives at Boston University, so I drop it from his credit list.

It's also extremely unlikely that he's in *Poison Pen* in 1939—a credit that appears everywhere on his list of films. It's a turgid drama about the revelation that a seemingly sensible and sensitive upstanding citizen is writing anonymous letters, ripping a village apart. The only time a young boy appears anywhere in the entire film is in the final scene. The guilty party hurls themself off a cliff when they're unmasked, and the vicar stands in front of his congregation flanked by choirboys. Although Roddy is credited online as a choirboy in the film, not one of those boys singing onscreen looks like Roddy. And with speaking parts in five films to his credit by this point, why would he be doing uncredited extra work? He also never mentions the film, and it never appears listed in *Spotlight*. So I'm dropping *Poison Pen* as well.

I have to say, never mind that Roddy isn't in it, *Yellow Sands* is a fantastic film, and there's still a Degree of Roddy McDowall in evidence: Coral Browne plays a village tart in *Yellow Sands* in 1938. She marries Vincent Price after they meet on the set of the 1973 film *Theatre of Blood*. Meanwhile, Vincent and Roddy star in *The Keys of the Kingdom* together in 1944. All three of them, Coral, Vincent, and Roddy, star together in a national tour of *Charley's Aunt* in 1976, thirty-eight years after *Yellow Sands*. There's even another Degree: *Poison Pen*. The script is adapted from a play by Richard Llewellyn, the author of the novel *How Green Was My Valley*. Even when credits are wrong, they can still have links to Roddy.

So many connections.

These connections are forged and nurtured throughout his life, as he leaves his childhood career in Hollywood behind and builds a theater and TV career in New York in the 1950s. He studies and blossoms, one week playing an Irish leprechaun, the next week a Cockney, or a Midwest American, or a Mexican innocent who turns cynical. There are limits, though. "Intellectually, I'd love to play Stanley Kowalski in *A Streetcar Named Desire*," he writes to his friend, the English film star Dirk Bogarde. "Can't you just imagine me down in the streets yelling, 'Stella! Stella!' God, the critics would have a lot of fun with that one. As Katharine Hepburn once said about Ethel Merman, 'She's never going to play Florence Nightingale.' Everybody has their limitations." He likes the Merman quip so much he uses it later in interviews, having tried it out on his friend Dirk first.

In the 1960s, he revives his Hollywood film career, becomes a world-renowned photographer, and opens a nightclub; in the 1970s, he makes more iconic films, works constantly in TV, and becomes a passionate proponent of film preservation, accumulating a massive private collection that prompts an FBI raid; in the 1980s, he continues acting, executive produces a huge Hollywood hit, and becomes a very public advocate for celebrating and protecting Hollywood elders; in the 1990s, he's one of the go-to voice actors for film and TV animation; and from the 1950s all the way through to the 1990s, he's the beloved friend and confidant to a galaxy of entertainment industry and literary giants—and also to many people who aren't famous for anything. You don't have to be Elizabeth Taylor to be his chum.

Just about everything written about Roddy talks about his amazing capacity for friendship. During the research process, in my interviews with friends and colleagues, the people still alive who knew him best often get emotional, but joyful. Happy tears are the norm. When people talk about how much he still means to them, how he stays imprinted forever in their hearts and memories, it leapfrogs gee-whiz showbiz positivity, landing in the realm of life-changing moments and epiphanies.

Correspondence from Roddy's archives also reveals extraordinarily close friendships. Along with deeply personal letters, he keeps up a constant stream of postcards, congratulating friends on good reviews, life milestones, birthdays, and anniversaries. The actor John Glover says he remembers one evening at a theater, taking his seat in the balcony, and there's Roddy in the orchestra section, scribbling away at his postcards before the show starts—the DMs of another age.

The number of saved letters is staggering. Originals of letters he receives are filed with carbon copies of the ones he sends. Elizabeth Taylor, one of his closest lifelong friends, doesn't generally write letters to anyone, though Roddy writes her often. The quote at the start of this book about Roddy's self-consciousness at seeing himself on screen, is taken from a five-page letter he writes Elizabeth after she believes her performance in *Cleopatra* is widely mocked in reviews, while his own is almost universally acclaimed. He seeks to reassure her about what he sees as the sublimity and fearlessness of her work. And almost all of her reviews are quite positive, but she's anxious about whether people will judge her acting or her affair with Richard Burton.

Roddy frequently trades newsy, unfiltered letters with Sybil Burton Christopher, Richard Burton's ex-wife. She becomes his business partner in a nightclub and is one of the last friends, along with Elizabeth, who's at his bedside before his death. It's the first time the two women have been together since *Cleopatra* and the implosion of the Burtons' marriage, when Richard's affair with Elizabeth makes worldwide headlines and is even condemned in the halls of Congress. Roddy has stayed best friends with both women, and one of his dying wishes is that the two women come together so as to bring one particular, beautiful goal of his to fruition. They agree. There is also a third person there as witness to their promise: Lauren Bacall, the third in this trio of extraordinary women.

Dirk Bogarde and Roddy exchange letters until Roddy's death. For some reason lost to history, they address each other as Gopher. "Dear Gopher . . . Love, Gopher." The legendary agent Robby Lantz and his wife, Sherlee, become especially close, and there are hundreds of letters and cards over the years, many suggesting—*demanding*—that Roddy return to New York immediately, where "we all love you desperately."

George Cukor sends things he finds funny, like a 1967 clipping about the Supreme Court of New Jersey lifting a Trenton city ban on homosexuals congregating in bars. The ruling notes that while homosexuals are "unfortunates," it's only fair that "well-behaved homosexuals" have the right to gather as they wish. "An historic decision for you and your kind!" writes George. "I'll wager you'll be giving up your flat on Central Park West. They have charming ways in Trenton, and there are taverns where you and other unfortunates may congregate if your public behavior conforms with currently acceptable standards of decency and morality. You can do it if you really try."

Noël Coward addresses Roddy as "Dear Evil Boy." Roddy and casting director Boaty Boatwright trade multipage single-spaced letters about their projects and their hopes. (Boaty and Dirk also write wittily disparaging things about each other, even as they're frequent houseguests in each other's homes and remain the best of friends. It's clear that Roddy never shares their thoughts about each other with either of them.)

Roddy, his sister, and their parents write constantly—often about finances, property, and legal matters—but also long letters about their daily lives and their love for one another. Thousands of letters. The shared legacies of his famous friends, but also of people who don't lead particularly public lives. For every Myrna Loy, Lee Remick, Tammy Grimes, or Laurence Olivier, there are friends like producer Alan Ladd Jr., the playwright

Peter Shaffer, his photo agent and friend Lee Gross, and acting coaches Bobby Lee and David Craig. One commonality is that just about everyone works in some aspect of show business or the arts. People are fond today of saying they "live in a bubble." Roddy definitely lives in a bubble, where everyone misses one another terribly. Everyone apologizes for not having written sooner. Mostly what comes through is how much affection these people have for one another and how they rarely complain or express anything like self-pity. They turn failures into funny stories, and triumphs into self-deprecating takes on how mortifying it is that anyone should call attention to their meager talents. It's a lovely bubble where people strive to be their best selves.

Many of the letters are actually itineraries, quick notes and telegrams about traveling for film, TV, and theater work, or for pleasure. They rattle off where they can meet up with Roddy; who else they plan to see; whom they plan to avoid; what they eat; and how frightfully busy and exhausted they are—a lot like Facebook. The actor Clive Brook, of "It's alive! It's alive!" *Frankenstein* fame, also sends wonderful cards and letters, all addressed, "Dear Baby Peggy."

No matter what Roddy accomplishes or how old he gets, his childhood career remains a part of his life. It's also a major force in his own personal development. As a kid, he navigates the incredibly complicated, sometimes crushing world of the entertainment industry. He balances his public role as the bravest, best little boy in the world, with his private role as the micromanaged child who has no power at all but is still expected to perform at a moment's notice. Make no mistake, his parents love and adore him. He and his sister are twinlike in their attachment to each other. Family bonds stay strong and intact. That is part of the conundrum that defines his life.

He loves his childhood and his family.

He's almost destroyed by his childhood and his family.

He owes everything to his childhood and his family.

He's shackled by his childhood and his family.

I believe that at a very young age Roddy makes a decision, perhaps subconsciously, though I suspect it's more mindful than that. I think he chooses to become a positive force in the world, whatever may come. He resolves to leave every situation and every person a little bit better than he finds them. He will accept contradictions and frailties, and act as a force for kindness and understanding whenever he can.

Don't get me wrong. There are plenty of instances where he gets royally pissed off, often as a result of perceived meanness or unfairness toward others. And there are many examples from his archives that show he's perfectly capable of the kind of hypocrisy that lubricates life. "Joseph Mankiewicz is terrific to work with," he says in interview after interview during and after the making of *Cleopatra*. "He's a genius." Yet in a 1961 letter to Montgomery Clift, he writes of arriving in Rome for the *Cleopatra* shoot. "I had an unforgettable supper with Mankiewicz, the Burtons, and Judy Garland. At least now I know first-hand what an incredible megalomaniacal, sadistic shit Mankiewicz is. Loathe him." Whatever his feelings, though, he acts as a peacemaker and cheerleader on and off the set of *Cleopatra*, helping and showing respect for Mankiewicz. Roddy makes the experience better.

The Roddy McDowall Collection at Boston University's Howard Gotlieb Archival Research Center is a treasure trove. The official archive inventory is 415 linear feet of material comprised of 520 boxes, packages, and film reels. The collection includes a lifetime of correspondence, scripts, notes, memorabilia, props, costumes, films, videos, and photos. The typed inventory of the collection is 221 pages. Just about everyone in print, online, and in person repeats the "fact" that Roddy's archives are sealed until 2098, for one hundred years after his death. Untrue. They are clearly marked to become available in 2020—a coincidental lucky break for me when I begin researching in 2023, first alone, then with the help of two able assistants, Diedre Flanagan and Daniel Kammer.

Roddy seemingly never touches a piece of paper he doesn't find worthy of preserving, including his voter identification cards; AMPAS, Actors Equity, AFTRA, and SAG membership cards; his driver's licenses, press books from his Fox films and from his later films at Monogram. There is an entire history crammed with autographs of the famous and the forgotten. He saves the complete German press book for *Holiday in Mexico*. Page after page after page. In German. There are thousands of press clippings from his career, as well as clippings about his friends' careers—Myrna Loy's itinerary for her national tour of *Barefoot in the Park*, Montgomery Clift's script for *From Here to Eternity*, reviews and articles about Ruth Gordon's 1971 memoir, and dozens of the wonderful reviews for Elizabeth Taylor in *Who's Afraid of Virginia Woolf?*

I'm unable to ascertain whether there are some other, more private materials that remain under the rumored century-long moratorium. There are no journals or diaries. No torrid love letters. By his own description, Roddy isn't a romantic leading man during his adult career, but a character actor. Once he gets past his teenaged years, there isn't a lot of press speculation about his love life. When he's occasionally asked, he usually says something about not having time for a relationship because he's married to his career. While an obfuscation, it's not untrue. Roddy's partners are all people who work in the business, and all are aware that Roddy prioritizes work over his personal life.

One of the happiest things I find in the available archives, however, is the complete normalization of Roddy's romantic partners. There's a big difference between a life of privacy and one of secrecy. While Roddy never publicly discusses his sexual identity, it's clear from decades of his correspondence that most of his family, friends, business associates, and domestic staff all know, like, and respect his companions.

"Give my love to John . . ." "Kiss Paul for me . . ." "My best to Steven . . ."

There are three longtime relationships I know about: John Valva in the 1960s, Paul Anderson in the 1970s, and Steven Jongeward in the late 1980s and into the 1990s. I'm told his caretaker during his final illness, a man named Dennis Osborne, regards himself as a partner too, but he declines to be interviewed, and I find no mention of him in Roddy's archives. John Valva is dead. I've been unable to discover anything about Paul Anderson's life after his relationship with Roddy. I've had some contact with Steven Jongeward, who has helped me get a few timeline things correct and guided me in some directions, but he only communicates with me via Instagram messages and doesn't want to be interviewed, intending to one day write his own account of their relationship.

I've learned about these partners via other interviews and research, but I don't speculate about intimate aspects of their lives together. If I mention something happening between them it's because there's a reference in Roddy's archives. Otherwise, I have no idea how they spoke to each other, what they talked about late at night in the dark, or how they felt about each other "deep down." The fact of using their names and calling them his partners isn't something I think of as "outing" anyone. The world has changed a lot since Roddy's birth in 1928 and his death in 1998. As unnerving as our current political and cultural moment may be, I don't think we're ever going back to the days when writing about someone having a partner of the same gender is in and of itself scandalous or spreading gossip.

If I were to explore why Roddy is regularly named in *Spy* magazine's "Spy List" in the late 1980s and early 1990s, that would be gossip. Even if it's true. Spoiler alert: I do talk about this, but only because Roddy does himself, laughing in exchanges with George Cukor about a 1969 article titled "The Biggest Tool in Show-Biz: Do You Feel Inferior?"

During his lifetime, Roddy is constantly told by everyone he knows that he should write a book. He's resolute in his refusal to do so, believing that the only book from him anyone will ever want to buy is one where he spills the tea on his famous friends in a tidal wave of scandal. Impossible. He will never write such a thing. He values the people in his life far too much to betray them.

I feel similarly. I don't wish to betray the people I love. And I have come to love him. I'm careful with his secrets. I'm also careful with the secrets of his friends. While reading materials from Roddy's archives, I look for ways to understand something of his inner life and to find out how much of a price he pays for his unyielding positivity and goodwill, and for his all-consuming love affair with his career.

Roddy's sister, Virginia, struggles with emotional issues for most of her life. In the early 1950s, she has an epiphany in therapy and writes an intense seven-page handwritten letter to Roddy about her profound realization that there's a fundamental difference between the siblings. Her problem, the thing that gnaws away at her, is an *inner* feeling that no one needs her and no one ever will. Roddy's problem is an *outer* feeling of always needing to be loved—a desire that can't and won't ever truly be fulfilled. She makes this prediction for her little brother's future as if it's something he already knows and accepts. Like she's referencing something they've talked about before.

The artist Adam Kurtzman becomes a friend of Roddy's through his husband John Glover, and Adam grows especially close with Virginia after Roddy's death. He believes she was afraid a book about Roddy might tarnish his reputation or damage his legacy. "She never wanted there to be a book about her brother," Adam says. "She was very clear about that."

If there's an afterlife, it's entirely possible Roddy McDowall hates the fact that I'm writing this book. But why save all your letters and commit them to a university archive if you don't want someone to one day read them and write about you? Maybe he doesn't hate the idea of a book about him after all. Maybe he actually loves it. I have a fantastical, if potentially embarrassing, reason for believing that such a possibility exists—a reason that might be completely bogus, a heady vote of confidence, or open me up to accusations of being a somewhat less than serious biographer.

I work on many projects at the same time, juggling different worlds and different lives, some real, some fictional. For a few months, in the middle of my Roddy research, my attention needs to turn back to Cesar Romero, the subject of the book that precedes this one. A Portuguese spiritualist I happen to know named José Pedras asks me out of the blue if Roddy McDowall smoked and whether he wore scarves.

For most of his life, Roddy smokes like a fiend (he dies in 1998 of metastatic lung cancer) and he amasses an enviable collection of Hermès scarves.

"Oh. Then, I think he was in my bedroom last night," José says, as if he's telling me the correct time or whether it will rain. He's not in the business of talking to the dead but, since childhood, he says, they come to him occasionally when they want to communicate. He drops another casual bombshell. Roddy wants to talk to me. Perhaps José is in touch with dead people, perhaps he isn't. How the hell do I know? But I figure, what have I got to lose? On a couple of nights that feel weirdly unspooky—not like séances, but like after-dinner chats—José says Roddy wants me to know that he has been waiting rather impatiently for someone to tell his story. Tired of waiting, he *chose* me for the task. "But with due respect and appreciation for the glorious Mr. Romero, perhaps it's time to return to *my* story?"

I really don't know what to think about this turn of events. I don't seriously propose that this book has a posthumous seal of approval from Roddy McDowall himself. That would be a batshit crazy and unbelievably self-serving thing to claim. (Even though I sort of believe it.) But I rely on no information coming from these events. Extensive interviews and research are the basis for this book. But I can say for sure that having these two nonséances is a fever dream worthy of a 1940s fan magazine. The idea fits right in with the circus of show business—the field of endeavor that shapes, defines, and fills much of Roddy's life.

Alive or dead, I hope Roddy might see this book as a celebration of his life and his career rather than an affront to his privacy. It's also something of a road map, a guide to a way of life that is almost unthinkable now, when an avalanche of negativity seems to define us on macro and micro levels, and when a desire for accomplishment is dwarfed by raging entitlement and lottery sized expectations. Fair enough. There are plenty of reasons for us to despair.

Or we can choose not to.

We can aspire to emulate Roddy's work ethic, his kindness, and his values—even while acknowledging our self-doubt and sadness. We can make fun of ourselves, like Roddy, who clips out a 1968 *Los Angeles Times* article about upcoming TV appearances by "two former kid stars" Roddy McDowall and Mickey Rooney. The headline is "Ex Moppets Busy."

Roddy gets an XMOPPET license plate for his red Alfa Romeo and uses the moniker gleefully in letters with friends and family.

The entertainment industry trade paper *Variety* is famous for its unique tongue-in-cheek shorthand. In *Variety*-speak, when someone leaves a job, they "ankle" it. And after reading that article in 1968, Roddy knows exactly how he wants the headline to read when he dies:

"Ex Moppet Star Ankles Life."

—Samuel Garza Bernstein

Chapter 1

This England

In a 1971 *Photoplay* interview, Roddy McDowall gets a question he's asked repeatedly in one variation or another, in just about every single interview he gives from the age of twenty to the age of seventy: "Do you think child actors of today are different from those of your time?" At this particular moment in showbiz history, 1971, two English child actors, Mark Lester and Jack Wild, come to mind for Roddy. They are treated as huge stars after the gargantuan success of *Oliver!* in 1968—Jack even gets an Oscar nomination. Now, Mark has one movie coming out soon, and Jack is in the middle of a two-year stint on the American children's TV show *H.R. Pufnstuf.* They're both working. Mark has eight films to his credit. Jack has five.

At the same point in his own career, Roddy had made twenty-seven films.

Yes, Roddy thinks child actors of "today" are in a completely different profession than the one created by the studio system. During the filming of *Son of Fury: The Story of Benjamin Blake*, a 1941 Fox press release trumpets that Roddy McDowall is beginning his 110th day of consecutive work—a new record that beats the previous record set by *Benjamin Blake*'s topline star Tyrone Power, who goes 82 days without a break while shooting *Blood and Sand.*

It's insane that a movie studio thinks crowing about exploiting a child so egregiously is a positive story for the press. And of course, the figure itself is ridiculous, almost certainly the concoction of someone toiling into the night, smoking and drinking while they hunt and peck on manual typewriter keys. (This isn't an arbitrary scenario. When *My Friend Flicka* is about to premiere, someone named Jerry in the Fox press department sends a late-night missive to Darryl F. Zanuck: "With a slight hangover already, and with each finger-move feeling like a blood test, I am finally able to type these words to you: Roddy and *Flicka* will be on the Sunday cover of *This Week Magazine*.")

However misguided or untrue that 110 days figure may or may not be, it tells (and sells) a story that is based in fact. Fox is making a $7 million bet on Roddy McDowall, casting him in five movies during his first year under contract. The roles he will play are critical to the success or failure of each of these projects. He's the chosen one because he's talented, he's mature beyond his years, he can work under the gun, and his soulful eyes pierce the heart of many a misanthrope.

It's the kind of pressure Roderick Andrew Anthony Jude McDowall seems to be under almost from the moment he's born on September 17, 1928, in the Herne Hill section of London.

The pressure comes first from his mother, Winefriede Lucinda McDowall, née Corcoran, known by some as Winnie and by some as Win; often misspelled as Winifrid or Winifriede, and by her children as Mother, or, in moments of tenderness, Mummy. Winefriede is born September 9, 1899, in Timahoe, County Kildare, Ireland. From childhood, little Winefriede wants to be a star. It doesn't matter which one or what kind: Mary Pickford, opera star Geraldine Farrar, or it could be Queen Marie of Romania, whose syndicated column, "Queen's Counsel," enthralls Winefriede. She loves the romantic tale of Queen Marie hitting the road after the Great War, traveling with a royal retinue and a massive amount of luggage across the United States to raise money for her beloved Romanian people. (The thought of selling any of her royal jewels to raise money for these cherished Romanians doesn't apparently occur to our Marie.)

Winefriede Corcoran's very wealthy Irish family loses their money, and at some point during her early childhood, they move to America, setting up shop in Philadelphia. Perhaps this reversal of fortune is the engine of Winefriede's drive and ambition.

Roddy's father, Thomas Andrew McDowall, born June 28, 1896, in London, is a merchant marine. (This civilian branch of service is a quasi-military operation, also sometimes referred to as the Merchant Navy.) Thomas visits Philadelphia in 1925, where he and Winefriede meet. He's enthralled by her passion and energy. In a whirlwind romance, her asks for her hand. She accepts, sensing in Thomas the ballast she needs. Thomas takes her back to London, and their first child, daughter Virginia, arrives on September 23, 1927, six days shy of one year before Roddy is born.

Prior to marriage, as she's becoming a young woman, Winefriede falls in love with the movies. She writes to Mary Pickford for advice, and receives a letter back, warning her of how difficult it is for girls to survive in the motion picture industry. Winefriede's starry-eyed hopes next land on a music career. She sings well enough, even once performing onstage with the "March King" himself, John Philip Sousa. The career roadblock is her appearance. She is plus-size and rather plain. Kate Smith, the "First Lady of Radio," isn't yet a star, so Kate's bulk and regular-gal countenance hasn't yet shown that singers don't have to be willowy and beautiful to become famous. Winefriede doesn't want a radio career anyway. She wants to be *seen*.

Once she marries and has children, her hopes for becoming a celebrity dim. She loves her children deeply and transfers her hopes for herself to them. She comes to believe that the greatest gift she can give them, aside from her motherly affection, is stardom. Every child's dream. She encourages Virginia and Roddy to think of themselves as twins, isolating them from other children. Later, it feels suffocating, and when Virginia grows into adolescence, her relationship with her mother sometimes turns brittle. When they're very young, however, they have no context to question the idea that becoming famous at some kind of artistic pursuit is their logical goal in life, or that having great ambition is morally correct. Winefriede encourages them to sing, dance, and playact from the time they can walk, and she starts teaching them to read when Roddy is just three and Virginia is four. Their father is no longer a merchant marine by this point, having begun building a road transport business, and he loves literature. He introduces his children first to fairy stories, myths, and adventures, and then, while they're still quite young, to English literature and history. Virginia and Roddy respond with tremendous enthusiasm, both happily losing themselves in books.

By the time the siblings are four and five, Winefriede arranges poetry, speech, and Shakespeare lessons. The schedule isn't solely focused on highbrow erudition, though, and Winefriede continues her childhood love affair with movies, taking her children to the pictures every Saturday for a matinee.

The movies make a huge impression on Roddy. All the books and plays that are a constant part of his life take magnificent form onscreen. The worlds he sees when he reads become real when captured on film and projected in the dark. Soon he comes to understand from the inside how movies are created. This early knowledge of how fantasy can be made real is one of the guiding ideas of Roddy's life.

Winefriede's ongoing fantasy of her children being twins, inseparable from each other and inseparable from her, is made to seem real. She dresses them the same way. Virginia is in a skirt and Roddy in pants, but essentially, they wear the same outfits, like dolls. And when Winefriede joins in with the children's make-believe games, she's a wonderful playmate, getting down on the floor with them, putting herself in the middle of their games. She takes charge, playing with them like they are dolls that belong to *her*.

Roddy's greatest solo enthusiasm—an activity where Winefriede and Virginia never become involved—is his love of creating miniature stage sets for reenacting the historical events in some of his favorite movies and books. One day, probably in 1934 or 1935, after reading about Napoleon's march on Moscow, Roddy builds a sort of diorama in a crate, depicting the whole saga. He sets it up on a table in the children's shared nursery, using cardboard to fashion the Russian hills and plains, gluing on cotton to be the snow, and putting red paper around the sides of the crate as a background to suggest the fires and explosions of the battle. But the paper doesn't look at all like fire. He aims a torch at the paper, hoping the light will make it look a bit fierier, but the batteries quickly die. He lights some candles, happy with the glow of the flickering flames behind the red paper. Then the paper catches on fire and quickly spreads to the cotton, the cardboard, the tablecloth, and finally the curtains. He yells for his parents, who quickly put out the blaze before it can spread any farther. Virginia's dolls and doll furniture are under the table, burnt to a crisp, completely destroyed. Roddy is very sorry and offers to give up some of his own toys to compensate for Virginia's loss. His parents, and even Virginia, are impressed with his show of empathy and contrition. Virginia's getting too old for dolls anyway.

On the weekends, Thomas sometimes takes Roddy sailing—an activity for men and boys for someone of Thomas's generation, not women and girls—and he gives Roddy a solid foundation in operating and caring for small boats. It's one of the few regular activities of Roddy's childhood when it's just him and his father. The sailing lessons also come in unexpectedly handy some five years later, at a public relations appearance where Roddy's task is to officiate at a dockside launch ceremony for a sailboat construction company and smile for the cameras. The company official gets cute, asking rather patronizingly if Roddy, now fourteen but looking younger, would like to sail the boat. He seems quite surprised when Roddy does just that.

Thomas is also an avid photographer, snapping photos throughout his life. In the Victorian era, there was a vogue for photographing the dead. Thomas keeps a photograph of his brother Edward, who died at nine years old in 1897, lying with flowers all around him, looking for all the world like he's merely asleep. The macabre image appeals to Roddy's sense of drama.

In 1935, Roddy and Virginia begin studying acting at the Hanover Academy of Dramatic Arts. A fanciful *Modern Screen* article in 1941 details a complex series of events whereby little Roddy makes history at the age of eight by becoming the youngest child ever admitted to the school, the youngest student ever awarded a medal for his acting, the only student to ever win a prize for elocution, and the only student to ever earn seventeen medals. The article also recounts Roddy's early introduction to the Bard.

"His passion for Shakespeare was born when he heard an older boy at dramatic school read King Henry's lines to Montjoy, beginning: 'Thou dost thy office fairly. Turn thee back and tell thy king I do not seek him now.' 'I'd like to be able to say poetry like that,' sighed Roddy. He was all of eight, so his mother said, 'Don't be absurd, my beautiful child.' 'I like the sound,' he persisted. 'Will you teach it to me so I can understand it?' "

You've gotta love the quotes, words that no human mother and son would ever say. Winefriede is also the last person on earth who would label the artistic ambition of one of her children "absurd." The fact is, Roddy's lessons in Shakespeare start before he's eight, the lessons are Winefriede's idea, and if anyone in the McDowall household has the wherewithal or urge to teach Shakespeare to Roddy, that person is Thomas, not Winefriede. But Roddy apparently does win seventeen medals, while Virginia wins fourteen, according to their *Spotlight* listings.

Roddy's first source of income has little to do with all this classical training, though. He becomes a print model. Some sources say it starts at age five. Roddy never remembers exactly. But by age seven, he pops up in various surviving newspapers and magazines. That's him in a Lifebuoy soap ad, covered in dirt, learning that he needs to use this wondrous soap every day because "the Lifebuoy habit protects health." And there he is grinning wildly over a bowl of Rice Krispies, because "a queer little noise makes Difficult Donald a hearty eater: Snap! Crackle! Pop!"

Winefriede is careful to treat Virginia as Roddy's equal in these pursuits, but there's no record of Virginia working until 1938, and when she does, the jobs are never more than bit parts. She doesn't attract the level of attention Roddy receives. It's likely, however, that both of them begin doing extra work in 1936 or 1937. By 1941, *Spotlight* lists Roddy with eighteen films and Virginia with six. These numbers are considerably higher than their known credits, which start in 1938. Roddy always remembers his career beginning with a lot of background roles, but few of his known credits are for extra work. His extra work probably happens earlier than 1938, before the children have agents, so Winefriede is the one who figures out how to get them working on film sets. She steps up her game in 1938 when she hears that Victor McLaglen is coming from America to star opposite Gracie Fields in a musical called *We're Going to Be Rich*, and the director, Monty Banks (Gracie's husband), is looking for a little boy to play an important role. Winefriede finds out Monty is lunching at the Dorchester Hotel, marches up to him, and declares that her son is perfect for the part.

Roddy doesn't get the job, but somehow or other he does get an agent—actually two agents: Felix de Wolfe and Derek Glyn, who get him twelve film jobs, one after the other over the next two years. The production dates for these films are tricky to figure out. British and American release dates for Roddy's early British projects bear no relationship to their actual production dates, particularly as World War II begins to play havoc with cinema release schedules. It's also hard to judge which of the many conflicting accounts from members of the McDowall family are the most credible. In interviews, Roddy sometimes says *Scruffy* is the first one that shoots of the twelve. This is credible. He also sometimes says that *Murder in the Family* is his first. This isn't credible. It's a larger role than the others, in a more important film than some of them, and he's more polished and camera savvy. Roddy's last film before coming to the US is verifiably *This England.*

A plausible production order is *Scruffy*, *I See Ice!*, *Saloon Bar*, *Convict 99*, *Hey! Hey! U.S.A.!*, *Dead Man's Shoes*, *The Outsider*, *John Halifax*, *Murder in the Family*, *Just William*, *You Will Remember*, and *This England.* This order is chosen for many reasons—some elaborated upon here, some too lengthy to go into—and some of the conclusions may be wrong. The order never seems important to Roddy. So much happens over such a short period of time, it feels to him like it's all happening at the same time.

Scruffy is the story of a young orphan who's forced to leave his beloved dog behind when he's adopted by a rich dog-hating woman. On Christmas Eve, two boys from the orphanage arrive with his dog, Scruffy, in tow. The three boys go on the lam together and take up with a pair of young thieves, making them a gang of five. Roddy is uncredited as a young boy they befriend, making the group of boys a gang of six. Shot some ten miles from the McDowall's London neighborhood, at Stoll Studios in Cricklewood, the film is a "quota quickie," a British film made on the cheap to comply with the Cinematograph Films Act 1927, which sets a minimum number of domestic films that must be made in order for films from the US to be exhibited in the UK.

The quickies are occasionally shot in a matter of days, and while some are still remembered, most are not. The regulation just states they need to be made, and then shown at least once. A lot of them are shown only in the early morning to a virtually empty house.

A film that is decidedly not a quota quickie is *I See Ice!* It's a comedy starring George Formby, a light comedian, good with physical shtick, who sings pleasantly while playing the ukulele or something called a banjolele. He's sometimes called the highest-paid performer in England, though it's hard to know the source or truth of the claim. In *I See Ice!*, he plays an aspiring news photographer who gets pictures by way of a spy camera in his bow tie. Comic confusion and chases arise from his inadvertently taking compromising snaps of an important editor. The merriment culminates with an on-ice confrontation with his figure-skating love interest's jealous boyfriend during a professional hockey match. Roddy has a very funny sequence on a train, doing an extended piece of comic business involving George Formby, a balloon, and an older gentleman who's asleep. Roddy holds his own in his two-shots. Also in the film is Cyril Ritchard, an actor and director Roddy isn't in a scene with here, so they may not meet, but Cyril becomes important in Roddy's life some fifteen years later.

Saloon Bar is one of those projects that is based on a single-set play and it shows. We never really get out of the bar, where, hoping for a Christmas miracle, a bookie and a motley collection of pub regulars seek to prove the innocence of a man scheduled for execution. Concurrently, the pub landlord expects the arrival of a new baby. Roddy McDowall has a bit as a busking, carol-singing urchin outside the pub. He has no lines of his own, but he gets a close-up while he sings.

He does bit parts in two films starring Will Hay as a hapless victim of ridiculous circumstances in *Convict 99* and *Hey! Hey! U.S.A.!* In the first, Roddy is Hay's bratty nephew, and in the second he's a smart-mouthed kid on the Southampton docks trying to make a buck by helping out an elderly porter. His comic outrage when the porter refuses to pay him makes its intended impact. There is no official list of what is or isn't a quota quickie, but these two films may qualify. His next three don't. They're considered important projects at the time.

Dead Man's Shoes, a forerunner of British film noir, is about an amnesiac who's blackmailed by someone claiming the amnesiac is actually a notorious criminal. Roddy's bit is as a kid at a party who happily declares that he can be a better tiger than the master of the house, Leslie Banks, the star of the picture. For the first time in his budding career, Roddy struggles on set. Directors usually seem quite pleased with what he does, but Roddy can't seem to figure out what director Thomas Bentley wants from him. Leslie Banks notices Roddy's anxiety and makes a point to let him know he needn't worry. The director is driving them *all* nuts, and *no one* knows what he wants. Leslie and Roddy never make another movie together, but Roddy always remembers this small act of kindness.

Roddy follows up *Dead Man's Shoes* with *The Outsider*, starring a very young George Sanders as a miracle-working osteopath with an indeterminate Eastern European accent. Shunned by the Harley Street medical community, he grows determined to cure lovely Mary Maguire's inoperable "congenital dislocation," whatever that is, and naturally they fall in love—a doctor-patient relationship that is apparently not a problem in 1938. Roddy memorably appears as a rambunctious youngster whom George cures after an eight-month stay. For good measure, the doctor waives his fee for Roddy's working-class parents.

John Halifax, Gentleman is a historic drama, based on a bestselling novel, that involves the Dickensian rise of a poor but honest man who achieves gentleman status through sacrifice and bravery. Roddy plays one of his children. His big scene is a pretend wedding where he performs the ceremony to marry his younger blind sister to the son of the picture's villain. The other two kids get close-ups, but Roddy has to settle for medium shots and the master. Roddy is offscreen when his blind sister is accidentally killed by John Halifax's villainous aristocratic nemesis, so there's no opportunity for Roddy to have a big, dramatic crying scene that might in any way compete with the big, dramatic crying scene of *Halifax* star John Warwick, which is a doozy.

Then one of the most important of the bunch—*Murder in the Family*. Roddy plays the young son of Barry Jones and Jessie Winter. His job is mainly to be the clueless comic foil to his much older siblings, Jessica Tandy, Evelyn Ankers, Glynis Johns, and David Markham, when they and their parents fall under suspicion for the murder of a foul-tempered, wealthy aunt. The narrative is unusual in that we know from the get-go that everyone in the family is innocent. The real story is how the family is almost destroyed by the viciousness of the reckless press and the misguided, self-righteous community at large.

Behind the scenes, Roddy is curious about everything. It's his ninth film, but the first where he's on the shoot virtually from start to finish. He's fascinated by the process of how the little pieces of the story are shot and then fit together in the editing room. He wonders whether he should be a director or a producer when he grows up. The cast and crew indulge his curiosity. He talks the continuity girl into letting him type some script pages and he asks director Albert Parker continual questions about making movies. The director doesn't condescend. He answers every question, treating Roddy like an intelligent human being—an adult. Cinematographer Ronald Neame is also a fan. Though the character Roddy plays isn't central to the action, Neame comments about how impressive it is that Roddy's constant awareness of everything going on around him allows him to anticipate what the filmmakers need from him. Three and a half decades later, Ronald Neame directs Roddy McDowall in one of the biggest hits of the early 1970s, *The Poseidon Adventure*, and Ronald is very sorry that the script calls for Roddy to be the first in the all-star cast to die. Roddy is a hell of a lot easier to work with than Shelley Winters.

Of course, whatever Roddy's preternatural gifts of maturity and curiosity on the *Murder in the Family* set, he's also still a ten-year-old boy. During breaks he sometimes pesters Glynis Johns to play with him. She agrees to occasionally (they become lifelong friends), but during the shoot she's already fifteen and no longer very interested in children's games.

Neither is most of the British public. England's 1939 declaration of war against the Axis powers isn't directly impactful on Roddy and Virginia at first. Their homelife changes little, even as their father's workday grows longer. His transport business becomes taken up with organizing the road delivery of vital supplies to the military and civilians alike. Although the government is encouraging evacuation of children, Thomas and Winefriede McDowall decide against acting immediately. Thomas is now in his forties, and since his transport business is considered part of the war effort (and as such, exempt from petrol rationing), Thomas isn't required to leave his family. Winefriede has her own reasons for wanting to stay. Roddy's career is showing real momentum. Why give that up? Especially when his next opportunity is so important: the first film adaptation of one of the *Just William* books.

Author Richmal Crompton's series of thirty-eight books eventually spans almost fifty years, from 1922 to 1970, and by the 1930s, the books are a national institution. Happy-go-lucky William is eleven years old in every story. Each tale starts with William having a simple intention, like putting on a neighborhood show, or gathering up scrap metal for the war effort. He sets out to accomplish his goal, but then, his good intentions notwithstanding, things go spectacularly wrong, over and over again, and hilarity reigns. His partners in crime are his best friend, Ginger, two other boys, named Henry and Douglas, and his scruffy dog, Jumble.

Press reports of producer Walter C. Mycroft interviewing three thousand boys for the *Just William* roles are probably overblown, but in terms of the project's stature in the marketplace, snagging the role of Ginger is Roddy's best opportunity since the start of his film career.

The movie begins with the boys hoping to unmask a spy, but they're repeatedly sidetracked as they sabotage a magician, knock down a fruit stand, cause chaos in a candy store, misplace a baby girl, abscond with several other random babies, thoroughly destroy a prized rose garden, get tangled up with a couple of burglars, foil some swindlers selling phony stock shares, and throw a wrench in the works of a Guy Fawkes celebration. Then William inadvertently saves the day, proving once again that he isn't really naughty after all. The exhausting hijinks keep the kids in constant motion, leaving Roddy and the rest of the boys with little opportunity to make an impact. But it's an important credit, viewed by all interested parties as a harbinger of big things to come.

His next role keeps the momentum going. *You Will Remember* is a musical biopic of songwriter Leslie Stuart, who achieves international success in the Victorian era. Once the Jazz Age hits, however, he sinks to poverty, obscurity, and even prison. A strikingly young Robert Morley is the lead. His costar is actor and writer Emlyn Williams, playing a bootblack and lifelong friend. Roddy is Emlyn Williams as a child, and he's central to several early sequences. Emlyn Williams is riveting on camera, and it's completely believable that Roddy is the boy who grows to be this magnetic man.

As the Blitz breaks out and scores of bombs start falling, Roddy, though old enough to understand the peril to his friends, family, and countrymen, finds it all a bit thrilling. Like the main character in John Boorman's 1987 semi-autobiographical film *Hope and Glory*, his fear is dwarfed by a magical sense that adventure may be around every corner. That death may also lie around every corner is too hypothetical at first to seem real. The family takes to sleeping on mattresses on the floor, in a large cupboard under the stairs. In the mornings, after nights of bombing, Roddy eagerly collects shrapnel. Virginia doesn't share his enthusiasm. The air raids frighten her horribly. One night she wakes up screaming and crying, fatigued by the bombings, and convinced they will all die. Roddy sits with her for the rest of the night, softly assuring her that they will be okay.

This is the backdrop as Roddy begins his final UK project. Though not well remembered now, *This England* is an important film in its moment. The opening titles set a heraldic tone with majestic Gothic writing: "The Earth of England is an old, old earth! / Her autumn mists, Her bramble-berry flame, / Her tangled, rain-soaked grass were still the same, / Time out of mind before the Romans came . . . Though from the skies men hurl their slaughter down, / Still there will be the bracken turning brown." Then the narrator intones: "This England—among whose hills and valleys, since the beginning of time, have stood old farms and quiet villages. The story of Rookby's Farm and the village of Cleveley, in peace and in war, is the story of them all."

Constance Cummings plays an American reporter, on a present-day visit to Cleveley, who learns of how its farm owners, villagers, and gentry strive for common ground in times of war, including during the Norman invasion, the Spanish Armada, the Napoleonic era, and World War I. You're forgiven for expecting a long slog through glorified English history-cum-propaganda, but what follows isn't at all rooted in pageantry or false nostalgia. Instead, screenwriters A. R. Rawlinson, Bridget Boland, and Roddy's *You Will Remember* costar Emlyn Williams construct multilayered stories that question many of the underlying assumptions of the aristocracy and that decry religious bigotry, misogyny, industrialization, and economic disparities.

In the first vignette, set twenty-two years after the Norman invasion, Roddy is the son of a Norman lord, jocularly asking his friends, the serfs in the village, "Do you hate my father?" They do—especially when they learn that the Norman lord of the manor has decreed that instead of reaping this year's harvest, they must build a roadway for the soon-to-be-visiting king, thereby letting their harvests go to waste, threatening them with starvation. This is a very good example of the lost sense of how important some of McDowall's early roles are. Most reference sources list Roddy as "Norman Boy," in the credits, which implies he might have a few lines. Not so. He plays the only son of the conqueror, who prefers spending time with the conquered villagers, instinctively treating them as human beings rather than little more than animals, as his father does. Tensions between the lord and the serfs come to a head, and Roddy is taken hostage. He doesn't see that his own dagger has been swiped from its hilt and is being wielded behind him by a serf rebel, played by Emlyn Willliams.

The rebels challenge the lord to a dangerous wrestling match between the lord and their hulking leader. Silently, Emlyn Williams makes it clear that Roddy will die if the lord doesn't accept the challenge. When Roddy sees his father killed in front of him, the desperate seriousness of the situation dawns on him. Despite his shock, his history of friendly and humane relations with the villagers, his sense of justice, and the inheritance of his father's title augurs a new era of goodwill and cooperation between the Normans and the Britons.

In one close-up, Roddy has to transition from a happy kid watching a wrestling match to a traumatized orphan who must immediately choose whether he wants to make peace with his father's murderers. That's a lot to put on the shoulders of a prepubescent boy, however forthright and endearing he may be, but Roddy is remarkable. He emerges as a believable embodiment of the hope that the British people will achieve peace through resistance. They may have to fight, and even fight dirty, but they can and they must win.

Production shuts down several times during shooting when German bombers are overhead and the cast and crew run for shelter—real-life events that mirror the life-or-death seriousness of the story. Yet Roddy remembers it all with great passion and excitement. It's his first costume picture, and here he is all decked out in an elaborate Norman getup, wearing a wig, and brandishing a dagger. Emlyn Williams is flush with creative inspiration, tearing off his wig between scenes and furiously rewriting the dialogue. Roddy is completely enamored with the cast, watching their every move, and drinking in their conversation and advice. He remembers the air raids, of course. But what he remembers most about them is beautiful Constance Cummings holding his hand and giving him sweets while they listen to the bombs above.

Soon after the film wraps production, one of Thomas McDowall's lorries is bombed while making a delivery, and the driver is killed. A few nights later, a German bomb rips a hole through the roof of the McDowall home. The front door is blown to pieces, and the window glass implodes. Virginia feels strangely vindicated. Her fears aren't unwarranted. Roddy doesn't want to leave London and the excitement of the war, but Thomas and Winefriede know it's time—long *past* time—for Winefriede and the kids to evacuate. Her brother and his family live in Washington, DC, but they aren't particularly close, so Winefriede prefers an offer from a friend of her family, a man named Hugh Carson, now living in White Plains, New York, who during World War I was befriended by Winefriede's mother when he served abroad with the American Expeditionary Forces. The families keep in touch over the twenty-seven years that follow, and he and his wife are happy to take in Winefriede and her children for the duration of the war if necessary.

Thomas manages to book passage to New York on the *Scythia*, a Cunard White Star liner, scheduled to depart on September 18, 1940, transporting evacuees in cooperation with the Children's

Overseas Reception Board (CORB), a British government sponsored organization that by the end of the war evacuates over 2,600 British children from England. Most of the children on board the *Scythia*, however, including Roddy and Virginia, are traveling as part of private arrangements that need no government assistance. Hopefully, Winefriede, Roddy, and Virginia will be safe in the US for the duration—if they can survive the journey. On September 13, 1940, five days before the *Scythia* is supposed to set sail, a German U-boat sinks the SS *City of Benares*. Over 400 evacuees are on the ship, including 90 children. Of those 90 children, 77 are killed, along with 181 other passengers.

As Thomas finalizes plans to evacuate his family, he makes a difficult decision. Though he's forty-four years old, an age that is considered rather advanced for war service in 1940, he feels that his World War I experience as a navigation and gunnery officer in the merchant marines is too valuable to waste. Protecting civilian convoys and military supply vessels is vital to the Allied cause. He puts one of his employees in charge of his transport business and makes plans to rejoin the crew of his former ship, now in active service. As bombs rain down on London, his last action as a civilian is driving his family in a flatbed lorry, with everything they can carry from their bombed-out house tied down in the back. He accompanies them on the train to Liverpool, then sees them off on their voyage to New York.

When Roddy is plastered across fan magazines in 1941 and 1942, much is made of the thrilling adventures he has with Virginia and his parents in the mad dash to Liverpool: the two days, three days, or six days of bombing they endure at the Liverpool docks, with Roddy pulling pranks and Virginia lovingly tutting about his youthful exuberance; their hijinks on board the *Scythia*, entertaining their fellow passengers with recitations of speeches and poems, acting out skits, and landing an American theatrical agent on board; Roddy proudly showing off his personal collection of shrapnel to anyone and everyone, telling tales of how he loves watching the bombs explode and doesn't like sheltering for too long. According to *Photoplay*, *Movie Life*, *Movie Star Parade*, *Hollywood Screen Life*, *Motion Picture*, *Movie Story*, *Modern Screen*, and *Screenland*, the scrappy McDowall family have an uncertain future, but they bravely laugh in the face of danger, and the lovable McDowall children spread happiness and entertainment wherever they go.

Or something like that.

Chapter 2

On the Sunny Side

Published stories about how Roddy McDowall is signed to Fox and is cast in *How Green Was My Valley* are quite colorful. Some of them may even be true. But a mountain of press clippings, letters, contracts, and cables in the Boston archives provides few clear answers about key events that are possibly discussed over the phone, in person, or in unsaved correspondence. The individuals involved don't recall the events the same way, and many of the participants, including Winefriede, Roddy, and Virginia McDowall, often get their own stories mixed up.

The first important moment is easily verifiable. Winefriede, Roddy, and Virginia arrive in New York on October 3, 1940. The passenger manifest of the *Scythia* confirms it, as does an article the next day in *The New York Times* about the "first large group of refugee British children to come direct to New York in more than a month." Among the "gay group of boys and girls, aged 5 to 16" is "Virginia and Roddy McDowall, aged 13 and 12." *The Times* knows nothing of Roddy's career and isn't selling a story about Hollywood magic.

From there on out, a lot of things get murky. We know Roddy tests for the role of Huw Morgan in *How Green Was My Valley* in New York almost immediately upon arrival and is then taken to Los Angeles, where William Wyler directs him in another test, opposite Alexander Knox playing Mr. Gruffydd, the role eventually played by Walter Pidgeon. At that time, Wyler is the film's director, later to be replaced by John Ford. The question is, how does a British refugee child arrive in New York with no friends or business contacts in Los Angeles, and find himself thirty-eight days later on the Fox lot being photographed for the world press showing a souvenir piece of shrapnel to Alice Faye, the reigning seventh most popular moneymaking star in the world?

The gist of the fairy tale–esque stories printed over the years is that the practically penniless McDowall trio arrives in New York with just $1, $20, or $42 in Winifrid's (*sic*) pocketbook. But she believes in her son. Instead of spending the last of her money on traveling to her official destination in White Plains, she checks into a hotel, or a boardinghouse, or they have no place to sleep and are presumably hours away from spending the night on a park bench. They eat a sandwich, a roast chicken dinner, or just a few crackers. She spends their last nickel, quarter, or half-dollar on a subway, streetcar, or taxi, to take Roddy, uninvited, to see every agent in the city. Ostensibly, every single one of the hundreds of theatrical agents who ply their trade in New York City. Whether this includes all five boroughs is never specified. It probably doesn't. In the fateful office of an agent who immediately disappears from the story, lightning strikes, the agent calls Fox, the studio makes a preliminary test, and Roddy is on the road to fame and fortune. This all happens in a single afternoon, one day, two days, or sometimes it's said that the process takes as long as a week.

Suggesting that almost all of the foregoing events, whichever details you choose, aren't entirely plausible doesn't negate how amazing it is that Roddy hits the big time so quickly; there are a number of scenarios where the adventure could turn out differently. Certainly, if Roddy didn't deliver in either test, the jig would've been up. Also, any number of financial and creative developments can stop a project in its tracks. In fact, *How Green Was My Valley* will be postponed, and is even temporarily canceled at one point.

In deconstructing some of the circumstances of Roddy ending up with a contract at Fox, there are a few things to consider. Financially, some try to rationalize the small amount of money in their possession upon arrival—most accounts settle on $42—as being the result of severe limits mandated by the British government on the amount of cash that citizens can take out of the country. It's true that the government doesn't wish people to leave with large amounts of cash. It's also true, however, that there's no specific rule or limit in September 1940, when the McDowalls leave England. At that time, $42 is about £10. While not impossible, it's unlikely that a middle-class mother of two, whose husband owns his own business, would leave the country with just £10, knowing it may be years before they can return.

That said, £10 goes pretty far in 1940.

Picking apart the stories detail-by-detail is fun but can quickly turn tedious. In sum, the underlying assumption in many versions of how Roddy ends up in *How Green Was My Valley* is that in an amazing, completely random turn of events, the part of Huw, a sensitive Welsh lad that seems tailor-made for someone just like Roddy McDowall, is by total coincidence being cast just as Roddy arrives in America. This is unlikely. There is a radical alternative theory also proposed at the time. England's *Daily Mail* goes so far as to say that Roddy knows the novel and is busy practicing the part of Huw before he leaves London—that his father even finds a Welsh man to teach Roddy the proper accent and that he has been rehearsing the part at home for months. This is also highly unlikely.

What *is* likely, however, is that Roddy is already on Fox's radar. He doesn't get on the *Scythia* with an offer of a contract by any means, but there are indications that people at Fox in

New York have seen his work in *Murder in the Family* and think he might be right for *How Green Was My Valley*, one of those indications being that *Murder in the Family* director Albert Parker's last twelve pictures have been for Fox, including *Murder in the Family*, produced by Fox's British arm. It's also true that Fox is looking at dozens of other little boys for the role who *also* might be right for it. Getting the part is absolutely the luckiest break of his life. It's not however a startling twist that comes completely out of thin air.

The account Roddy gives Gavin Lambert for *Interview* is undoubtedly a scrupulously accurate rendering of what Roddy says he remembers. Gavin and Roddy are longtime friends and sometime colleagues. It stands to reason that the quotes are accurate, because if Gavin misquotes Roddy, he will never hear the end of it.

"We were to live in White Plains, New York, for the duration of the war. But on the boat, old Mom got us two kids to give a concert, and somehow, she got some newspaperman on the boat to be there. She wasn't going to live in White Plains, you see. No dust on her. And within two weeks she had found an agent in New York, who told us that MGM was going to make a film called *The Yearling*. I was taken to MGM, and they said I wasn't right—after all, I had this terrible English accent, but they suggested Mom take me over to Fox at 56th Street, because they were looking for a child for *How Green Was My Valley*. I made the test within three days, went to Washington, DC, to visit with my uncle, and got a telegram telling me to come to California to make another test. Fox put us up at the Beverly Wilshire Hotel, and I made the test with William Wyler, who at that time was going to direct the picture. I got the contract, and was asked to leave the Beverly Wilshire at once, because I was no longer on company expenses."

But Roddy's recollections in 1989 are of events from almost

fifty years prior, and memory is a slippery thing, especially when the story of your life has been sliced, diced, and repackaged so often, over so many years, by people with so many different agendas (and deadlines).

At first glance, Roddy's memory of being seen for *The Yearling* seems suspect since the film isn't released until six years later, in 1946. Yet it's indeed originally scheduled to shoot in 1940. Those plans are abandoned when MGM can't find a boy they like to play the lead. There is no record of journalists being on the *Scythia*, so the newspaperman he remembers is probably the *New York Times* reporter who meets the ship, whose interview has nothing to do specifically with Roddy and Virginia or show business. The agent Winefriede "somehow finds" could be a referral from his London agents Felix de Wolfe and Derek Glyn, who already have Roddy poised on the brink of stardom in England.

One thing we can be absolutely sure of is that when Winefriede, Roddy, and Virginia McDowall arrive in Los Angeles on Sunday, November 10, 1940, he's bug-eyed with excitement. His only images of the city before this come from black-and-white projections on movie screens. Nothing prepares him for the sun-drenched color of the place, the already dominant car culture, and the fantastic, eclectic building styles of the houses.

He's on the Fox lot with his mother and sister the day after they arrive. It's also an exotic new land, unlike anything he has ever seen and nothing like the studios that exist in London at the time. To start with, Fox is huge. The backlot extends into much of what's now Century City. The atmosphere at the studio isn't quite like the meta scenes in movies about movies—where every time someone steps outside a soundstage they're met with Roman guards, feathered showgirls, cavemen, Western outlaws, and a medieval damsel or two—but the range of films in production in November 1940 is impressive, including *Tall, Dark and Handsome* starring Cesar Romero and Virginia Gilmore,

Tobacco Road directed by John Ford and starring Charley Grapewin, Marjorie Rambeau, and Gene Tierney, *Golden Hoofs* starring Jane Withers and Charles "Buddy" Rogers, *Murder Among Friends* starring Marjorie Weaver and John Hubbard, *Western Union* starring Robert Young and Randolph Scott, *Sleepers West* starring Lloyd Nolan and Lynn Bari, *Hudson's Bay* starring Paul Muni and Gene Tierney, and *Scotland Yard* starring Nancy Kelly and Edmund Gwenn.

In the days that follow, though, studio life quickly becomes an orderly routine. He goes to the studio every day at eight or nine in the morning, Monday through Saturday, for tests, publicity meetings, and studio schoolroom classes on weekdays, with Saturdays focused only on film-related activities. Once he starts shooting his first picture, his call time will be earlier. It's nothing like his nomadic London experience of revolving studios and new coworkers from film to film. This is a factory. Many of the people he meets on his first day will be familiar faces every day for the next six years.

The ethos of the studio world is a feeling of family—however ephemeral or forced it may turn out to be. At age twelve, Roddy definitely feels welcomed as a new member of the family. Winefriede quickly adapts as well. She is a strong advocate for her children, but she's very careful to never interfere. Instead, she becomes a colorful member of the family in her own right, bringing little gifts to people as Roddy begins working, and she carefully keeps up with the personal lives of executives up and down the food chain, sending congratulatory notes and cards on births and marriage.

Virginia is lost from the moment she arrives. In deference to Winefriede and Roddy, the studio throws her a few bit parts here and there, and they readily agree to Winefriede's request that Virginia join Roddy at the studio school, a situation that will soon become a daily reminder to Virginia of her failure to thrive at Fox. Roddy is a remarkably empathetic brother, and their bond survives throughout, but her self-esteem diminishes bit by bit.

Roddy's first picture, of course, is supposed to be *How Green Was My Valley.* Based on the bestselling novel by Richard Llewellyn, it's originally intended as a Technicolor spectacular to rival *Gone With the Wind*, the previous year's biggest hit, in fact, by some measures, the biggest hit in the history of cinema. Tyrone Power, one of the studio's most popular box-office attractions, is considered for the lead, Huw Morgan as an adult. Originally, his childhood self is only in the first section of the film. The adult version of the character is the one taking center stage in a story about his passion and bravery under the strain of repeated battles to protect the exploited miners in the village who live and die year after year in poverty, beaten down but unwilling to step back from their fight for fair wages and decent living and working conditions.

The planned film adaptation will run close to four hours and cost a fortune.

During preproduction, the Fox board of directors makes an unusually intrusive decision to cancel the project. The cost is too high and they consider its pro-union message anti-American. More important, they find the message tedious and potentially off-putting to audiences. An expensive, subversive, Technicolor period piece set in Wales isn't going to be on Fox's 1941 release schedule. The board action comes completely out of the blue, and Darryl F. Zanuck is enraged by their interference. He resolves to make the film anyway. He will slash the budget, address their concerns, and then, if they don't agree to finance the film, he will raise the money and make it outside the studio—no idle threat, and a wildly revolutionary action for a studio head to contemplate.

Roddy is diverted to *Man Hunt* and a much smaller role. Shooting starts in early March 1941. It's a chase film set before the start of World War II, with Walter Pidgeon starring as a posh

Englishman who tries to kill Hitler, misses, and is then caught, tortured, and sentenced to death. He manages to escape, bruised, bedraggled, and desperate. Joan Bennett is the Cockney cutie who falls hard for Walter but pays with her life. Roddy's former costar from *The Outsider*, George Sanders, and his sidekick, John Carradine, are the Nazis on the deadly manhunt. They will get Walter Pidgeon or die trying. Spoiler alert: They die trying.

Director Fritz Lang is quite the character to Roddy, what with his pirate-like eye patch, his penetrating intensity, and his harsh German accent. Lang is said to be cruel, even physically abusive. (Hollywood lore has it that he once secretly puts dairy into the food of a crew member with a severe allergy just to laugh as he watches the man's face swell and turn blue.) He's brusque but affable enough with Roddy. Perhaps Fritz Lang draws the line at torturing children. In truth, with Roddy, he has no "reason" to, since he's quite pleased with Roddy's ability to respond naturally in front of the camera. It gives his scenes a feeling of improvisational humor and enthusiasm. It's Roddy's first time working with Walter Pidgeon, his future *How Green Was My Valley* costar, and the two have an immediate onscreen connection.

Roddy plays an English cabin boy on a Danish merchant ship who hides Walter from the Nazis. It's an extended sequence where Roddy must outwit his own captain and the Nazi bad guys. His dialogue is liberally strewn with Hollywood's idea of how the English speak. *I say! My word! Rah-THER!* These bits of silliness aside, the performance comes to life the instant his little face flashes on screen. Upon learning that Walter is on the lam, Roddy cocks his head, absentmindedly rolls his tongue, thinking, and then leans in: "Have you committed a crime, sir?" Walter says no, and Roddy responds with a knowing look, hilariously playing the serious man of the world: "Was it about a woman?" It's meant to be funny, and it absolutely is. Roddy is kinetic as he plots his next move, finding the moments of peril thrilling rather than scary. It's a more conventionally recognizable portrayal of a precocious kid, without the ethereal seriousness to come in *How Green Was My Valley*—closer to who Roddy is in his "real" life.

The rest of the cast is terrific once you get past their accents. Walter doesn't even try to sound British, Joan's Cockney is downright terrible, and George Sanders as a German character speaks with the plummy tones of a member of the House of Lords. Uneven vocal inflections notwithstanding, the film is tense and nuanced, trying its best not to stack the deck in the Brits' favor while the US is still officially neutral, but skillfully getting its anti-Nazi point across.

Virginia also makes her American screen debut in *Man Hunt* in an uncredited role as a girl rushing to get the authorities for her postmistress mother when Walter is still on the lam—but this time from English authorities. She has no lines in the final cut, and whether she has any while shooting is unknown. But at least now she can have an official reason to go to school on the lot.

During the two months *Man Hunt* is shooting, Zanuck is hard at work resuscitating and reworking *How Green Was My Valley*. He jettisons the expensive plans for Technicolor. The vibrant colors of California plants and flowers look nothing like anything found in Wales anyway. The location in Brent's Crags, near Malibu, where Zanuck plans to build the Welsh mining village of the story, will look much more authentic in black-and-white.

Another idea begins to crystallize that can solve a lot of problems. Roddy McDowall is so terrific, with those big, soulful brown eyes: What if he never grows up? His weekly salary, charged against the picture's budget, is also a fraction of what Tyrone Power gets. At Zanuck's bidding, screenwriter Philip Dunne cuts the script almost in half, and transforms the adult Huw's best scenes, rewriting them so they happen from the vantage point of a little boy. This naturally softens the pro-union message, because seen from a child's perspective, what the men want from the mine owner seems like basic fairness rather than anything political. Director John Ford becomes a third member of the makeover team when William Wyler drops out to direct Bette Davis in *The Little Foxes*. William Wyler has been a Roddy McDowall cheerleader throughout the process. John Ford's enthusiasm proves even greater. His entire directorial approach becomes using the camera to filter everything through the eyes of Huw.

What Daryll F. Zanuck regards as Fox's most important film of the year will be told entirely through the eyes of Roddy McDowall.

With the intense concentration of a child who notices everything as it happens around him, Roddy will be the eyes and ears of the audience as a string of harrowing events come to pass. This isn't to imply that his role is passive. He's central to the action, as he's called upon to learn how to box; rescue his drowning mother; become crippled and learn to walk again; withstand savage, almost life-threatening beatings; leave school and toil to the point of exhaustion in the coal mines; finally holding his dying father in his arms. If this sounds over the top, that isn't how it will ultimately play under John Ford's spare, masterful approach. The events unspool with a sense of restrained, aching inevitability.

The revamping of the project works. The Fox board still isn't particularly impressed with the screenplay, believing it will be neither a good movie nor a successful one, but they agree to step out of Zanuck's way. On June 10, 1941, production starts on *How Green Was My Valley*.

Roddy feels safe with John Ford, a director who's considered brilliant but whose reputation for cruelty, like Fritz Lang's, is legendary. At the time, this sense of abusiveness is often highly valued. Many people seem to feel it signifies genius rather than sadism. (This attitude persists in the entertainment industry through the rest of the century, into the next. Only now are we questioning the notion, and yet it still endures, even as it becomes far less acceptable, and the careers of some directors and TV showrunners are adversely affected.)

Director John Ford and Roddy McDowall prove a good match. Ford can be a very happy director when he gets what he wants, and Roddy has an unerring sense of how to give people just that. The brilliance of the performance isn't about Roddy understanding the craft of acting, it's about his understanding of how to please the adults around him.

"John Ford was shrewd. He was a titan. He drew things out of me like a conductor, masterful with an enormous dexterity. He made me feel as if I was doing it myself," Roddy later says. "When children act, they don't know what they're doing, they don't have any craft. I certainly didn't know what I was doing. I was just responding. . . . As many times as I've seen that film, I really am astonished at the performance that he got out of me. . . . He just played me like a harp. . . . A really amazing experience. There were never more than two takes. So very little rehearsal. No retakes."

It isn't all seriousness and cinematic suffering. One scene is set against a backdrop of a hillside full of daffodils. Every one of them is fake, cut out from pieces of paper. Roddy isn't busy the morning the set decorators put the daffodils in place. He has a wonderful time romping through the hills setting out daffodils. It's like building scenes in his childhood nursery—instead of cotton snow for Napoleon's Russian march, Roddy, along with an entire crew, uses paper flowers to turn Malibu into Wales. Costar Maureen O'Hara takes Roddy and Virginia on long drives up and down the California coast on Sunday afternoons, cementing a bond that will last the rest of his life. Anna Lee, who plays the bride of one of Roddy's older brothers, also becomes a lifelong friend.

The casting up and down the call sheet of *How Green Was My Valley* is perfect. Donald Crisp as Roddy's father just seems to *be* this man caught between his traditional sense of honor and his loyalty to his family and neighbors, and Sara Allgood as his mother has a speech that brings down the house, when she faces a crowd of violent, angry villagers—her own people—and shames them about their treatment of her husband, whom they turn into a pariah for arguing against unionization, even when the mine lowers pay rates. Donald fears a fight for a union will result in the mine shutting down, with all of them left to starve. His five grown sons bitterly disagree and resolve to support the union. Donald warns them that no son who goes against him can stay in the family home. All five leave the family dinner table to pack their things and go. When they abandon their father, Roddy is the only one who stays at the dinner table. Stoic but devastated, Donald Crisp can only stare down at the table. Roddy rattles his cutlery, letting it drop on his plate, once, twice, urgently wanting his father to see that he still has support, even if it's from only one of his sons. His father still can't look up. "Yes, my son," he says. "I know you are there." Roddy understands his father's sadness and responds. It's such a small moment in the tide of drama, but it's heartbreaking. (Actress Joanna Gleason—who will join Roddy, Vincent Price, and Coral Browne in their 1976 tour of *Charley's Aunt*—says it's her father, legendary *Let's Make a Deal* presenter Monty Hall's favorite scene in the history of the movies. He watches *How Green Was My Valley* again and again throughout his life and breaks into tears every time Roddy looks over at his father.)

Maureen O'Hara, as the one female among seven siblings, has her own tragic story arc. She is a traditionally obedient daughter but is outspoken and passionate within the village, daring to shout down a clergyman who shames a fallen young woman in front of the whole flock. Marriage to a rich man is proposed. Her father agrees. Against her own desires, Maureen goes along with it. It's a disastrous marriage, and she runs away from her cruel, abusive husband, intent on divorce—an almost unthinkable decision. Roddy watches in horror when her chaste but very real love for the town minister, Walter Pidgeon, turns her into a village pariah too, just like their father. Walter is Roddy's mentor and best friend, who nurses him through his crippling illness and teaches him there's an outside world with broader ways of looking at morality, loyalty, and love than the ones embraced by the villagers—even than the beliefs and customs embraced by his own family.

The film also offers one of the most satisfying moments of justified revenge in cinema history. Roddy is brutally beaten by the English schoolmaster who's prejudiced against the Welsh. Boxer Rhys Williams and his cohort Barry Fitzgerald, friends of the family, decide to teach the schoolmaster a lesson. Rhys gives the class a pseudo-educational demonstration of boxing techniques with Barry providing colorful commentary. The boxer beats the schoolmaster to unconsciousness, demonstrating the nonregulation punches the students should avoid. Rhys leaves the schoolmaster twisted and bent on the floor in front of his students. When the film is released, audiences cheer the carnage.

Over the subsequent decades, the Welsh have a love-hate relationship with the film. They are justifiably mortified by the terrible accents. Rhys Williams is the only actual Welsh person in the cast, and it sounds like it. The Morgan family home seems quintuple the size it should be and impossibly sunny and clean. The vast outdoor set looks nothing like an actual Welsh mining village. Still, audiences in the 1940s don't expect realism from Hollywood films, and to have Wales as even a misrepresented location in such an important movie is a point of pride, particularly in the era of the film's original release, possibly a bit less so to those modern-day Welsh people who know the film.

Ten days into the *How Green Was My Valley* shoot, *Man*

Hunt is released to good notices and solid business. Roddy isn't singled out in the reviews, but industry response to his work is decidedly positive, and Zanuck's faith in Roddy seems well placed. The shooting schedule of *How Green Was My Valley* overlaps with Roddy's next film, *Confirm or Deny.* In turn, *Confirm or Deny*'s shooting schedule overlaps with *Son of Fury: The Story of Benjamin Blake.* The three films are made over five months, between June 10 and November 15, 1941. That Fox press release about Roddy working 110 consecutive days in a row suddenly doesn't seem quite so hyperbolic. Actually, according to *Movie Star Parade*, the most pressing problem of Roddy's whole Hollywood adventure so far is his hair.

"Roddy was told to let his hair grow long for the filming of *How Green Was My Valley.* Before he had finished his role, though, he received notice that he was to play with Don Ameche and Joan Bennett in *Confirm or Deny*, for which it would be necessary to have his locks shorn. It was fortunate that he put off his visit to the barber shop for a day, because another message arrived, advising him that he would go into *Son of Fury* with Tyrone Power, and would again need extra-length hair. He had to go into a huddle with studio executives on how much hair he could bare for *Confirm or Deny* and how quickly he could grow it back again for *Son of Fury.* It all got to be a hopeless impasse. After some sort of a compromise, Roddy was allowed a slight trim, but the shearings of his hair were saved for any and all emergencies. Glamour boy? Not Roddy McDowall!"

Movie magazines manage to make everything sound ridiculous. And yet . . . There really are worried meetings among directors and executives trying to figure out what to do about Roddy's hair due to the scheduling conflicts of the three films. Whatever the state of his hair length, *Confirm or Deny* starts shooting just as *How Green Was My Valley* is winding down. It's a fast-paced story of love during the London Blitz as American newspaperman Don Ameche falls for English teletype operator Joan Bennett, while enlisting clever, industrious, eager-to-please office boy Roddy McDowall to help him get coded messages about the possibility of a German invasion. Roddy's office boy character never seems to go home. You wonder if his parents have been killed and he's on his own, possibly even sleeping rough somewhere, or camped out in the basement of the newspaper offices. Joan and Don "meet cute" in the tube during a bomb raid, and the two have chemistry for days, with some surprisingly racy sequences: They spend the night together, his arms around her, while the bombs fall, and he's quite candid about his liaisons with other women all over London. Don Ameche's machine-gun delivery recalls *His Girl Friday*, shot the year before, but it takes on a different kind of urgency here, when, instead of being played for comedy, the speed is dictated by life-threatening events.

Joan is the very definition of a movie star, gliding through the action with elegant aplomb, a droll smirk always at the ready, until dire circumstances cause her to take desperate actions. She certainly rises to the occasion. It's one of the best performances of her career, and her character is more upscale than the Cockney girl she plays in *Man Hunt*, so her clipped, mid-Atlantic accent, while not exactly authentic, isn't distracting.

Roddy is a revelation, with his brave smile looking out from the bombed-out remains of the newspaper's office, as he asks how he can be of help. The plot hinges on whether Don Ameche will be able to transmit what he considers the scoop of a lifetime—the top-secret report of an imminent Nazi invasion of England. There will be hell to pay with the British war department. Censorship of war information is tightly enforced. But he will face the consequences and get the news to his paper in America. Joan Bennett, on the other hand, will do anything to stop him, since reporting the story will let the Nazis know that the British have broken their codes and will be prepared for the German invasion rather than sitting ducks. Don and Joan are physically fighting over the point as, elsewhere, Roddy is perched on the top of a building, directly in the line of fire, surrounded by sandbags, awaiting two carrier pigeons. He's gleeful when the first bird finally arrives. Then just after relaying the message from the second bird through to Don Ameche, Roddy is shot to death.

A heroic child actually *dies*—a shocking event in an American movie of this era.

Roddy's death proves the pivotal moment in the film. As Don transmits his story, ostensibly, the story Joan fears will lead to catastrophe for her country, she pleads with him to stop but he won't listen. He keeps typing, savagely beating down on the keys. He sends the story. But as Joan discovers when she tears away the printout, it's not the story she's dreading. Don has written a bitter, furious report of the latest "glorious" Nazi "victory."

Joan reads it out loud. "Single-handed, one of the Nazi squadrons has mowed down an Englishman called Albert Perkins [Roddy], aged 12. Albert Perkins, a volunteer, stuck to his post through the greatest bombardment in history. He will not be given a citation or a Victoria Cross, but when they find his body"—Joan falters, stifling tears—"and bury it in the ground of England, the soil over his grave will be free soil!"

On the page here, the dialogue may come across as melodramatic, but onscreen it plays as deeply emotional, albeit expertly manipulative. And world events turn on such movie scenes. Roddy's personal story of childhood fame takes on a meaning that goes far beyond Hollywood history or legend. While his work onscreen is the result of creative forces coming together to produce a piece of filmed entertainment, one of fifty movies Fox releases in 1941, it's also extremely effective national propaganda that is a vital part of convincing the American public that sacrifice is ennobling and moral. In his string of films released in 1941 and 1942, Roddy becomes the face of the British children America must help save.

Confirm or Deny and *Man Hunt* take a definite stand on the war, coming down squarely against the Nazis, though they are made before Pearl Harbor, when the US is still officially neutral. Some Hollywood historians note that gentile Fox studio head Darryl F. Zanuck doesn't seem to have the same concerns about ruffling the feathers of the anti-Semitic "America First" crowd as his fellow studio heads, most of whom are Jewish, and often shy away from anything that might highlight their "otherness." It's telling that Zanuck is also the one who makes the groundbreaking *Gentleman's Agreement*, a searing (and incredibly profitable) 1947 film about anti-Semitism. Louis B. Mayer at MGM is on record by then arguing that the war is over, and no one cares anymore about anything to do with the Jews. He's wrong.

Roddy has little sense of his own place in a larger global story. For him, making movies is about his interactions with the adults who surround him all day. The two most impactful events during the making of *Confirm or Deny* are, first, when director Fritz Lang has a gallbladder attack ten days into the shoot and is replaced by Archie Mayo, a veteran director whose career begins in the silent era. Archie Mayo lacks the colorful appeal of Fritz Lang—no pirate eye patch—but Roddy finds him easy to please. The second event is falling off a bicycle.

A *Screenland* piece about the making of *Confirm or Deny* prints a story that is essentially true, though the supposedly quoted dialogue itself reads like fan magazine prose. It's all about the day director Archie Mayo decides he wants Roddy to ride a bicycle in a particular scene. An assistant director dutifully finds a bike. The story continues: "[Roddy] was ordered to ride a bicycle. He mounted and quickly crashed into a wall. 'You're a terrible rider,' said the frightened assistant director, fearful of broken bones. 'Naturally, I never rode before.' 'But all English boys ride bikes.' 'I know you thought that sir, so I didn't want to disappoint you.' "

Roddy aims to please, no matter what.

Son of Fury: The Story of Benjamin Blake takes place during the reign of George III. A gunsmith cares for his orphaned young grandson, the title character, played by Roddy as a boy and Tyrone Power as a man. Roddy is assumed to be the illegitimate son of a baronet, whose brother, slithery George Sanders, greedily enjoys the inheritance that by rights should be Roddy's. George aims to keep his "enemy" close, however, and after an exhaustive search, he finds Roddy and demands he live with him as his bonded servant.

Roddy is again called upon to be noble and self-sacrificing, but he gets the opportunity to raise a little hell. He has a terrific, no-holds-barred fight in the stables with an older, bigger boy who bullies him. Roddy is knocked back again and again but continually comes back for more. The kindly stable master finds him filthy and bleeding on the ground. "Are you bad hurt?" Roddy shakes his head. "If you're wise, you'll submit. Like the rest of us."

Roddy runs away, back to his grandfather, and they plan to flee. They will be breaking the law. George is a titled gentleman with the legal right to take Roddy. The penalty if they're caught could be dire for his grandfather. Roddy won't turn his beloved grandfather into a wanted criminal. He resolves to return to George Sanders. "I'll go back. And he can do with me as he pleases. But I'll never submit." And you believe him. The film is much less interesting once Roddy grows up and becomes Tyrone Power, who falls in love with Frances Farmer and, after a South Seas adventure, ultimately vanquishes George Sanders.

As Roddy settles into this new life at the studio, he also settles into a new home life, one that is surprisingly not that different from the one back in London. With Thomas away at sea, though, Winefriede's control over their lives is unfettered. From a child's perspective, it's just how things are—there's nothing else to compare it to. Yet Winefriede's influence is a form of gaslighting, where Roddy and Virginia must pretend to be choosing activities and meals of their own free will, all the while acceding to their mother's wishes. Sometimes, if Winefriede doesn't get her way she feigns a heart attack or apoplexy, miraculously rising from near death immediately if the phone or the doorbell rings. Her insistence on getting her own way often isn't about anything that matters, particularly. Winefriede isn't asking them to do things they hate to do or eat things they don't like. And mercifully, she stops trying to dress them as twins. The issue is that Winefriede can't seem to function unless her desires prevail, so everything Roddy and Virginia do is micromanaged. She arranges for other industry kids and children of people who work at the studio to come over to visit, and sometimes to spend the night. On nights when the three of them are alone, Winefriede often asks Roddy to sleep in her room with her, in her bed, citing worries over kidnapping threats. Winefriede's attachment to Roddy grows all the more suffocating, further crowding out Virginia, who comes to feel as an adult that their mother's insistence that Virginia be treated as a professional, just like Roddy, is a way of overcompensating. She believes that as Roddy's star rises, Winefriede loses interest in her entirely.

In interview after interview, Roddy describes Winefriede as a fun-loving yet motherly force of nature. When Virginia is asked to participate, she says the same. Carefully positioned stories about Winefriede McDowall as the good-natured opposite of a stage mother appear in the press. Though Winefriede is relatively hands-off at the studio—she believes it's vital that Fox sees her as an ally rather than a pest—publicity is another matter entirely. With the press, Winefriede believes she can control the narrative. For her children, living in a company town where the business is making and selling dreams further confuses the truth.

A *Modern Screen* article gives readers an inside peek into Roddy's home life. "The children have never disobeyed, not because they're goody-goods, but because the need to assert themselves through revolt hasn't arisen. Allowed every fair latitude, they take it for granted that their mother doesn't say no except for sufficient reason, so they don't argue. Mrs. McDowall doesn't give orders. She makes a suggestion, and it's followed." Winefriede doubtless believes the story emphasizes her children's free will and that she comes across as a free-thinking, affectionate mother.

Whose children have *never* disobeyed and don't argue? Ever?

The fantasy of the laissez-faire childrearing methods she supposedly employs is contradicted by the reality of her need for iron control.

When Roddy is in his own imaginary universe, though, he's free. He starts creating this universe back when he begins drama school in London. He calls it the city of Loin. The name is a transposition of lion. Loin is the hub of the Kingdom of Scotta, which in turn is part of the Royal Empire of Lane, which is a part of the planet Fidelis. He draws a detailed, ever-growing blueprint of Loin, while also writing the adventures of its inhabitants. Within a few years, a vast movie studio takes center stage in his city, where in addition to imagining the layout of all the buildings and soundstages, he constructs a creative and financial empire. Roddy invents screenwriters, scripts, best-selling novels that can be adapted into films, studio executives, and a roster of stars. He tracks box-office results and popularity polls of his stars. Things turn three-dimensional when studio songwriter Harry Revel creates a miniature movie theater with places for Roddy to display his own posters and change the marquee. In one sense, Roddy is turning fantasy into real life. In another sense, he's turning real life into fantasy. The two are one and the same.

This blending of reality and fantasy is also a major part of something much more far-reaching: packaging Roddy as the face of British resistance. It starts from the moment he hits town, with that photo of him, on the Fox lot, showing a piece of shrapnel to Alice Faye. Every story in the massive wave of publicity that accompanies *How Green Was My Valley* connects Roddy to England's heroic fight to stay in existence; every story highlights his scrappy dismissal of the dangers involved back when he and his family are dodging bombs in London; every story reminds the reader that while Roddy is sensitive and soulful, he's also manly and willing to fight. The messages get distilled into a four-page spread in *Screenland* proclaiming Roddy McDowall as a clever boy who has been "Bombed Into Stardom!"

"Roddy didn't want to come to America. It wasn't that he doesn't like the United States, because he does, very much. His hero is President Roosevelt, and his favorite subject at school is American history. But Roddy didn't want to leave the excitement behind. 'I had a spy glass and used to run out on the porch when I heard the air raid signal,' he said. 'I'd watch the R.A.F. go after the Jerries. Sometimes I saw them get a Jerry's plane and he'd come parachuting down.' Yes, sir, it was exciting in London, especially when you were before the movie cameras and about to say your piece, and the wail of the banshees would start, and you would dash for an air raid shelter. Roddy's father, though, said they had to go to America—Roddy, his mother and his sister. The government too was urging mothers and children to leave London for safer areas. 'Father stayed,' said Roddy. 'He's got to help them get rid of the Jerries!'"

While *Son of Fury* is still shooting, *How Green Was My Valley* is released with an avalanche of marketing and advertising materials. The studio publicity department's press book proudly proclaims the film is "presold in every corner of the land with headline-crashing showmanship and attention-grabbing national advertising. Over 50 million readers will see and absorb Fox's full-page two-color picture ads, selling messages in these mass circulation magazines: *Ladies' Home Journal*, *Look*, *Life*, *Christian Herald*, *Christian Science Monitor*, *Movie Life*, *Movie Star Parade*, *Hollywood Screen Life*, *Motion Picture*, *Movie Story*,

Your Charm, *Screen Romances*, *Modern Screen*, *Screenland*, *Screen Guide*, *Movie and Radio Guide*, and *Photoplay Movie Mirror*." Interviews and articles on the principal cast members report about their career highlights, their thoughts on Welsh rarebits, and their messages to the American troops who soon will be shipping out to the Pacific.

Roddy has never experienced this level of excitement with any of his other pictures. He's in the eye of the storm—and mostly, he likes it just fine—though he still finds it confusing that so many members of the public are interested in him. His fan mail grows every week. Virginia is sometimes tasked with answering the special requests the studio sends over that call for a personal response. Winefriede and Virginia don't always accompany him to *How Green Was My Valley* press events. Often, he attends with Maureen O'Hara, vowing that once he's twenty-one years old, he will marry her.

The reception from critics and the public surpasses even Darryl F. Zanuck's wildest hopes. It isn't a movie, it's a phenomenon. It becomes the third-highest-grossing film of the year. (*Gone With the Wind*, still in theaters since the end of 1939, is in the second-place slot, and *Sergeant York*, the Gary Cooper drama about a World War I pacifist who becomes a battle-scarred war hero, is at the top.) Right after *How Green Was My Valley*'s release, on November 11, 1941, Winefriede files for Roddy's American citizenship. "Roddy and I feel that since we are living in the United States and benefitting so much from this country that the very least we can do is to become good citizens," she tells Louella Parsons. "We expect to make our home in Los Angeles and Roddy hopes to go to an American university when the time comes. The American people have been so good to us, and we are more than just grateful."

This England makes its American premiere two weeks after the release of *How Green Was My Valley*. Fox sends Roddy, Winefriede, and Virginia to New York to be guests of honor at a benefit for the British War Relief Society, where he meets Mayor Fiorello La Guardia. *How Green Was My Valley* is nominated for ten Oscars and wins five, including the first Best Picture Oscar awarded to 20th Century-Fox and Darryl F. Zanuck. John Ford wins his third Best Director Oscar, Donald Crisp wins for Best Supporting Actor, and the film wins for black-and-white cinematography and black-and-white art direction—with all those paper daffodils getting the credit they deserve.

Between wrapping *Son of Fury* and starting his next picture, *The Pied Piper*, Pearl Harbor is bombed, and the US enters World War II. *Confirm or Deny* opens seven days later. The public watches Roddy McDowall die—shot down on the newspaper office's roof, with his messenger pigeons nearby—perishing for the sake of his home country, now America's ally in the fight for freedom.

The start of America's involvement in the conflict doesn't feel as momentous to Roddy and his family as it does to most Americans. The McDowalls have been living with the war for almost two years already, with Thomas now serving in the Pacific. As Fox steps up Roddy's wartime personal appearances, a seemingly innocuous introduction occurs. At a war bond rally in Pershing Square in Los Angeles, Roddy meets a very young Ava Gardner. He remembers her as one of the most beautiful girls he has ever seen in his life. "Her body was absolutely extraordinary," he says, almost thirty years later when he's directing her in a film called *Tam Lin*. "The way all her facial features were placed was perfect. She was classically beautiful, and her spirit was quite adorable. It's very strange to see that sort of tenderness radiating out of somebody that exquisitely beautiful."

He asks for her autograph. She signs it, "Mrs. Mickey Rooney." Mickey is her first husband. She isn't yet famous—she hasn't really done much yet. Roddy is only thirteen, but he sees something quite special in her, and when her star rises, he isn't a bit surprised.

Roddy wins acting awards from the National Board of Review, *Box Office*, *Fame*, *Parents* magazine, and *Photoplay*. "Little Roddy McDowall is superb," says *The New York Times*, along with just about every critic in the US, Canada, and the UK. The best review of all comes, perhaps, from *How Green Was My Valley* screenwriter Philip Dunne: "The warp and woof of comedy and tragedy were expertly knit into a single glowing tapestry of drama, and the frame that held it all in place was the superlative performance of a boy of 12. Roddy McDowall proved to be all that we had hoped for, and more."

The Pied Piper starts shooting in 1942, soon after *How Green Was My Valley*'s Oscar wins. It's a wartime story set during the Nazi invasion of France. Eccentric Englishman Monty Woolley is vacationing in the south of France, in 1940, as the evacuation of Dunkirk begins. He must get home. A couple vacationing with their two children persuades the extremely reluctant Monty to take their kids, Roddy McDowall and Peggy Ann Garner, safely back to England with him. With France under Nazi control, the parents have important League of Nations business to attend to in Switzerland and must get there as quickly as possible. Monty Woolley takes a comic dislike to all children but finds himself the unexpected escort of still more refugee children: A French girl, a French boy who's Jewish, a Dutch boy, a German girl who's half-Jewish, and a kitten. At first, Roddy plays genial straight man to wisecracking Woolley, but once they're on their journey, Roddy's role broadens, and he's the catalyst for bringing other children into the fold after each loses their parents. Roddy comforts the traumatized children with a pragmatic solemnity.

The real surprise is Monty Woolley. If you know him primarily from *The Man Who Came to Dinner*, you're prepared for his way with a witticism, but here he's also called upon to use his dramatic chops. Lives are at stake, and he rises to the challenge. There are multiple languages spoken throughout, and unlike the

Hollywood custom of the time, where foreign characters speak in English with haphazard accents as if they're speaking a foreign language, here, when Anne Baxter (as a Frenchwoman who helps the group find a way across the English Channel) speaks in English with a French accent, it's because she's speaking English. When she speaks to other French people, she speaks French. The same with soldiers speaking German. Roddy and some of the other children speak multiple languages, but Monty only speaks English. Sometimes he has no idea what anyone is saying, and neither does most of the audience. When it becomes necessary to hide his Englishness, he pretends to be a deaf, doddering Frenchman. The filmmakers' choice to incorporate the language issue adds a layer that enhances Monty's growing awareness of how much danger he and the children are in. Otto Preminger shows up as a Nazi officer with a secret who provides an unexpected denouement.

The direct mention of the Jewishness of two of the children is still rare for an American movie, even as the plight of the Jews in Europe is becoming clear, if not the true horrors of their deaths. It's another example of Fox having the courage to confront Hitler's anti-Semitism. There is a running gag about whether Rochester is a state or merely a city. Monty insists it's a state. Roddy knows better, but once they're traveling companions, he chooses to humor Monty in an act of solidarity. Fox ultimately premieres the film in Rochester and garners a ton of press throughout New York.

Monty and Roddy develop a camaraderie over their shared love of books, but Monty is intent on getting Roddy to read more of the classics and fewer books about Hollywood history. He's horrified to learn that a young boy with Roddy's literary capacity wastes his time reading about silent stars like Pola Negri, and worse, writes to her asking for her autograph.

Instead of responding by mail, Pola sees the return address on Roddy's letter and shows up at his door with a signed picture.

Soon after, Roddy meets a drunk John Barrymore. Later he meets Tallulah Bankhead—another idol—and takes to doing impressions of her. (Pointing out that few little boys who love doing Tallullah impressions grow up to be straight men may be fostering a stereotype, but sometimes stereotypes exist for a reason.)

During the *Pied Piper* shoot, when Roddy comes down with the mumps and is bedridden for a few days, Monty sends over a stack of books, writing an inscription on one: "There's practically nothing I can criticize about you except your unending desire to collect undesirable autographs."

After *The Pied Piper* wraps, Thomas McDowall unexpectedly arrives on leave for a two-week visit, on the heels of receiving a medal for rescuing twenty-seven American seamen, adrift for ten days when their freighter is torpedoed. Thomas is a real-life hero, and though a stiff upper lip attitude is always present (another stereotype that exists for a reason), this is a very emotional homecoming. It's the first time his family has seen him in almost two years, and Roddy and Virginia are deeply attached to their father. His usual role in the McDowall household historically doesn't include openly opposing or in any way undermining Winefriede. He's too captivated by the force of personality. Yet in his quiet way, he traditionally provides a counterbalance that his children sorely miss during his absence at sea.

Thomas isn't a man to indulge his anxieties, but contemplating his son's new worldwide fame is unnerving. It's so much bigger than he can truly understand, and he has no idea what he will find in Los Angeles. It's a relief to see that Roddy and Virginia are relatively unchanged. Virginia is a bit more withdrawn, but Roddy is doing extremely well. Already confident and forthright back in England, it seems Roddy is now maturing into an extraordinarily self-possessed young man.

Hollywood, on the other hand, will take some getting used to. Their home is in Cheviot Hills, equidistant between Fox and

MGM. Winefriede courts the press, often putting together big meals, entertaining grandly on their son's earnings. And Roddy is almost always "on," performing whatever is expected of him. Thomas finds himself at the Hollywood Canteen smiling awkwardly at what seems to him like a hundred photographers and reporters, while Roddy greets the reporters and photographers by name, chatting easily about his father's heroism, answering questions about his next movie, and posing for pictures set up for him where he clears tables while servicemen have coffee and doughnuts, and he poses with a broom as he pretends to sweep up.

Roddy and Winefriede have a lot of obligations, leaving Thomas and Virginia alone for some of Thomas's leave. Virginia has a mission. She has had a couple of walk-ons, and Winefriede doggedly continues making her a part of Roddy's public life, but at age fifteen, Virginia wants to build a life for herself by leaving the studio school at Fox and going to regular high school. Winefriede McDowall still talks as if her daughter is a potential star. Can Thomas intervene? It's unclear who says what to whom, but Virginia gets her wish. Winefriede agrees that next semester, Virginia may transfer to high school in Beverly Hills.

Thomas returns to sea, Virginia dreams about her new life to come, Winefriede plans her next dinner party, and Roddy begins preparing for his next film by taking riding lessons.

My Friend Flicka is Roddy's first film shot on location, three months in Utah. The gist of the story is that clumsy, unfocused Roddy wants a colt of his own, and he falls in love with a horse he names Flicka (Swedish for "little girl"). The complication is that Flicka is the daughter of Rocket, a "loco" horse that is untrainable. There is a lot of talk about getting rid of bad bloodlines—so much so that it starts to feel a bit like a pro-eugenics argument. And "breaking" the horses is presented unsentimentally at first, but then his dad says, "You're her whole life now. Make her like it." The sequence is extremely effective, as Roddy gently uses his own bandana and belt to coax Flicka into the notion of wearing a bridle and being led. She's "broken," though essentially made whole by her bond with Roddy. In the tradition of other boy-and-his-animal-pal films, the horse is (almost) put to death, but everything turns out happily, with Roddy learning responsibility, his father, Preston Foster, learning that sometimes it pays off when you hope for the impossible, and his mother, Rita Johnson, engineering most of the plot twists, while looking ravishing in her high-waisted, thin-belted riding pants that wouldn't last a minute on an actual ranch. Roddy rides well, appears at home in the rural environment, and is utterly convincing as a boy passionately in love with his horse—his first real friend. Considering how much Roddy hates the horse in real life, his performance is even more laudable. Roddy thinks the animal gets pleasure from constantly stepping on his feet and pushing him.

On a day off from shooting, Roddy and Virginia decide they'd like to go up in an airplane, and uncharacteristically, on their own, they find a man who will do it, and they make the arrangements themselves. When the studio gets wind of the plan, they hit the roof. Never mind flying, Roddy isn't allowed to even go to the airport lest something happen to the star of the film. He's so disappointed, and Virginia doesn't want to go alone, so she decides not to go either. Roddy won't hear of it. He gets angry—a very unusual occurrence—and demands that he be allowed to take Virginia to the airport. He won't argue with the studio about going up in the plane himself, but he won't let Virginia miss out, and he will be there to see her do it. He's quite polite about the words he chooses, but he makes clear the implication. He's the star of the picture, and if he wants to go watch his sister do something that makes her happy on his day off, no one is going to stop him. It's not exactly storming the barricades, but for the Best Little Boy in the World, it's a truly revolutionary act. Virginia remembers that moment for the rest of her life, telling the story often. He stands up for both of them that day. Thank God Winefriede is having lunch with a reporter at the time, or they would never have gotten away with it.

My Friend Flicka has a plot point involving a mountain lion that's a linchpin of the story. Mountain lions aren't rare, but the production has trouble finding one that's trained. Someone knows a guy who knows a guy, and they locate an animal trainer in New Mexico. He's been working with a captured lion for about two months, and he's confident the lion is tamed. A few days later the lion arrives in Utah and is carefully let loose, with the trainer ready to step in if anything goes wrong.

Something goes wrong.

The lion looks up at the maze of lights aimed at it, someone makes a loud noise, and the animal leaps away. The trainer tries in vain to calm the animal down, but it goes on the attack, in a frenzy of biting, clawing, and shredding. Thankfully it's attacking set pieces, wires, lights, and camera equipment rather than people. Cast and crew, already at a fairly safe remove, scamper away quickly to an even safer remove. Several hours of shooting is postponed as the trainer works with the lion, acclimating it to the set, while keeping it securely chained. Camera and lighting technicians work with the trainer to devise ways of keeping the lion secure during its scenes with hidden restraints, and camera angles are modified so the actors spend as little time as possible in the same shot with the lion. It's too dangerous for Roddy to go to the airport, but letting a wild animal loose on set is apparently perfectly acceptable.

At the same time Roddy is tangling with a horse and a mountain lion, a dog is patiently waiting at MGM, where for two months the cast and crew have been shooting scenes that don't involve the main character in *Lassie Come Home*, a role slated for Roddy to start shooting the minute *Flicka* wraps. MGM is happy to schedule around Roddy, believing he's the only one who can bring the role to life. They're right. *Lassie* is the second movie Roddy makes as a kid that today qualifies officially as a classic. That isn't a subjective judgment. Since 1988, up to twenty-five films are chosen each year for preservation in the United States National Film Registry of the Library of Congress as being "culturally, historically, or aesthetically significant." In 1990, on the third induction, *How Green Was My Valley* is selected. *Lassie Come Home* joins the list in 1993, and Roddy's 1968 classic *Planet of the Apes* is added in 2001.

Just before starting *Lassie*, Roddy visits a site in Woodland Hills that he doesn't yet know much about. He and Virginia, along with three thousand members of the film community, gather for the dedication of the Motion Picture Country House, an ambitious project of the Motion Picture Relief Fund, where elderly members of the film community can be cared for if and when they can no longer care for themselves. Jean Hersholt, the actor who spearheads the project, personally reaches out to Winefriede to ask that Roddy attend. (The Academy honors Herscholt with three Special Oscars over the years for his charitable activities, and the Jean Hersholt Humanitarian Award is created in his name.)

Jean Hersholt has a special reason for wanting Roddy there. He hopes that as an important, very visible member of the younger generation of actors, Roddy will help his peers understand the necessity of having a place to honor and protect the people who have devoted their lives to the industry. Jean Hersholt may or may not know the prophetic wisdom of reaching out to Roddy McDowall, who's already unusually fascinated by Hollywood history, and who has an enormous capacity for empathy. The Motion Picture Country House, and its umbrella organization (that is later known as MPTF—the Motion Picture Television Fund) becomes and will remain an essential part of Roddy's life. It's the charity that means the most to him and the one he works the hardest to nurture and protect. His legacy lives on there to this day.

Lassie Come Home may not have the Oscar credentials of *How Green Was My Valley*, but its emotional impact hits just as hard, if not harder, particularly to a modern audience. Roddy is the boy, a dog called Pal plays Lassie, and the rest is magic. Donald Crisp is Roddy's father again and Elsa Lanchester is his mother. They live in Yorkshire, scratching out a bare-bones existence in the moors. Roddy and Lassie have a remarkable friendship, with an almost telepathic bond. When his parents are forced to sell her—it's that or starve—Roddy is devastated, but he bravely compartmentalizes his sorrow, ultimately not wishing to bring further pain to his parents. The buyer is aristocrat Nigel Bruce, who gives Lassie to his beloved granddaughter, the impossibly tiny, impossibly beautiful Elizabeth Taylor. Lassie has other ideas. She keeps escaping and running back to Roddy. Nigel realizes the dog will never stay put since she knows the way to her former home so well. He sends her to his estate far away in Scotland.

Lassie is undaunted. Her harrowing journey finding her way back to Roddy is remarkable, both in terms of the filming itself, and the ability of Pal to convey a sense of emotional connection. It may be our own anthropomorphizing that makes Lassie seem so expressive, but no matter, it works.

In 1993, when the American Film Institute salutes Elizabeth Taylor, Roddy remembers their first meeting fifty years previous.

"Well now, Bessie, when first we met, I was twelve and you were eight. And the lighting cameraman on *Lassie Come Home* was requesting you to please remove your false eyelashes. And you were demurely trying to explain that you weren't wearing any. And it was then I realized that there are some people—not too many to be sure—but there are some people who are born with a double set of lashes. And I began to giggle, because you were the most exquisite thing I had ever seen in my life and about the nicest. And it has been wonderful to watch you over the years matriculate as a human being, as an actress, and as a major contributor to the welfare of mankind. It makes this friend feel very proud. I value each one of those years of our friendship more than I can ever express."

Roddy isn't twelve and Elizabeth isn't eight—he's fourteen and she's ten, but Hollywood is so intent on keeping Roddy a child that he himself forgets that when he makes *Lassie*, still believably boyish, he is, if not yet on the cusp of manhood, certainly on the cusp of the cusp.

While *Lassie* is in production at MGM, *The White Cliffs of Dover* is shooting at Fox. In fact, both films have approximately the same start and wrap dates. Roddy is in both movies. So is Elizabeth. (Call back to *Photoplay* in 1971. "Do you think child actors of today are different from those of your time?" "Yes.") *The White Cliffs of Dover* is the epic wartime story of Irene Dunne as an American woman who marries English nobleman Alan Marshal only to lose him in World War I. Roddy McDowall is the son who never meets his father—a pint-sized Lord of the Manor bravely becoming the man of the house for his mother. Elizabeth Taylor is adorable as a little girl mooning over Roddy. An unpleasant encounter with some German boys claiming the Great War was not lost by their country, just unfinished, convinces Irene Dunne that one day another war in Europe is inevitable. She tries to take Roddy back to America to keep him out of harm's way. He asks her, "Do you think Father would want me to run away?" They stay in England, and all too soon Roddy McDowall and Elizabeth Taylor grow up to become Peter Lawford and June Lockhart. Peter dies in battle, just like his father, leaving Irene Dunne alone, certain in the knowledge that her husband and son's sacrifice is meaningful, but tragically missing them all the same. It's a giant hit—the fifth-highest-grossing film of the year. (Bing Crosby as a priest in *Going My*

Way is number one.) Today *The White Cliffs of Dover* comes across as a bit turgid and slow moving. Irene is as magnetic as ever—she's one of Roddy's favorite people, personally and professionally—but the film is a tough slog.

Roddy seems even younger in his next project, *On the Sunny Side*, as a British schoolboy sent from England to stay for the duration with family friends in Ohio. The "sunny side" of the Atlantic right now is America, while England fights for her life. The film utilizes documentary footage of child evacuees arriving in New York in the summer of 1940, intercutting it with Roddy standing on deck with some other evacuee children, all of them looking in awe across the water at the Statue of Liberty. "Isn't she splendid?" he says, then explaining to the other kids that France gave the statue to America as a birthday gift on the hundredth anniversary of American independence.

When he arrives at the home of his host family and meets their son, Freddie Mercer, fresh from a scrap with the class bully, proudly sporting a shiner, Roddy is impressed. "I say, that *is* a beauty. That must have been a jolly good scrap, *rah-THER*!" In interviews, Roddy peppers his speech with added Britishisms, sounding the same onscreen and off. It's not that British people don't use the phrases "Old chap," "My word," "I say," and "Rah-THER." It's that they don't tend to use all four in the same sentence.

Lots of scenes are written to gel with Roddy's public image. The other boys are fascinated by Roddy's bombing souvenir: a bullet-riddled propeller. When the boys in the gang ask Roddy about the air raids, which in truth he has nightmares about, he puts on a jocular, brave front, saying proudly, "Oh, London can take it!"

But can Roddy?

When *My Friend Flicka* is released, Roddy sets off on the usual press tour, which includes live appearances at movie theaters in larger cities where the film is playing. William Ragsdale, Roddy's costar forty years later on *Fright Night* remembers Roddy laughing one night at one of his famous dinner parties, telling the story of how, at one theater while he's introducing *Flicka*, some guy up in the balcony starts shouting, "Go fuck Flicka! Go fuck Flicka!" Roddy isn't quite sure how to respond so he doesn't. He keeps going. William is still incredulous thinking about it in 2025, forty years after Roddy tells the story in 1985, which is forty years after the fact. "He was just a kid, you know?" says William. "I mean, my God, how awful to experience that kind of bullying in front of a whole crowd of people when you're that young."

Critical and box office response to *My Friend Flicka* is positive, and over the years, it retains its magic, prompting Pauline Kael of *The New Yorker* to write, in 1982, "As a piece of moviemaking it's ordinary—and that's putting it kindly. But when Roddy McDowall is on the screen, that doesn't seem to matter; he has a magical seriousness. . . . It's one of the rare children's films—old or new—that doesn't make you choke up with rage."

Personal appearances to publicize film releases are paired with photo ops and publicity activities surrounding the war. The stars promote their films; they promote themselves; they promote the war; they sell war bonds. Often, they are presented with an honorary war bond as "payment" for their services. They then buy some war bonds themselves in a show of gratitude and generosity. In one sense it's all playacting. Yet it's also entirely sincere and deadly serious. Hollywood stars like Tyrone Power, Clark Gable, Jimmy Stewart, Henry Fonda, and Cesar Romero do a million photo ops visiting war factories and bolstering civilian morale. Each of these stars, and many more, also go into battle, risking their lives for real. Marlene Dietrich and Martha Raye risk their lives as well, entertaining the troops in Europe and sometimes finding themselves under enemy fire. Carole Lombard dies flying home from a war bond rally. Bette

Davis, Joan Crawford, Betty Grable, Lana Turner, Judy Garland, and Greer Garson pour coffee, serve doughnuts, and dance with servicemen at the Hollywood Canteen, where Winefriede and Virginia McDowall serve coffee and doughnuts right along with them, and where Roddy also does his part when he isn't shooting.

Back when his father is visiting, Roddy appears in those photo ops at the Hollywood Canteen with Thomas, just pretending to clear tables, empty ashtrays, and sweep up so that the photographers can get what they need. And those shots are printed and reprinted in newspapers and fan magazines from coast to coast. But what is make-believe for publicity for that day is also a real, continuing part of what Roddy contributes to the war effort.

Hollywood publicity is all fake. And it's all real.

Roddy's next two projects, *Keys of the Kingdom* and *Thunderhead: Son of Flicka* have script problems and are delayed several times. So Roddy hits the road. The headline in Dallas, Texas: "Youthful Star Gets a Typical Texas Greeting," with a photo of Roddy surrounded by a group of Women's Army Corps (WAC) servicewomen and standing in an Amphibious Jeep; he speaks to the Navy Mothers Clubs of America in Santa Ana, California; he kicks off a National Scrap Drive in Bayonne, New Jersey; he becomes an honorary chief of the Cheyenne tribe.

"Know ye that reposing special trust and confidence in the integrity and tolerance of our pale faced friend, I hereby make Roddy McDowall an Honorary Chief of the Cheyenne Tribe and do authorize and empower said friend to use the above title and fulfill the duties of that office, according to the laws of the five civilized Tribes of North America. In testimony whereof, I have caused the scribe of our tribe to attest this certificate and cause these letters to be made patent and the great Seal of our tribe situated in the state of Oklahoma, Indian territory to be hereafter affixed—signed and sealed by Chief Red Bird, attested to by Indian agent George Daransoll."

It's typical through much of the twentieth century for kids to play at being cowboys and Indians. How many of them become an authentic, certified Indian chief?

The Keys of the Kingdom depicts the life story of an unconventional Catholic priest who travels to China to start a mission. In flashback, the priest is Roddy McDowall, the son of Ruth Nelson, his Protestant mother, and Dennis Hoey, his Catholic father. An anti-Catholic mob beats Dennis near to death during a storm. As Ruth helps her battered husband home, a hanging footbridge over a raging river gives way. Roddy watches helplessly as both of his parents drown. Orphaned, he keeps a brave face with his young friend Peggy Ann Garner, who wants only to comfort him, but when alone, with the coffins of his parents brought to their home, he collapses, sobbing against the outside of the house. He grows up to be Gregory Peck and the story continues. (It has to be said that by this point, any actor finding out that Roddy McDowall is playing their kid knows they will probably get to play a death scene.)

Three films starring Roddy McDowall are released in 1943. *My Friend Flicka*, *Lassie Come Home*, and *On the Sunny Side.* If you're one of the moviegoing public, you imagine it's a pretty busy year for him, but it isn't. Those films were shot in 1942. He doesn't start shooting *Keys of the Kingdom* until February 1944, some fifteen months later—an eternity in terms of a boy on the verge of becoming a man. He stays busy with a Red Cross drive and then a war bond tour, with visits to Kansas City, Dallas, Chicago, Pittsburgh, Cleveland, Toledo, Salt Lake City, and Toronto. He raises $11 million in war bonds, and $2 million for British war relief. He appears in Boston with Carole Landis and Dana Andrews; with Carmen Miranda and Lynn Bari in New York; and the *Hollywood Reporter* reveals that in a poll among young movie fans under eighteen, Roddy McDowall has beaten

Mickey Rooney to take first place among their favorite young stars. And Macy's is very sorry to report that they are completely sold out of their entire range of Roddy McDowall children's ties.

Radio broadcasts are a routine part of life at this point. Often the shows are abridged versions of his films. Sometimes they are interviews at premieres or other events. There are also special broadcasts that go over the Armed Forces Radio Network to American troops. These are usually tightly scripted comedy skits acted out under a meta guise of Hollywood stars being "just regular folks."

In a *Command Performance USA* broadcast, Frank Sinatra sings and banters with Frances Langford. Little Elizabeth Taylor shows up asking for an autograph from her very favorite singer . . . "Miss Langford." She doesn't want Frank Sinatra's autograph. He's too scrawny. Then tiny Margaret O'Brien arrives, also insulting Frank Sinatra about his thinness. Roddy McDowall and Peggy Ann Garner pop in saying they have been engaged for nine years, since nursery school, but Roddy is tired of how much she likes listening to Frank Sinatra records. He hopes if she gets a look at how weak and skinny he is, she will get over her infatuation. "Better move your chair," Roddy warns. "Unless you get him at the right angle, you can't see him at all!" Roddy McDowall and Elizabeth Taylor are irrepressible, cheeky kids teasing the young Sinatra. Fast forward four decades and Elizabeth Taylor and Frank Sinatra are American national treasures showing up at the same events to receive various life achievement awards, often with Roddy McDowall in attendance, all tearful smiles handing Elizabeth an award, or standing in an ovation, clapping and beaming for Frank. Elizabeth hands Roddy a couple of awards too. While making this broadcast, the three of them can't possibly conceive how their lives will remain intertwined.

Roddy finishes up his raft of personal appearances and reports back to the studio.

In his first scene in *Kingdom*, he's almost unrecognizable until he starts to speak. Then the voice is unmistakably his. He does a wonderful job. The problem is that he doesn't look like a little boy anymore. And through a Hollywood lens, the problem isn't only that he's growing up, it's also that he looks decidedly awkward from some angles. He's fifteen going on sixteen, and by movie star standards, he suddenly isn't as attractive. By any normal, reasonable standard, he's still very good-looking, but the entertainment industry doesn't trade in "normal" or "reasonable." The magnetic quality that made it impossible to turn away from him as recently as his last two films is suddenly missing. Roddy and his family are as yet unaware of any big shift. They know Roddy is growing up, of course, but his box-office popularity is solid, and his fan mail is robust.

He's also popular among his own age group in real life. Throughout the war, Winefriede enlarges her gatherings, going from relatively formal affairs for the press and people from the studio to weekends and evenings with Roddy's young studio friends. Winefriede invites everybody.

"But I don't think *Roddy* really ever invited anybody," actor Farley Granger remembers in his autobiography. In 1944, Farley is shooting *The Purple Heart* at Fox with Dana Andrews and Richard Conte. He's seventeen and working on just this one picture, without the safety of a long-term contract. "The fact that we were all supposed to be very sophisticated and well-known, so therefore we must be leading these wonderful glamorous social lives was a total fiction. None of us had any place to go, and few of us had many friends. But Roddy's mother created this atmosphere in their home. It was kind of the gathering place."

Winefriede is a warm, fun hostess to their guests. She always has plenty of food, and the attitude is the more the merrier. For Roddy and Virginia, though, it's more of the same. Winefriede stays in charge, controlling what happens in their lives, even if it's when and with whom they swim or who gets paired for badminton. Winefriede is at the center of every interaction. It's why they seldom go out to anyone else's house. She can't control things that aren't under her own roof.

For Farley, it's an oasis from his own dysfunctional family. When the invitations come to stay for dinner and spend the night, he jumps at the chance to be in an atmosphere without the drinking and fighting during meals at home. And it's so close to the studio, where they both have early calls. Roddy and Farley grow very close during this time, and an inference can be drawn from some of their later correspondence over the years that their nights together might include a bit of sexual experimentation. They remain friends throughout Roddy's life.

Later, after appearing in *Holiday in Mexico*, Jane Powell becomes a regular. "If it hadn't been for the Sundays at Roddy's, I don't know what I'd have done. I think he saw the loneliness in me," she tells Dickie Moore for his memoir. "Elizabeth [Taylor] was younger than I was. And, of course, she was very sophisticated, but she never went any place either."

Farley Granger's film, *The Purple Heart* is the gritty story of a downed bomber crew imprisoned in a brutal war camp in Japan. During the shoot, Farley turns eighteen and must begin his real military service once the film wraps. If Fox wants to offer him a contract, he can likely stay out of the military for all practical purposes. There are ways for Hollywood personalities to serve while staying well clear of combat. Landing a studio contract really can be a life-or-death proposition.

Soon after Farley goes into the service, Fox puts Roddy into a sequel, *Thunderhead: Son of Flicka.* It hits a lot of the same beats as its predecessor, with the addition of an exciting horse race with Roddy as the jockey (and someone else in the dangerous long shots). It opens with a seal of approval from the Humane Society, but there are some truly brutal scenes of horses stomping and beating other horses to death. It's incredibly violent for what's intended as a film for the whole family. Virginia, now eighteen and a high school graduate, works on the shoot with Roddy, as a stand-in for Rita Johnson, his mother. Roddy loves the horse that plays Thunderhead, as opposed to his dislike of Flicka, and he gives virtually the same performance he gives in the first film, which is exactly what's asked of him.

It does fine at the box office but isn't a big hit. Perhaps Jane Withers can point the way.

Generally forgotten, though some Boomers and Gen-Xers may remember her as Josephine the plumber in a series of TV ads for Comet cleanser, Jane Withers is one of Fox's most profitable stars of the late 1930s and early 1940s. She comes to the McDowall Sunday get-togethers occasionally but isn't one of the regulars. She hosts her own weekend gatherings, also with swimming and badminton. Where most of Roddy's friends are trying to find their way toward adulthood, Jane is firmly entrenched in a kind of parody of girlhood. She relishes showing off her giant well-publicized doll collection to friends and acquaintances, turning every visit into a veritable tour. Some of her contemporaries, including Farley Granger, remember these tours as rather weird, creepy experiences. Jane carves out a niche as the topline star of a series of B pictures at Fox and Republic that never rack up the kind of grosses that Roddy's A pictures do, but because they're so cheap, they make a lot of money for the studios. Jane churns out film after film—popular fare like *Her First Beau*, *A Very Young Lady*, *Small Town Deb*, *My Best Gal*, and *Kitty O'Hara, Performer.*

Jane's big hits are screwball comedies mostly (some would say "cornball") and miles away from anything Roddy has done since *Just William* in 1938. But maybe her kind of film is a path forward for Roddy. When Winefriede takes it upon herself in 1937 to push director Monty Banks to cast Roddy in the musical *We're Going to Be Rich*, the star of that film is Gracie Fields, who also just happens to have an upcoming project at Fox, a screwball comedy, *Molly and Me*, with Roddy's friend Monty Woolley. While it's not strictly analogous to a Jane Withers vehicle, its emphasis on physical comedy and visual humor puts it in a very different realm than Roddy's other Fox films.

Gracie Fields is Molly, an actress desperate for work. Tired of the ups and downs of life in the theater, she decides to play a very different kind of part—that of an experienced housekeeper to Monty Woolley, a stuffy and tyrannical retired member of Parliament, who's ostensibly a widower, and who has a strained relationship with his son, Roddy McDowall. Reginald Gardiner is the butler with a drinking problem, who it turns out is also an actor. Monty and Roddy need some life in their lives, and Gracie is just the woman to do it. She encourages Monty to return to politics, his first love, and she inspires Roddy to let his hair down. Gracie fires the rest of the staff when she realizes they're robbing their employer blind, and she replaces them all with fellow actors. Roddy gets a chance to do a hilarious impression of his father and has some fine comic moments below stairs with the actors masquerading as staff. The final set piece is Gracie staging a murder, which for complicated plot-related reasons successfully protects Monty and Roddy from a blackmail attempt they know nothing about.

It's set in 1937 to avoid having to deal with World War II. Roddy manages to rise above the trap of feeling sorry for himself, though it's really the role's only function. Particularly when he opines about his father not liking him because he reminds his father of his sainted dead mother, who unbeknownst to Roddy is very much alive and a floozy. *She's the blackmailer.* Roddy never finds out, and more is the pity, since a revelation like that would give him something more interesting to do. Everyone else has a whale of a time, but although third billed above the title, Roddy's role is written as a plot device rather than a character. He gets a change of pace in a screwball comedy, but Fox wastes the opportunity.

A typical blurring of fantasy and reality occurs one day at the studio school on the lot. The teacher takes him and the other students on a field trip to the set of *Wilson*, a movie on the life of President Woodrow Wilson. The teacher treats the set as if they're in the real White House, like it's an actual educational opportunity. The kids are a little dubious. It's just a set, after all. But later, when Roddy visits the actual White House, he can't tell the difference. "The set for the movie was so accurate, right down to the doorknobs," he tells the *Boston Globe* in 1987. "You really couldn't tell the difference between the make-believe and the real." The confusion doesn't end there. Add the haze of memory and the blur gets more pronounced. When Roddy gives this interview to the *Boston Globe*, they print his quote and his version of the events without checking. Roddy says he visited that set at MGM with Elizabeth Taylor and Debbie Reynolds by his side. Debbie Reynolds doesn't sign with MGM until 1948, several years after the making of *Wilson*, when Roddy is twenty and no longer in school or at Fox. And *Wilson* is a Fox film (that loses a boatload of money). There is no MGM film about Woodrow Wilson. The *Boston Globe*'s headline is "MGM's Woodrow Wilson Tour." This isn't to throw shade on anyone at the *Boston Globe.* Someone may find something similar in this book. Memory is changeable. That's why eyewitness testimony can be so fallible.

Following *Molly and Me*, Roddy makes more personal appearances at war bond rallies and other war-related events. His next assignment isn't for another several months, a loan-out to MGM for *Holiday in Mexico*. In the interim, a few other events come up. Germany surrenders. A few months later, so does Japan. In between the two events, Roddy has costume fittings for *Holiday in Mexico.* This isn't in any way to suggest that Roddy isn't as deeply affected as everyone else by the war finally coming to an end. It means his father will come home. It means . . . so many things. The war has been such a huge part of life and his career that he can't really imagine what life will be like without it. He celebrates with Winefriede and Virginia. They attend parties and galas. They honor the returning servicemen and servicewomen.

And Roddy hopes for a career boost with *Holiday in Mexico.*

But he has the grace to keep such personal concerns to himself. He knows his anxieties about his work are small potatoes in the face of world events, but the anxieties don't just go away. And Hollywood is a place where putting your career above all other concerns isn't just tolerated, it's celebrated.

Apart from the excitement and relief of the war ending, Winefriede is business as usual when it comes to Roddy's career and their lives in Los Angeles. Roddy, however, sees some warning signs. It isn't that he doesn't like the scripts Fox is sending him. It's that they aren't sending him *any* scripts. Everyone including Zanuck himself assures him that he has a bright future at Fox, that he's one of the family, beloved by all.

But there are no scripts. Just the loan-out to MGM. He's seventeen years old and clearly on the verge of actual manhood. At least *Holiday in Mexico* gives him an opportunity to play, if not an adult, a character his own age: A wealthy, young, somewhat nerdy young man, son of the British ambassador to Mexico, who gets into romantic complications with Jane Powell, the wealthy, young, strong-willed daughter of the American ambassador. And she sings a little. The cast also includes Roddy's friend Walter Pidgeon, bandleaders José Iturbi and Xavier Cugat, and Ilona Massey. The stakes aren't high. Roddy and Jane will obviously remain sweethearts, even as she becomes comically convinced that her destiny is with José Iturbi, a man pushing fifty. Roddy does a fantastic series of pratfalls, exhibiting physical comedy skills that are a happy surprise. He gets the girl and then, for no apparent reason, with no connection to the plot whatsoever, Jane sings "Ave Maria" to an audience of thousands (a painted backdrop) and everyone is so happy that it feels like a "Holiday." In Mexico.

Winefriede makes a point of sending *Holiday in Mexico* director George Sidney a birthday card. He writes back: "Dear mommy in a million. Thanks for your very thoughtful card on my birthday. Let me in turn congratulate you on having raised such a wonderful young man. We are all reflections of our surroundings and our parents, and Roddy certainly reflects all the goodness and kindness that is you. I think this is very wonderful. Good luck to you both. Love George Sidney." It's a reassuring letter, as is a similar letter from producer Joe Pasternak.

"Dear 'Mommy' (for Mrs. McDowall), I appreciate your note. Not only do I think and feel that Roddy is a wonderful artist, but it was a pleasure to have him on the picture, because he's a perfect gentleman. Which we so seldom can say about some of our other artists, young or old."

Roddy goes on the *Holiday in Mexico* press tour with optimism and determination. MGM says they love his work in the film, and Jane Powell seems poised on the verge of a major career. Perhaps *Holiday in Mexico* will be the shot in the arm he's hoping for. Under Roddy's byline, a piece appears in *The Saturday Evening Post.*

"The Role I Liked Best—by Roddy McDowall. To me the role of Stanley Owen in *Holiday in Mexico* was tops. Right from the first the set was as gay as the title. We all started off, in the Pasternak tradition, by sipping some champagne, and after each take was finished, Xavier Cugat would play a rumba. Walter Pidgeon was just as nice to me as he can be, and that means very nice indeed. Jane Powell was as bubbling as that champagne we sipped the first day. And José Iturbi was just as pleasant in a quieter way, except when he had difficulty phrasing some thought clearly. That always worried him and surprised me, because if I could play the piano like Iturbi, I wouldn't worry about anything else!"

Roddy gets good reviews. Typical is the notice from *The New York Herald Tribune*: "A brash young man named McDowall is neither oppressively British nor offensively juvenile and provides the principal comedy of the falling and clattering variety." Funnier, but with a nod to Roddy's age, is *The New Yorker*'s John McCarten. "Into this atmosphere of determined Latin gaiety, the producers have plunged Roddy McDowall, who was only the other day, mooning childishly over Lassie the dog and Flicka the horse. Master McDowall is getting to be a big boy now, but it still doesn't seem as if he ought to be chasing girls, even girls as young as Jane Powell, the little songbird of *Holiday in Mexico*, who warbles with the persistence of a canary. Perhaps to make Roddy feel at home, the picture includes a Saint Bernard and a Chihuahua, but neither of them is up to the canine artistic standard set by the ineffable Lassie."

Holiday in Mexico does well if not spectacularly at the box office. It's sort of a precursor to *A Date with Judy*, MGM's 1948 all-star extravaganza, again starring Jane Powell and featuring Xavier Cugat; this time with a lineup that includes Wallace Beery, Elizabeth Taylor, Carmen Miranda, and Robert Stack, plus Scotty Beckett in the Roddy McDowall role: A rich, young, slightly geeky "regular" guy who still gets the girl. A case can be made that Scotty Beckett, a poised young man with conventionally good looks, who *pretends* to be awkward and nerdy, is more romantically appealing than Roddy McDowall, who at this transitional moment in his life, actually *is* awkward and nerdy.

Roddy's breathtaking ability to communicate loss and grief, the emotional magnetism that can move audiences to tears with a single close-up, is just not as relevant or marketable at age eighteen as it was at age twelve. Joe Pasternak, his producer on *Holiday in Mexico*, continues to be very complimentary—as well he should be, Roddy is very good in the film—and he talks about how much he hopes Roddy will come and work at MGM again. Certainly, he means it. Roddy is terrific to work with.

Then Winefriede makes a fatal error. Things at Fox may not

be going well, but Roddy has a year left on his contract. Somehow, she misunderstands Joe Pasternak's compliments and thinks he's making an actual offer. Then Winefriede persuades Fox to let Roddy out of his seven-year contract early so he can sign with MGM. Joe Pasternak, however, isn't in charge of deciding who the studio puts under contract. When Roddy is released from Fox, MGM isn't interested. Neither is any other studio. No one wants to add an expensive, awkward adolescent to their list of contract players.

Roddy is his family's sole breadwinner, and thanks to his mother, he's unemployed.

Chapter 3

Remains to Be Seen

Thomas McDowall arrives in Los Angeles just after *Holiday in Mexico* wraps, but before Roddy leaves Fox. He's thrilled to be reunited with his family, but in one sense, it isn't a homecoming at all. Other than his two-week leave, he has no knowledge of the city and nothing other than his family to anchor him to such a strange place.

The manners and dress of Hollywood people in 1945 are far more formal than the twenty-first century's aggressively casual customs. But to a Brit born in the nineteenth century, the way people behave in California post–World War II is incomprehensible. They're so overly familiar, taking for granted that anyone and everyone wants to hear about their latest films, their latest romances, and their latest purchases. There are some aspects of it he loves. Like most Brits, he regards the endless sunshine as a daily miracle. And the cheerfulness of the place may be a bit surreal at times, but it beats returning to London, where the city is in ruins.

The Hollywood entertainment industry is the thing he can't wrap his head around.

In England, his children working on film sets emerged naturally from their lessons at their drama school. Unusual, certainly, but easy to understand. The studios there were part of the city. They seemed *normal*. The MGM and Fox lots are massive cities of their own devising, filled with people who believe they're at the very center of the universe. Nothing is more important than what they do. No war, or scientific advance, or act of real-life bravery can compete. It's deeply troubling.

He sees Roddy on a frantic hamster wheel, with little understanding yet of some of the reasons underpinning of his son's sense of urgency. His wife is drunk with the excitement of her own constant motion. Everything seems an emergency. What if such and such reporter thinks Roddy isn't talented anymore? Someone isn't returning her call, what does it mean? What if Virginia doesn't get her acting career back on track?

Winefriede sent Thomas press clippings throughout the war, but in looking at the scrapbooks about Roddy that she and Virginia have created, Thomas is struck by the immensity of what his son has accomplished in his five years in America. Understanding that a film has done well and won an award, or that another film gives Roddy a chance to be some kind of Indian chief—these are digestible. Seeing all of it compiled, though, is another matter. It's overwhelming. Thomas feels unnecessary to the operation and unsure what his next steps are to make these strange circumstances feel like home.

Roddy and Winefriede travel to New York for one of his *Holiday in Mexico* appearances, and Thomas is bewildered at being on his own. He writes to a friend, "I do not pretend to be able to understand the show business and so cannot tell you why just as I've returned, they left and will not be back until next week. . . . Virginia is quite well, however, and keeping house very successfully for me."

One thing that *is* familiar to Thomas is a sense of isolation. Not just during the time when Roddy and Winefriede are out of town, but even when the house is full of people. The McDowall family's life here is nothing like it was back in London, with the four of them on their own so much. Thomas recognizes many though not all of the friends and acquaintances at the McDowall house swimming on a Sunday or eating dinner with them during the week. It seems all of young Hollywood is there: You could bump into Elizabeth Taylor, Peggy Ann Garner, Darryl Hickman, Jane Powell, Donald O'Connor, Jane Withers, Bonita Granville, Natalie Wood, Gloria Jean, Dickie Moore, Scotty Beckett, Ann Rutherford, Jackie Cooper, Mickey Rooney, Margaret O'Brien, Freddie Bartholomew, and occasionally, a very young Dean Stockwell (who later becomes part of a very different phase of Roddy's life and career).

Yet Winefriede is so intent on things playing out with a story in her mind of how it's all supposed to go that it feels a bit like they're all under glass. The sense of it being like a cocoon is part of what makes it feel safe to these young performers, all of whom cope with public and private pressures that their civilian peers don't encounter. But cocoons can feel stifling if you're never allowed to emerge. This is the sense of isolation Thomas feels. He never communicates it explicitly or in those terms, yet when he resorts to a phrase like "you know what your mother is like," as he often does in response to his children's growing frustrations over the next few years, this sense of her need to control them is clearly what he's referring to. Winefriede's children do love her dearly, but they also long for freedom.

Freedom isn't yet in the cards for Roddy. When he leaves Fox, now, instead of the studio dictating his professional activities, Winefriede leaps in to fill the vacuum. Just like the old days in London. She works closely with his agent, Wynn Rocamora, to fill Roddy's life with as many paying gigs as possible. Being unemployed is shocking to Roddy without actually being surprising. He has had some warnings. While at MGM making *Holiday in Mexico*, the studio drama coach is blunt, saying, "Until you're twenty-seven, nothing is ever going to happen to you again." Wynn Rocamora is willing to work hard with Winefriede but responds to Roddy's sudden lack of a studio contract with a stark observation: "Just remember, it's possible you might never work again."

Roddy feels he's failing everyone.

In Dickie Moore's memoir, he quotes Roddy comparing himself to his friend Natalie Wood, who also experiences serious growing pains upon hitting adolescence. "Many of us shared Natalie's inordinate sense of responsibility, not just for ourselves, but for the pictures we were in," says Roddy. "When we saw ourselves on screen, we thought we could have improved our performances. I had a sense of wanting to do better, but I didn't know what 'better' was."

In Roddy's mind, if he could make his performances better, maybe MGM would want him. Maybe Fox would keep giving him scripts. Maybe he wouldn't be out of work, feeling strangely helpless. He's very good at compartmentalizing this fall from grace. In later interviews, and in letters with friends, he identifies it as a simple question of growing up. The upheaval is down to circumstances entirely outside of his control. This isn't how he internalizes the situation at the time, however. Not only does he have the pressure of believing everything is his fault, but he's also absolutely certain that he mustn't show any sign of struggle or fear. Virginia is perhaps the only one who understands. Not that he shows his struggle or fear to Virginia either. She understands it without discussion, because she feels it too. She writes about it many years later, acknowledging the perils he faces at this tumultuous time of transition.

He idly wonders what it would be like to go to college. It's not a deep desire by any means—Roddy loves learning but isn't particularly keen on doing it in a classroom setting. Still, isn't college what kids his age are doing now? "How could I go to college? There wasn't enough money," he says to Gavin Lambert. "Who was going to do the work?" When he brings up the idea of college to Winefriede, she stays true to form, telling him that of course he can go to college, he can do anything he wants to do. No one is stopping him. She then slowly and painfully explains the way things will collapse in the family's life together if Roddy doesn't continue bringing home the bacon.

The split from Fox has unintended benefits for Winefriede as she takes the bull by the horns. She likes having control of Roddy's career again. She has missed it. And Winefriede does have an excellent idea. Theater. She reads all the sections of the trades, combing through the articles on film, radio, theater, and vaudeville. There's money in theater and the experience will be good for Roddy. They start by putting Roddy in *Young Woodley* for the summer stock circuit of 1946. The production will continue on past the summer season, through the winter, eight months into 1947, with gaps in the schedule at different points for Roddy to fulfill various other commitments.

One of those commitments is complying with the Selective Service Act of 1946. He goes on the books in the Organized Reserve Corps as a private in the 67th Armored Infantry Battalion Division. This typically requires one drill weekend per month which involves a combination of physical training, weapons instruction, tactical exercises, and administrative duties. Then in the summer, a two-week field training exercise is required. There is no record in his archives of any such activities. Local commanding officers have wide latitude at the time in how reserve obligations are enforced. In Los Angeles and New York, commanders often accommodate filming schedules, promotional tours, and theater engagements.

Young Woodley is the play that launches Roddy's stage career. It's also the play that launches Douglas Fairbanks Jr. on the Hollywood scene in 1927 (and it's how he meets first wife, Joan Crawford, who becomes something of a groupie, seeing the show a number of times). Its plot of a British student struggling with his infatuation for his headmaster's wife and the headmaster's subsequent plan for revenge is a logical step for Roddy, allowing him to broaden his film persona from sensitive kid, to sensitive kid with a libido. Stock isn't a comedown. Stars like Helen Hayes, Gertrude Lawrence, Gregory Peck, Freddie Bartholomew, and Tallulah Bankhead are on the boards the same season.

The selling point to the theaters is that the same star or stars agree to appear in a show at a number of venues, with each venue hiring a local supporting cast, and staging the show after a short rehearsal period—often as little as one week. The money is fairly good. Winefriede adds a twist though, stipulating that she function as the company manager, responsible for approving the casts at each theater and sitting in on auditions. At two of the East Coast theaters, Westport Country Playhouse in Connecticut and the North Shore Players in Massachusetts, a very young Jack Lemmon auditions and is cast in a supporting role. His accent is so good Winifriede thinks he's English. He vividly remembers Winefriede's obsessive concern for detail as the company manager and how she seems in charge of everything. Estelle Parsons plays a bit part. The tour culminates in Mexico City. Photographers capture Roddy's arrival in every city, staging pictures of him with local high school girls and young debutantes at parties.

The McDowalls hire their own publicist, and another idea pops up. A vaudeville tour. Live entertainment in between movie showings is still popular. (Disney revives the practice to great success in the 1990s at the El Capitan Theatre in Hollywood.) A six-month national vaudeville tour is laid out, dovetailing with Roddy's appearances in *Young Woodley.* He often gets booked into theaters splitting the week with Mickey Rooney, who's also finding the transition to adulthood problematic, with Roddy headlining a show for three days followed by Mickey Rooney and a singer named Connie Haines for four days. The poster for one of Roddy's typical shows promises: "Direct from Hollywood, On Stage and in Person, Roddy McDowall, Youthful Screen Star in *A Gala Vaudeville Show* with Joe, Lou & Marilyn Gaites: *The Past and Present in Dancing*, Jack Leonard: *A Ton of Laughs*, The Atlas Trio: *Acrobatic Novelties*, and Extra Attraction in Person, Glamorous Singing Star of Pictures, Ruth Terry!" Four stage shows daily starting at eleven o'clock in the morning. *The Courier-Journal* approves: "Tall, dark, and 18, actor Roddy McDowall is in Louisville this week and now we know why Lassie came home. The movie star, appearing on the National Theatre stage today through Sunday, is an irresistible combination of sophistication and bright-eyed boyishness." Roddy doesn't remember it happily, later kidding that he's so awful, he's probably the sole reason vaudeville dies.

In between his vaudeville appearances and theater performances, he heads to New York or back to Los Angeles to star in radio dramas like *Suspense* ("Sponsored by Roma Wine, the better-tasting California wine!") and entertainment programs like *The Kate Smith Hour*. Roddy also starts a multiyear stint as a guest host of a radio anthology series called *Family Theater*. At the opening of each broadcast, an announcer intones, "More things are wrought by prayer than this world dreams of." The vibe is family oriented, religious, and morally upright. Roddy usually acts as a host but occasionally he acts in various stories as well, along with stars like Ann Blyth, John Sutton, and Patricia Morrison.

Thomas occasionally becomes a public part of the circus. He goes on the radio with Roddy for a "Keep Up with the Kids" quiz segment that pits a parent against one of their children; he also appears at the Shrine Auditorium in the *Father and Son* show, benefiting the Los Angeles Junior Chamber of Commerce. Overall, though, Thomas isn't particularly interested in any sort of public life, nor does he seek to call attention to himself when Winefriede entertains. That reticence on his part helps Roddy regard his father as a touchstone to the days of Thomas reading classic literature and Roddy learning Shakespeare passages, at home and then at drama school.

Roddy still dreams of performing classical roles, and he's

overjoyed when Orson Welles approaches him about taking on the role of Malcolm in a production of *Macbeth* in mid-1947. Orson will stage the show first at the University of Utah for four days as part of Salt Lake City's Centennial Festival, then shoot a condensed, experimental, surreal version of the story on film over twenty-three days on the lot at Republic Studios in Studio City. Roddy views it as a marvelous opportunity, and the chance to stretch his wings proves a positive harbinger of things to come. His childhood familiarity with Shakespeare gives him confidence. A key decision Orson Welles makes is to have the cast perform with Scottish accents—a request the actors respond to with differing degrees of proficiency. Orson Welles exhibits great inconsistency with his own.

The stage production is well received in its few performances. After screenings of the film version, however, in Denver, Salt Lake City, and San Francisco, many complain that the Scottish accents render the dialogue incomprehensible, and Republic makes the drastic decision to rerecord 65 percent of the film. The accents are actually pretty good, especially considering the nonexacting standards of the era, and the dialogue is understandable. Roddy handles the language very well, but he can't seem to convey Malcolm's sense of righteous anger at the murder of his father or his aching need for revenge. Although the project is a critical and commercial disaster when it's released domestically and in the UK in 1948, it's successful in many non-English-speaking countries, especially France, where critics laud Welles's highly stylized approach. They are right. Even with the feeling of distance that comes with so much dialogue looping, there's such immediacy, and so much energy and movement. The film sustains its air of breathless dread and horror, due to its clear vision and, in no small measure as well, to Jeanette Nolan's brilliant film debut as Lady Macbeth.

Working with Orson Welles is intriguing. Roddy admires the director's approach to *Macbeth* but comes to believe that his sense of self-importance dooms the project. "As the English say, he was ultimately too clever by half," Roddy says in the 1988 *Films in Review* piece. "He did a lot of damage to his own genius for some perverse reason, which I don't particularly understand."

Roddy signs a five-year contract with producer Lindsley Parsons for two pictures per year, released through Allied Artists, at Monogram Pictures. Parsons tends to have the better product among the "poverty row" producers at Monogram, and he has high ambitions to make a dent in the stranglehold that the "Big Six" studios (20th Century-Fox, Columbia, MGM, Paramount, Universal, and Warner Bros.) have on the marketplace. Roddy will get associate producer credits on all ten of the films, and although much is made in the press about him being the youngest producer ever and what his important responsibilities will be, it's a vanity credit. Roddy has no hand in producing the projects.

His proposed Monogram projects are more high-profile than the studio's usual releases, and Monogram believes strongly that their box-office prospects will benefit greatly from Roddy's continued stardom. That's also one of the ironies of Roddy's life at present. Even as the studios show no interest, the consumer and trade press, the fans, and the fan magazines still treat him like it's 1944. It could be lingering goodwill because of the beauty and simplicity of his early screen work. Everyone seems to wish him well, with none of the schadenfreude that can turn people like Louella Parsons and Hedda Hopper into vultures circling a fresh kill. Louella and Hedda keep writing about his exciting new projects, how grown-up he is, and how he has his pick of the girls.

Monogram films, even the high-profile ones, are shot sometimes in as little as ten days, and lack sophistication, both narratively and technically. Roddy's first, *Rocky*, is a canine retread of *Flicka* with a plot revolving around the offspring of a sheep-killing wild dog instead of the offspring of a "loco" horse. Critical comparisons with *Lassie* and *My Friend Flicka* in the press aren't particularly snarky. They note the similarities without making it seem like Roddy's career is on the rocks, as they might do for other stars facing career downturns. Monogram is happy to have any press, good or bad. It's a new experience for them, knowing that anything they release with Roddy will get treated in the trades and the major dailies with much the same attention as a film of his has always gotten. Their bet on Roddy pays off almost immediately.

His next film, Robert Louis Stevenson's *Kidnapped*, is the familiar story of an eighteenth-century Scottish orphan who tries to claim his inheritance but is kidnapped and sold into slavery by his nefarious uncle, who wants the inheritance for himself. From a filmmaking standpoint, rather than comparing it to its literary source, *Kidnapped* is basically a low-rent *Son of Fury* with Roddy in the Tyrone Power role. For a Monogram film, though, this period piece is quite expensive, and the shoot lasts almost a month.

Winefriede gets a happy surprise when Roddy arranges a small bit part for her as an innkeeper's wife. She handles the scene well enough, describing the meal on offer. Roddy feels increasingly insecure about his performance, however, believing his work is uneven, and he isn't wrong. His performance is perfectly serviceable, but no different from that of any other moderately talented male ingenue. Crucially, it lacks true believability. There is a tiny moment that illustrates the problem: As he heads to meet his uncle for the first time, he narrates in voice-over. "The sun began to shine on the hilltops as I went down the road." (The fact that the hills are clearly California, not Scotland, doesn't help the believability issue.) He stops and asks for directions. "If you take my word for it, you'll steer clear of the house of Shaws," the man says ominously. Roddy is supposed to be confused by this comment. So he *shows* us how confused he is by doing a double take and shaking his head. He's so busy *showing* us that he's confused, he doesn't take the time to actually *be* confused. He's trying too hard, and it robs him of the magic that makes his childhood roles so memorable.

His early acting training in England, a very presentational style of performing, isn't transferable to the screen at all. And his experience in films as a child feels evanescent. There is no technique to those performances—they're the work of a very observant, impressionable child, able to translate the desires of the adults around him into flesh-and-blood characters by a kind of alchemy. He intuits what they want and becomes that person.

There is no way to sustain that method into adulthood. The intentions and desires of adult characters are complex, and their actions and motivations are rarely straightforward, adding layers of subtext to the process. This is an oversimplification to an extent, but take a moment in a scene where love needs to be conveyed. Generally speaking, what a child actor needs to do is tap into a feeling of love and say something clear and declarative, or more often, say nothing at all. Just look at the other character with their big, innocent eyes and wait for the director to say, "Cut." This isn't to suggest that it's easy. It's extraordinary if a child has the capacity to communicate emotion that way, but the *process* is usually (though certainly not always) relatively unencumbered by subtext. Conversely, adult acting is sometimes more about subtext than about the text itself. And achieving it takes technique—which is what Roddy believes he lacks. Couple that with his self-consciousness about his looks in these transitional years. He feels thin, awkward, and ugly. That's what he sees when he looks in the mirror, regardless of what anyone else sees.

He does his job and gives a performance, often excellently, but he doesn't feel satisfied, because he doesn't know how he achieves anything good or what he's doing wrong when he's unhappy with his performance. And he often finds the narratives of his current projects reductive. They push the same buttons over and over, looking at coming of age as a problem unto itself. It's not the path to building a career with any staying power.

A little more than a week before his nineteenth birthday, Roddy is in a serious collision in the early hours of the morning coming home from a party with Virginia, a friend, actor Dick Long, and Dick's sister, Barbara. Detour and construction signs erected during construction work cause the roadway to narrow, and the other driver crosses into Roddy's path. Though Roddy isn't cited or accused of being at fault, it makes for bad publicity. It may be the first negative publicity of his life, the inference being that a group of teenagers shouldn't be driving around at two o'clock in the morning. They all suffer multiple cuts and bruises, with Virginia also losing some teeth and Barbara spraining her ankle and fracturing her thumb. On September 10, the *Los Angeles Times* reports that two men in the other car are suing Roddy, accusing him of being to blame for their injuries and lost wages. The outcome is unknown. There is apparently no record of the lawsuit being adjudicated one way or the other and no record of any financial payouts in the McDowall archives.

Perhaps it's a little specious to draw a comparison between losing control of his car and having no control over his career, but he has essentially returned to his days as a ten-year-old child, his mother controlling everything at home and at work. He feels like a windup doll. No stone is unturned. Harkening back to his days doing print ads for Rice Krispies and Lifebuoy, here is Roddy in a supermarket point-of-purchase ad, posing with a kitchen gadget:

"Roddy McDowall, a friendly, young cinema star, demonstrates cutting equipment that any homemaker would enjoy owning. Here, Roddy shows how easy it is to slice cucumbers and potatoes paper-thin yet crisp, and how to grate carrots and cabbage to perfection with no loss of juice. . . . Mr. McDowall is starring currently in Monogram's *Kidnapped*, the Robert Lewis Stevenson story."

Now that Winefriede is back in charge on the career front, she resurrects the idea that Virginia will become a successful actor too. After her bit in *Man Hunt*, three other uncredited appearances with no dialogue and the *Thunderhead* stand-in job are the only work she has had. Winefriede's resolve actually pays off this time, with an incredibly exciting opportunity. While in New York with Roddy doing one of his vaudeville shows, Winefriede wangles an invitation for Virginia and Roddy to meet the great British actress, Dame May Whitty. Uncertain of his future prospects, Roddy asks the venerable actress whether she thinks he has any talent. She asks him to do a scene for her, right there and then.

Roddy and Virginia do the balcony scene from *Romeo and Juliet*, a piece they learned backward and forward in their days at the Hanover Academy. When they're finished Dame May turns to Roddy and says, "Your sister is very talented." She asks if she might arrange for Virginia to audition for the Margaret Webster Shakespeare Company. They are casting for a company of twenty-two actors to embark on a college campus tour of *Hamlet* and *Macbeth*. Elated, Virginia says yes immediately. Roddy is excited for his sister, but he has more questions. He explains that he wants to be a great actor, like Laurence Olivier, but isn't sure how to go about it. Dame May assures him that "Larry is capable of being a tremendously bad actor." She remembers him as quite bad in his early days. "[But] he had the greatest gift anyone can have: He never stopped learning." That's the advice Dame May has to offer: Don't stop learning. Roddy writes that down and thinks about it often. He likes to learn too.

Virginia prepares for the audition. The Margaret Webster Shakespeare Company is a very big deal. Margaret Webster, a well-regarded theater actress, producer, and director, is "the best director of the plays of Shakespeare that we have," according to critic George Jean Nathan. Virginia gets the job. It's one of the happiest events of her career—of her life. She plays Ophelia and Lady Macduff, for a thirty-week tour through twenty states and Canada. *The New York Times* prints an article announcing the tour and highlights the fact that Virginia is chosen from among three hundred actors auditioning. Winefriede is over the moon of course—all her confidence in Virginia is proved justified. Roddy couldn't be happier that Virginia gets a chance to shine. He hopes it's a harbinger of many successes to come.

Meanwhile, Thomas starts handling much of the endless correspondence going back and forth surrounding all of Roddy's various jobs. Thomas takes great care, spending a lot of time, treating things quite literally. When an "answer man" radio program gets in touch, requesting information for a listener who writes in asking for a list of magazines with articles on Roddy McDowall, Thomas's answer is a two-page, single-spaced letter explaining in tedious, plodding detail why he can't answer the question with complete accuracy. Monogram's publicity department proposes a fan magazine column for Roddy and Virginia, answering requests for advice from readers. Things like, should you accept a date with a boy when you know you aren't the first one he has asked; whether it's proper to give a Christmas gift to a girl you frequently date; and how do you get an older sibling to stop treating you like a little kid. Thomas replies, again with pages and pages of his thoughts, on why the proposal is unsuitable. How can Roddy and Virginia be expected to answer such questions with no context, and without knowing anything meaningful about the people requesting advice?

Roddy doesn't care whether or not he has a fan magazine column. He's busy.

In *Tuna Clipper*, Roddy stars as a young law student who takes a tuna-fishing job to work off a debt. With friend and fellow former child actor Dickie Moore along for the ride, it's a story that also involves gambling, blackmail schemes, and family loyalty. Incredibly—some might add puzzlingly—François Truffaut, then still working as a film critic, admires the film, writing that it's "charm lies in its modesty and honesty." Another boy-and-his-horse story, *Black Midnight*, has the familiar beats of taming a horse, the horse being accused of doing something terrible, and Roddy saving the horse from someone who wants to kill it, with boy and horse living happily ever after. *Killer Shark* is the tale of a college student who must take over his father's shark-hunting boat and fails miserably before manning up and turning things around.

The benefit to Monogram is they know that if a Roddy McDowall film is on the top of the bill on a double feature, an audience is going to show up. If it's the second half on a double bill, the audience will stay to see it and eat more popcorn and candy. Everybody wins.

Roddy scrapes the bottom of the barrel with *Everybody's Dancin'*, a musical Western for a different low-budget indie outfit, Lippert Pictures. Los Angeles TV personality Spade Cooley is a fiddle-playing bandleader who's determined to keep away from phonies when he goes to Hollywood to make a movie. Roddy shows up as himself in a scene at the studio and plugs his new real-life radio show at KMPC, a mix of music and entertainment industry guests that runs for most of 1950. Spade bails out an old friend whose dance hall is in danger of going bust, creating an atmosphere of such merriment that, before you know it, Everybody's Dancin'—rather badly, truth to tell. The acting is as wooden as performances in an Ed Wood movie, even Roddy's.

"I just did it for the money," he admits anytime someone has the bad manners to bring it up. "Better not to talk about it."

A much happier event occurs when his parents throw him a huge party for his twenty-first birthday. It's like one of their Sunday parties but much bigger. Winefriede sees it as an opportunity to show everyone that his career is thriving. Maybe someone at one of the big studios will see how well he's doing and want to put him under contract. Soon after, Roddy signs his citizenship papers and buys himself a new Studebaker Champion convertible with red leather upholstery and a red leather roof treatment. There have to be some perks to working so hard. Elizabeth Taylor is no longer a kid by this time, and they go on long drives together, talking late into the night when one or the other doesn't have an early call.

One place in his life where he's exerting control is his time off. He has precious little of it, but when he wants to spend time with his friends, he takes to doing it away from home. The Sunday gatherings become less frequent. He and his pals go to clubs and parties, take long drives, hang out at the beach. He becomes friends with other gay and bisexual young men his own age. Some aren't yet famous. Roddy is out with Dick Clayton, then an actor, but soon to become a talent agent, and he meets Tab Hunter when Tab serves him at a soda fountain in 1948. They meet again after Tab is signed by manager Henry Willson and a publicity buildup starts. Roddy and Tab are featured in "eligible bachelor" layouts as shirtless buddies just looking for the right girl. Roddy is self-conscious about his body and doesn't like the photos. He meets another Henry Willson client, Rock Hudson, and they hit it off as well. His friendship with Farley Granger resumes, and in the early 1950s he becomes friends with Anthony Perkins. While the press angle is always of the "bachelors on the make" variety, Roddy doesn't try to build a straight facade. If he's at a premiere with Elizabeth Taylor or Jane Powell, he doesn't try to overtly make it seem they're on dates. He will always be discreet in public. Yet there's no indication that Roddy ever feels conflicted or ashamed of his sexual orientation. He accepts himself.

This is part of a series of choices he begins to make as he enters adulthood, as he maneuvers through his career difficulties, and as he grapples with his relationship with his parents. It likely doesn't seem to him like he's making choices at all, but he is, even as it may feel to him like simple logic. It's logical that he should accept and embrace his own nature. It's logical that he should acknowledge the need to grow as an actor rather than wallow in the memory of his childhood success. It's logical that his love for his family endures regardless of the financial and emotional complications involved. These choices are logical. But they *are* choices. There are high-profile instances where people in similar circumstances make *other* choices. There are gay actors who marry women. There are former child actors who overdose. There are former child actors who turn bitter toward their families, often justifiably so, but to whose benefit? There is a saying that harboring resentment is like taking poison and expecting the other person to die. Roddy chooses not to dwell in resentment. "Never harbor a grudge," is how he puts it in letters and interviews—reminding others, reminding himself.

That's how Don Bachardy, Christopher Isherwood's young lover, remembers Roddy when they meet. "He was lovely," Don says in a 2024 interview. "I was so impressed to meet a real movie star, but Roddy was so genuine and nice—the exact same man, the same person he would be 20, 30, and 40 years later when Chris and I would see him."

While continuing to make his Monogram films, hosting his own radio show, and keeping up a heavy personal appearance schedule, Roddy tours in six plays. Following *Young Woodley*, he stars in Philip Barry's *The Youngest*, as the misunderstood heir to his father's business, opposite real-life friend and former costar Peggy Ann Garner, *The First Mrs. Fraser*, as the impudent son of a divorced couple, *The Hasty Heart*, as a dying young veteran, *O Mistress Mine*, as the left-wing son of a mother set to marry a capitalist, and *Remains to Be Seen*, as a zany drummer in a comedy that kicks off with the murder of a pornographer. Written by Howard Lindsay and Russell Crouse, the playwrights of *Life with Father*, one of the longest-running plays in Broadway history, *Remains to Be Seen* isn't a particularly great play, nor is it demonstrably more successful critically or financially for Roddy compared with his other summer stock shows. What's notable is that he finally plays a stage role that isn't some variation of his former screen image struggling to grow up. *Remains to Be Seen* gives him sexy, farcical scenes that get laughs, pointing the way toward different roles and a different kind of future.

Roddy makes two more pictures for Monogram. The first is called *Big Timber*. He plays a young tree surgeon whose romantic entanglements get in the way of him finding work as a logger. It isn't terrible. Then comes the best of his Monogram projects, a thriller called *The Steel Fist*, shot in 1951. Set in an unnamed Eastern European country ostensibly behind the Iron Curtain, it's a spare production that makes a surefooted emotional impact, alternating sequences of tight, propulsive action with scenes of very little movement, where the tension hangs in the air and the characters hold their breath. Roddy is a student protest leader whose antigovernment activities could get him killed unless he flees the country. A network of resistance spies aids his escape. The complications are believable and frightening. And for the first time in a long time, Roddy finds the power of stillness. Not the stillness of a child facing adult situations he can't quite fathom, but the stillness of a man realizing that if he doesn't figure out his next move quickly, people he cares about will die.

Roddy also needs to figure out his next move in real life.

He works constantly—*earns* constantly—but he never really knows what happens to his money. He gets a certain amount regularly for himself. No one calls it his allowance . . . but it's basically his allowance. And his parents handle everything else. So Roddy doesn't really ask a lot of questions.

The problem is that by 1950 and 1951, unbeknownst to Roddy, the math stops working. Money is coming in, but after Roddy's agent takes 10 percent, the publicist takes 10 percent, his parents take 7 percent for managing his career, and Uncle Sam takes around 40 percent, there isn't much left to cover everything else, including his considerable travel expenses, which are always first class per Winefriede. Roddy must always look like a star in public. There is also little left to maintain the big house with a pool and the costs of all the entertaining Winefriede does to keep up appearances. Bills start coming in that can't be paid, and Thomas insists that it's time for Roddy to become aware of their dire circumstances.

Learning the true extent of their financial problems is demoralizing for Roddy. How is it possible that his exhaustive and exhausting work schedule isn't enough? He's killing himself, saying yes to any and every job. He made *Everybody's Dancin'* for Christ's sake! How can *that* not be *enough*?

Chapter 4

The Fighting Cock

Sometimes going broke is a good thing.

Roddy is by nature pragmatic. The McDowall family's way of life is on the verge of financial collapse. Something must change. So why not change things for the better?

He thinks often of his visit with Dame May Whitty and about the power of learning. What is he learning? What does he *want* to learn? He wants to learn how to act. Properly. Not with the hit-or-miss way he approaches each new character, where sometimes he finds the right beats, sometimes not. He needs to gain technique.

New York is the place for that kind of training.

Jane Powell is heartily in favor of Roddy moving to New York. She is still riding a wave of popularity at MGM and the money is rolling in, but her parents spend it as fast as she makes it. She knows the strain Roddy is under. Jane is unusually perceptive, seeing how the stress eats at him. The money situation is a real problem, but the deeper issue is the constant pressure of being what he thinks his parents want him to be. She believes if Roddy doesn't get away from them, he will have a nervous breakdown. And though it's another story for another book, Jane Powell knows a thing or two about nervous breakdowns.

Elizabeth Taylor also thinks Roddy needs to go. And someone

new in Roddy's life agrees. The actor Montgomery Clift. He makes Roddy feel that anything and everything is possible if he finds the courage to follow his own instincts. Monty can be an extremely persuasive man when he wants to be, moving in close, with the kind of intense immediacy that movie stars sometimes have, where they look into your eyes and make you feel like you're the only person in the world.

At this juncture in showbiz history, many people believe Monty will be even bigger than Brando. He's just thirty-one years old and has two Oscar nominations for Best Actor. His deal with Paramount allows him the freedom to turn down any script and any director. His own life may be messy, but he believes he can clearly see the actions people need to take to fulfill what he thinks is their destiny. He likes being a catalyst for change in the lives of the people he cares about.

When Monty and Elizabeth Taylor work together on *A Place in the Sun*, she credits him with making her understand that she isn't just a beautiful movie star. She's an actress who can connect deeply to her material if she chooses to. Without *A Place in the Sun*, there's no *Cat on a Hot Tin Roof*, no *Suddenly, Last Summer*, and without those films there's no *Who's Afraid of Virginia Woolf?*

Elizabeth loves Monty. It's different than her love for Roddy, who doesn't *need* her in the same way Monty does and is like a safe harbor where she's never judged or made to feel like she's not enough. Roddy adores her without judgment. Monty needs to be protected and cherished, *mothered*, though she's twelve years younger. Monty, however, isn't necessarily a safe harbor—he challenges her to be better, sometimes quite forcefully. Elizabeth needs both influences in her life. She needs the two of them equally. And she has a feeling that Monty and Roddy might need each other. So she introduces them.

It's perhaps somewhat speculative to say that for Roddy,

meeting Monty is love at first sight. The nature of that love isn't entirely quantifiable. Many biographies treat their sexual relationship as a given. It's almost certainly true, yet there's no definitive confirmation in Roddy's archives. They aren't living together. They don't wear matching rings, as Roddy does with a partner he meets in the early 1960s. That Roddy loves Monty, however, is inarguable. His correspondence and his private and public descriptions of Monty and of his feelings about Monty as a person and as an actor are filled with deep, passionate admiration and connection. He credits Monty with opening the door to the blossoming of his New York life and what becomes a remarkable career renaissance.

The *Washington Daily News*, however, is also on the case, linking Monty and Roddy in what to their readers is a far more important issue: their eligible bachelorhood.

"Montgomery Clift has inherited Jimmy Stewart's crown as Hollywood's No. 1 bachelor, but he won it almost by default. There are only eight eligible genuine bachelors left here. From Roddy McDowall, 20, to Caesar (sic) Romero, a veteran 42—and to share them are two dozen just as famous glamour girls who've never tied the knot . . ."

The Washington Daily News reporters and readers aren't the only ones who regard Monty and Roddy as eligible bachelors. Virginia is unaware of their sexuality and their relationship. Imagining her brother as gay isn't part of her lexicon yet. What she *does* know is that Roddy needs to pull the plug on his Hollywood hamster wheel.

Roddy knows it too.

He isn't quite ready to pull the rug out from under his parents though. He takes it upon himself to learn all the things Winefriede never wanted him to know about his finances. The full extent of her evident mismanagement and overspending becomes clear. There is also an element of her spending that seems good-hearted. She is everyone's fairy godmother. Sometimes it's fans with a hard luck story who get a bit of help from the McDowall coffers. She is also the actual godmother to the children of various people she views as important for Roddy's career and to the children of people who aren't well known or influential. She genuinely enjoys helping people and being mommy to all. It also seems true that giving herself this role in so many people's lives feeds her sense of self-importance.

At the height of his childhood acting career, Roddy is making over $100,000 a year. That's huge money in the 1940s, roughly indexed at about $2 million in 2025. The McDowalls do own several properties in Los Angeles, so at least there's still something to show for all those earnings. To Roddy's dismay, he learns that there are mortgages and second loans on those properties. The bitter pill is realizing his scrupulously honest father is so mesmerized by his mother that he never puts a stop to any of it.

He discusses the situation with Virginia. She is also hungry for change and hopes to build on her success with the Margaret Webster Shakespeare Company to carve out her own career in New York. The news that they both want to leave California hits Winefriede like a sledgehammer. But it gets worse. Winefriede can't believe that her children want to sell the family home—an unbearable idea. There is fainting. Attacks of apoplexy. The facts don't change, however. They can no longer afford their current lifestyle. Roddy and Virginia take a reconnaissance trip to New York.

Monty, now already back in New York, is firmly a part of Roddy's life by this point. There is an element of hero worship on both sides. Each starts his career as a child, but Roddy's success when he's young dwarfs Monty's. To Monty, Roddy's screen performances as a kid are legendary. For Roddy, Monty represents everything he wants to be—part of an exciting new breed of actors. He's also physically beautiful. Roddy sees himself as scrawny and unattractive. Monty is perfection.

When Roddy and Virginia arrive in New York, Monty forges a close connection with Virginia as well. He introduces them to real estate and financial people who agree to help Roddy and Virginia find a solution to their family's situation. They devise a plan to sell everything in Los Angeles and move the entire family to New York, intending to buy a small apartment building where the family can take three apartments, and the remaining units can be income property. They bring up the idea on a very long, very expensive long-distance call.

More tears. More feigned heart and nervous problems. Winifriede argues that their detractors will portray selling the Los Angeles home in order to move to New York as Roddy running away in shame. These "witch-hunters" are lying in wait. They will pounce gleefully on the McDowall family's misfortune, laughing at them over their morning newspapers. Who are these witch-hunting detractors hoping to torment them? The press? The same people who have been avid supporters of Roddy through the years, so much so that they even talk up his movies at Monogram? *Those* witch-hunters? Roddy and Virginia counter that Winefriede's arguments make little sense. In the last several weeks there have been trade articles about Dorothy McGuire, Gloria De Haven, and Gene Tierney all selling their homes in Los Angeles and moving to New York. The press is positive, cheering the actresses on for spreading their wings.

Roddy and Virginia get nowhere with Winefriede. So they compose an excruciatingly long but incredibly revealing letter that carefully and specifically lays out the entire proposition to their parents, hoping that communicating the details in writing will give Winefriede a chance to absorb everything without the need for a dramatic performance. Their letter is of course addressed to both parents, but Winefriede is the obstacle to moving forward. Thomas will be onboard, if Winefriede is convinced.

Virginia writes that she and Roddy are composing the letter together in the hopes that they will be able to make themselves clear and not confuse the issues anymore, as they continually try to figure out a solution that will offer the best answer to their situation. She writes that they believe the McDowall clan must move to New York. This, after thinking over the problems involved in selling the West Coast house, Roddy's career issues, the low possibility of finding substantial income property in the West, and the slim chance of any employment for their father in California. She is also very mindful of public appearances. They can position the move in the press as a change that is in response to the demand for Roddy on stage in New York, that is seeking brighter opportunities for Virginia, and that gives their parents a new adventure.

She painstakingly acknowledges the dreadful shocks she and Roddy know both Winefriede and Thomas will suffer as a result of leaving their wonderful California way of life but that the entire ship will collapse if they don't take action. She wants to detail the actual numbers involved but can only come up with "an imaginary figure due to our lack of complete knowledge of the various liabilities involved." Winefriede is thus far unwilling to disclose the full amount of the existing loans against the house, so Roddy and Virginia don't know the exact amount of how much money will remain after selling it. Nor can they figure out exactly how much the taxes will be.

But page after page lays out the various financial details, utilizing what numbers they're privy to so far, and filtering that through the advice they gain from Monty's people. They continue the letter by outlining the career advantages of moving to New York. Virginia will be able to seek acting work. If she isn't acting, she can support herself with secretarial work. Hopping back and forth between the two at a moment's notice is common and easily accomplished in New York. They argue it's impossible for her to do the same in Los Angeles, that she will have to choose one or the other, and secretarial work is the only guaranteed income between the two. Do their parents want to force Virginia to give up on her own theatrical ambitions?

The letter continues: "As for Roddy, we have been over that

so many times that he looks like ground round. Certainly in the New York area, there's more immediate money to be made, and any films that may come up can be met, made, and completed, and after tucking money in his pocket, he can sprint with the aid of track shoes and a good many thousands richer, back to the fold. At the present time, we are primarily concerned with just plain existing, without a complete collapse of everything."

The letter accomplishes nothing. Winefriede still doesn't want to sell the house. And under no circumstances will she and Thomas move to New York.

Roddy is secretly relieved his parents won't move. No one can say he hasn't tried. And Winefriede's choice not to come to New York means he can create his new life without being under her watchful eyes, without having a daily sense of responsibility for her happiness.

He hires a business manager named Stephen Weinrib to sort out the financial side of his life while he turns his attention elsewhere. Roddy gives Stephen Weinrib power of attorney—in essence transferring parental authority over his finances from his actual parents to a different kind of parent. It's an association that lasts almost three decades. Roddy does become more involved over time and learns about money and business. Stephen Weinrib comes to function like a member of the family. He's the go-between when Roddy's parents or Virginia need money.

Stephen Weinrib gives Winefriede and Thomas no choice about the house. It's sold. Winefriede and Thomas move into a smaller, more affordable house, and Roddy and Virginia each rent small apartments in New York. These changes happen in an almost surreal aura of goodwill. Letters between different parties are strikingly different in tone about the same events. Somewhat to Winefriede's credit, she channels her animosity via Thomas, who expresses her displeasure to Stephen, rather than to her children. The family acts like nothing at all has changed, even as Roddy begins to fashion a life that is entirely separate from his parents, and even as the need to be careful with money becomes a daily part of Winefriede and Thomas McDowall's existence.

Monty encourages the distancing, advising Roddy to do the very thing that Monty himself can't do: Cut the apron strings. Monty's own mother is a great deal more toxic than Winefriede, and her hold over him has sinister overtones. Whatever Monty's own emotional baggage, though, he acts as a vital force for Roddy's transition from an uncertain former movie star into an adult actor, in command of his craft and confident in his abilities. Roddy is the veteran of almost forty films at this point. It's humbling to begin his training all over again with Monty's omnipresent acting coach, the teacher Mira Rostova. She has her own cult of personality and an aura of influence that is temperamentally the polar opposite of Winefriede's gregarious approach but is just as controlling. Roddy doesn't fall into the trap of making her indispensable. During this time that he looks at as a kind of rebirth, he also studies with Bobby Lewis and David Craig. The three coaches employ different approaches to finding truth and specificity, some of it emotional and Method-based, some of it more cerebral and logical, breaking down the intentions of a character in terms of how that role fits into the whole story of a script. Roddy feels free to take what he considers to be the best from each of the three teachers. He begins a strict process of analyzing his scripts and writing detailed notes about his characters' motivations and intentions—especially their subtextual thoughts, those that are conscious, and those that are subconscious. It's a habit he retains for the rest of his life. The pages of his archived scripts are often marked up with his notes to the point of illegibility, whatever the material. He makes as many notes on *That Darn Cat* as he does for *The Tempest.* Roddy comes to believe that exhaustive preparation is what can allow him to respond honestly in the moment, throwing out his preparation if the scene goes a different way but using it as a foundational tool to root his performance.

Roddy's apartment on the East Side near Bloomingdale's is

close to many of the people who become important in this stage of his life. There's Monty; Peggy Ann Garner is also trying to transition to adult roles and is living in New York; an up-and-coming young singer Roddy befriends named Merv Griffin; Farley Granger moves into a nearby apartment; Roddy's acting coach David Craig and his wife, actress Nancy Walker (who falls deeply in love with Monty at one point during her marriage); he meets the actor Jack Larson through Monty and also becomes close with another of Monty's friends, the former singer Libby Holman, best known for the late-1920s hit song "Moanin' Low" and for the veil of suspicion surrounding her wealthy husband's death twenty years before. Although many in this circle of friends are connected to Monty, Roddy's relationships with these individuals endure because his connections to them become personal. They always have Monty in common, but he's not what cements these ties. Roddy's talent for friendship grows naturally out of his curiosity about people. It's also undoubtedly propelled by emotional needs developed in childhood—his desire for approval and his eagerness to please, which in turn coexist with his own decisions about who he wants to be and how he wants to live.

The search for understanding his own inner life is a pathway to understanding the inner lives of the characters he plays. "I wanted to learn to act while I had a few years of my name left—the part of my name, that is, which had not been whittled away," he tells Louella Parsons in 1965. "It was a shattering and revealing experience." He's quite focused on his acting classes, but he doesn't have the luxury of taking a break from working professionally. Biographies of some of Roddy's friends from this era often repeat the idea that Roddy is out of work for many months, or even as long as several years, when he moves to New York. This isn't the case. He starts booking jobs the moment he arrives and never stops. From 1951 to 1960, Roddy has just six film credits, but sixty-two TV credits.

This is a time when live TV is centered in New York. A golden age of anthology programs is beginning. Roddy couldn't have chosen a more perfect time. His celebrity is highly valued in the early 1950s, when film stars are loath or forbidden by their studios from appearing on TV. His first important role is in "When We Are Married" for *Robert Montgomery Presents* in 1951, as a church organist who falls for a young woman in the congregation, incurring the disapproval of three pompous church elders. When they try to lecture Roddy about his "inappropriate" behavior, he reveals secrets he knows about each of their marriages. As a live broadcast, the performance feels more like theater to him than film—sink or swim, with no retakes.

It's the bridge to a new period in his career, pointing the way to the next stage of his life. Roddy commits fully to New York. He moves his Army Reserves placement from Los Angeles, though there's no record of him participating in any Reserves activities there either, despite the draft going into full effect as the US launches military action in Korea.

The jobs keep coming. The money isn't spectacular. The American Federation of Television and Radio Artists (AFTRA) minimum rate for a one-hour drama is $100 in 1952. Roddy is a star, so his pay is closer to $160. It's enough. Roddy works for *Lux Video Theatre*, *Broadway Television Theatre*, *Kraft Television Theatre*, *U.S. Steel Hour*, *Campbell Television Soundstage*, *Goodyear Television Playhouse*, *Medallion Theatre*, *Pond's Theater*, *General Electric Theater*, *Hallmark Hall of Fame*, *The Kaiser Aluminum Hour*, *NBC Matinee Theater*, *The Alcoa Hour*, *Playhouse 90*, *DuPont Show of the Month*, *Oldsmobile Music Theatre*, *Sunday Showcase*, and *The Twilight Zone*. As happens with *Robert Montgomery Presents*, many of these shows invite him back multiple times.

The range of roles is extraordinary—from Shakespeare to kitchen-sink drama and everything in between. At first, he tends to be cast as young men with romantic problems, in original scripts as well as adaptations, where classic roles include characters like Richard in "Ah, Wilderness!" for *Celanese Theatre*, Pip in "Great Expectations" for *Robert Montgomery Presents*, and Mr. Elton in "Emma" for *Kraft Television Theatre.* Soon the range of roles broadens, as producers realize he has much more to offer than playing a male ingénue. He takes on antiheroes, villains, and magical creatures. As he gains experience and visibility, he plays Squeak in "Billy Budd" for *DuPont Show of the Month*, Ariel in "The Tempest" for *Hallmark Hall of Fame*, and Marlow in "Heart of Darkness" for *Playhouse 90.* It's not all high-profile excellence. He also stars in something called "Too Bad About Sheila Troy" for *Oldsmobile Music Theatre*, a live show that awkwardly incorporates existing popular music into half-hour stories. Its ratings put it in 114th place out of the 125 shows on TV at the time.

Steady work in TV gives Roddy enough financial stability so that he can build upon his theater work. His stage career previously was based on marketing plays regionally on the strength of his celebrity. Now he enters the Broadway and off-Broadway arenas, where no one is going to build a show around him, and he will often have to audition if he wants to get a job. He hates auditions—they make him nervous—yet he doesn't expect to be exempt. He could look at having to audition as a step backward. Not since 1941 and *How Green Was My Valley* has he needed to test or audition. Roddy views it as a step forward. He wants to earn his place in the New York theater world.

His first important stage opportunity is working for Cyril Ritchard, who was also in the 1938 George Formby vehicle *I See Ice!* The production is a revival of George Bernard Shaw's *Misalliance*, with Tamara Geva and Richard Kiley, and another familiar face, Barry Jones, Roddy's father in *Murder in the Family.* In *Misalliance*, playwright Shaw puts marriage, the role of women, and social justice up for debate. On a summer afternoon, a pilot and a Polish acrobat crash their plane onto an English country estate, disrupting a garden party where Roddy McDowall plays the spoiled, entitled fiancé of the daughter of the lord of the manor. The show itself and the working environment are miles away from summer stock.

The trick is figuring out how to apply the acting techniques he's learning into an approach that makes sense for the role, discovering how to harness his passions and focus them effectively. Roddy can't really relate to the selfish, narrow-minded *Misalliance* character through the lens of his own experience, because Roddy lives his life in a diametrically opposite way, striving for generosity of spirit, decorum, and making others happy. Going through his lines, he naturally wonders, what would it be like to be able to voice every selfish thought of his own? To express his own whims like a two-year-old kid, grabbing at things, yelling out, "Mine!" Wondering what a different life would be like is the starting point for most actors. The lightning bolt moment for Roddy is linking the idea of behaving like this other person to a sense of childlike excitement, giving himself over to that sense of play with total focus—*that* is the oxygen that will give life to the characters he plays.

He needs to allow acting to become fun.

Such a simple idea, really. But momentous in terms of Roddy moving forward. It's in his nature to be studious and thoughtful, to approach his work with a sense of purpose and commitment. That's good. It's useful. It's vital. And it's enough to get him to a place where every performance is acceptable. To the best of his knowledge, he has never gotten a truly bad review in his career. He always shows up and does his job. But if he can find the element that makes him light up like a kid at Christmas, then he's got something. That element can be anything—tragic, comic, happy, sad—it doesn't matter, as long as he finds a way for it to spark with his own sense of wonder and play.

With *Misalliance*, that means wholeheartedly embracing his inner two-year-old child and daring to take his performance to a place where he might feel a bit ridiculous. Ridiculous is okay. Ridiculous is *wonderful*. Roddy throws himself into the role, utilizing some of the physical comedy skills on display back in *Holiday in Mexico* but filtered through the exacting demands of Shaw's text and Cyril Ritchard's direction. It works. John Chapman in the *Daily News* singles out Roddy. "I particularly enjoyed the performance of Roddy McDowall, a former film moppet, as an overbred youth who lies down on the floor and has a tantrum whenever affairs don't suit him."

Lying on the floor and having a tantrum is *fun*.

The four-month run for *Misalliance* is the longest time Roddy has spent playing one role on one stage. He loves the work and is enthralled with the cast. He wants to record his feelings about these extraordinary people and hits on the idea of buying a camera, hoping to catch his colleagues in moments where he can capture what he sees as their essence. He wonders if he can know them differently, perhaps even better, if he sees them through a camera lens. He hopes that they might see themselves as he sees them—special and multifaceted. Roddy begins snapping photos constantly, everywhere he goes. When he can disarm his subjects and make them feel natural and at ease, he sees sides of them that are surprising.

A lab technician at the place where Roddy gets his film developed encourages him to nurture his skill, telling Roddy he has a real eye. When he isn't at the theater or shooting a TV show, for six months, Roddy takes to shadowing the technician in his darkroom, learning the fundamentals of photography from the inside out. Here's where being a celebrity comes in handy. Roddy has the contacts to be able to reach out to two noted photographers with very different points of view. Fashion photographer Richard Avedon and photojournalist Eliot Elisofon. Roddy shows his work to both men. They become mentors, giving their insights as Roddy broadens his skills, mixing his eye for beauty with his desire to show something of the inner core of the people he shoots. He's fascinated with the sense, especially among actors, that there can be layer upon layer of authenticity and facade, one blending into the other. A beautiful person can appear beautiful. They can also appear ugly. Or best of all, they can appear as both in the same picture. He continues working and learning, as the idea of having a parallel career begins to take hold and then to take shape. And snapping photos is *fun*. It makes him think of his father and that terrible Victorian photo of his dead uncle.

When *Misalliance* closes, Roddy goes into *Charley's Aunt* as Lord Fancourt Babberley at Playhouse in the Park in Philadelphia before getting his next Broadway role, in a British import called *Escapade*, with Brian Aherne, Ursula Jeans, and Carroll Baker in her Broadway debut. The plot contrasts Brian as a father with Roddy as his son. Brian blusters incessantly about promoting international peace, while Roddy takes action in a spectacular way. He escapes school, steals a plane, and flies to Geneva with a peace petition and a plan. Roddy has a wonderful time—again finding the way to indulge his own sense of joyful purpose with the character's actions. Though the show is poorly reviewed and closes after only thirteen performances, he views it as a positive experience, and his notices are good. In a decidedly mixed review, *The New York Times* singles him out. "As the schoolboy wise beyond his years, Roddy McDowall is thoroughly winning, managing in some fashion to keep the precociousness innocent and modest." He wishes he didn't care so much about the reviews and audience approval, but it does matter to him, and it always will. He can look to satisfy himself creatively all he wants, that doesn't change the fact that he will always be eager to please. Steady income from TV, though, means Roddy can afford to be in stage shows that flop as he sharpens his craft.

Among many TV appearances, he plays a shy young man who faints from hunger on Patricia Collinge's doorstep, in "The

Shy One" for *Campbell Television Soundstage* on NBC; Otto Kruger's son, determined not to follow in his footsteps, in "A Suitable Marriage" for *Medallion Theatre* on CBS; and a law student who gets caught up in a case of international intrigue involving a Scottie dog and a Pekingese in "My Client, McDuff" for *Armstrong Circle Theatre* on NBC. He utilizes the techniques he's exploring. At first glance, it may seem like there isn't a lot of fun to be had in fainting on someone's doorstep. But fun is relative. For Roddy, someone who never gives up, who rarely asks for help, and who looks after himself, the idea of giving himself over to his feelings can seem rather wondrous, even when those feelings are hunger and powerlessness. What a giddy relief it might be to just fall over and expect someone else to pick up the pieces. It doesn't matter if his inner reaction wouldn't literally be the case if the character were a real person. "Giddy relief" is almost certainly not what a starving person feels in real life when they faint. But this isn't real life. It's playing pretend. Certainly, he also works to connect to the pain of hunger, the specific motivations that drive the character, and all the homework that grounds the performance in reality. That's the foundation. Giving in to the excitement of creation is what propels the work into something that feels magical to him.

Roddy also participates in a very unusual WABC local TV show called *Angel Auditions*, a program that examines how stage plays are produced and financed. The episode's focus is *The Homeward Look*, an off-Broadway domestic comedy featuring Roddy. Viewers can see Roddy performing in a scene from the show on the air and then go see the show in person when it opens. *The Homeward Look* isn't a hit, but it has the distinction of being the show that forces the far more successful production of *The Threepenny Opera* to close after just ninety-six performances. *The Homeward Look* has a guaranteed opening date. A combination of scathingly negative reviews for the play if not the performances closes the show quickly, allowing *The Threepenny*

Opera to reopen for one of the longest runs in off-Broadway history, over six years.

Slowly, Roddy transitions from playing the role of someone's son to also playing characters whose conflicts and concerns are broader than that of parent and child. Roddy always cites 1955 as the turning point. Playing a devious, bongo-thumping warlock in *Bell, Book and Candle* in Stamford, Connecticut, is a happy stretch. His second Shaw experience, *The Doctor's Dilemma*, provides the opportunity to play an immoral tubercular patient. He gives himself over to the idea of satisfying his darkest desires and risking death by showing his true colors. The summer season takes him to Stratford for the American Shakespeare Festival as Octavius Caesar in *Julius Caesar* and best of all, Ariel, in *The Tempest*, in a cast that includes Jack Palance as Caliban, Raymond Massey as Prospero, Joan Chandler as Miranda, Christopher Plummer as Ferdinand, Fritz Weaver as Antonio, and Jerry Stiller as Trinculo, the Jester—with a ballet masque created by George Balanchine.

Roddy auditions for the season already hatching a plan to play Ariel. At first glance, the odds aren't in his favor. Since the mid-nineteenth century, Ariel is traditionally played by women, and no one has ever seen Roddy play anything like this magical creature, who hovers in an emotional netherworld, trapped in servitude yet sometimes drunk with its own power. It's physically demanding, by turns balletic then gymnastic, and demands a fearless willingness to skate on the edge of the outrageous. Roddy prepares studiously for the audition. He grounds the character in a sense of realism he imagines might exist in a magical realm and gets the part.

Then he turns to the physicality of Ariel. What would it be like to be in Ariel's body?

When Roddy first arrives in New York, he makes a lot of changes, often urged on by Montgomery Clift, who believes Roddy can accomplish whatever he sets his mind to. One of the most important changes Roddy wants to make is to his body. He wants to get rid of whatever is left of his awkward, skinny adolescent self and become stronger, more physically present. He starts working out with weights, determined to transform it into what he believes will be more appealing. He wants to be able to take off his shirt for a role without feeling scrawny. He also works on his movement skills, building confidence.

With Ariel, the language of Shakespeare is easy—it's been a part of Roddy's life since early childhood. Imbuing that language with surprise and passion allows him to soar. His sense of his own creative power is flowering. And it shows. A scene from the play survives from an appearance the cast makes performing two scenes on *The Ed Sullivan Show.* Roddy's physicality gives the performance a surprising sexual power, without a trace of a sensitive little boy. His pure enjoyment is marvelously on display.

In a mixed review of *The Tempest*, Brooks Atkinson in *The New York Times* writes: "Best of all, Roddy McDowall plays the difficult part of Ariel with genuine skill. Made up like a sprite, sprinkled with stardust, he has a trim and eager look. But he also gets around the stage with effortless agility, speaks his lines ardently and sings his catches well. With an excellent Ariel, a production of *The Tempest* cannot go wholly awry." The *Daily News* agrees: "As the spriteliest of all sprites, Roddy McDowall makes a splendid Ariel, quick of body and spirit. His is the best performance." United Press syndicates its review nationwide: "The outstanding player in the cast by quite a bit is Roddy McDowall, playing Ariel. . . . This young man, who has come a long way as a stage actor in the past five years, makes one wonder why anyone ever thought the role should be played by a woman, as it usually is." *The Bridgeport Telegram* compares him to Nijinsky, no less.

A month later, Roddy also performs scenes on *The Ed Sullivan Show* from his next stage appearance, *No Time for Ser-*

Roddy McDowall, *How Green Was My Valley*, 20th Century-Fox (1941).

Roddy McDowall, *Son of Fury: The Story of Benjamin Blake*, 20th Century-Fox (1941).
Photo courtesy 20th Century Studios, Inc. © 1941. All rights reserved.

Fleurette Zama, Merrill Rodin, Roddy McDowall, Peggy Ann Garner, Maurice Tauzin,
The Pied Piper, 20th Century-Fox (1942). *Photo courtesy the Everett Collection.*

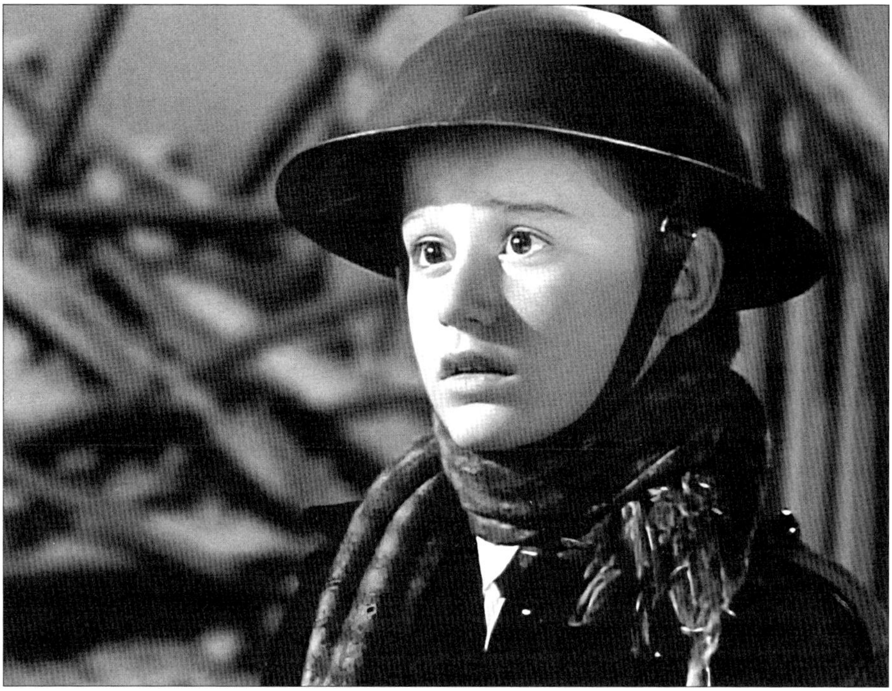

Roddy McDowall, *Confirm or Deny*, 20th Century-Fox (1941).

Wahana, Roddy McDowall, *My Friend Flicka*, 20th Century-Fox (1943).

Pal, Roddy McDowall, *Lassie Come Home*, MGM (1943).
Photo courtesy the Everett Collection.

Virginia McDowall, Roddy McDowall, Winefriede McDowall (circa 1944).
Photo courtesy the Everett Collection.

Roddy McDowall, Peggy Ann Garner, *The Keys of the Kingdom*, 20th Century-Fox (1944). *Photo courtesy the Everett Collection.*

Jane Powell, Roddy McDowall (1947). *Photo courtesy the Everett Collection.*

Elizabeth Taylor, Roddy McDowall (circa 1947). *Photo courtesy the Everett Collection.*

Roddy McDowall, Virginia McDowall (circa 1948). *Photo courtesy the Everett Collection.*

Barry Jones, Jerome Kilty, Jan Farrand, Richard Kiley, Roddy McDowall, Dorothy Sands, *Misalliance* (1953).
Photo by Friedman-Abeles © The New York Public Library for the Performing Arts.

Margaret Hamilton, Roddy McDowall, *The Diary of a Scoundrel* (1956).
Photo by Friedman-Abeles © The New York Public Library for the Performing Arts.

Roddy McDowall, *Compulsion* (1957).
Photo by Friedman-Abeles
© The New York Public Library
for the Performing Arts.

Roddy McDowall, *Camelot* (1960).
Photo by Friedman-Abeles
© The New York Public Library
for the Performing Arts.

Tammy Grimes, Roddy McDowall, Jack Gilford, *Look After Lulu* (1959).
Photo by Friedman-Abeles © The New York Public Library for the Performing Arts.

Roddy McDowall, *Cleopatra*, 20th Century-Fox (1963). *Photo courtesy the Everett Collection.*

Roddy McDowall (1966). *Photo courtesy Alamy.*

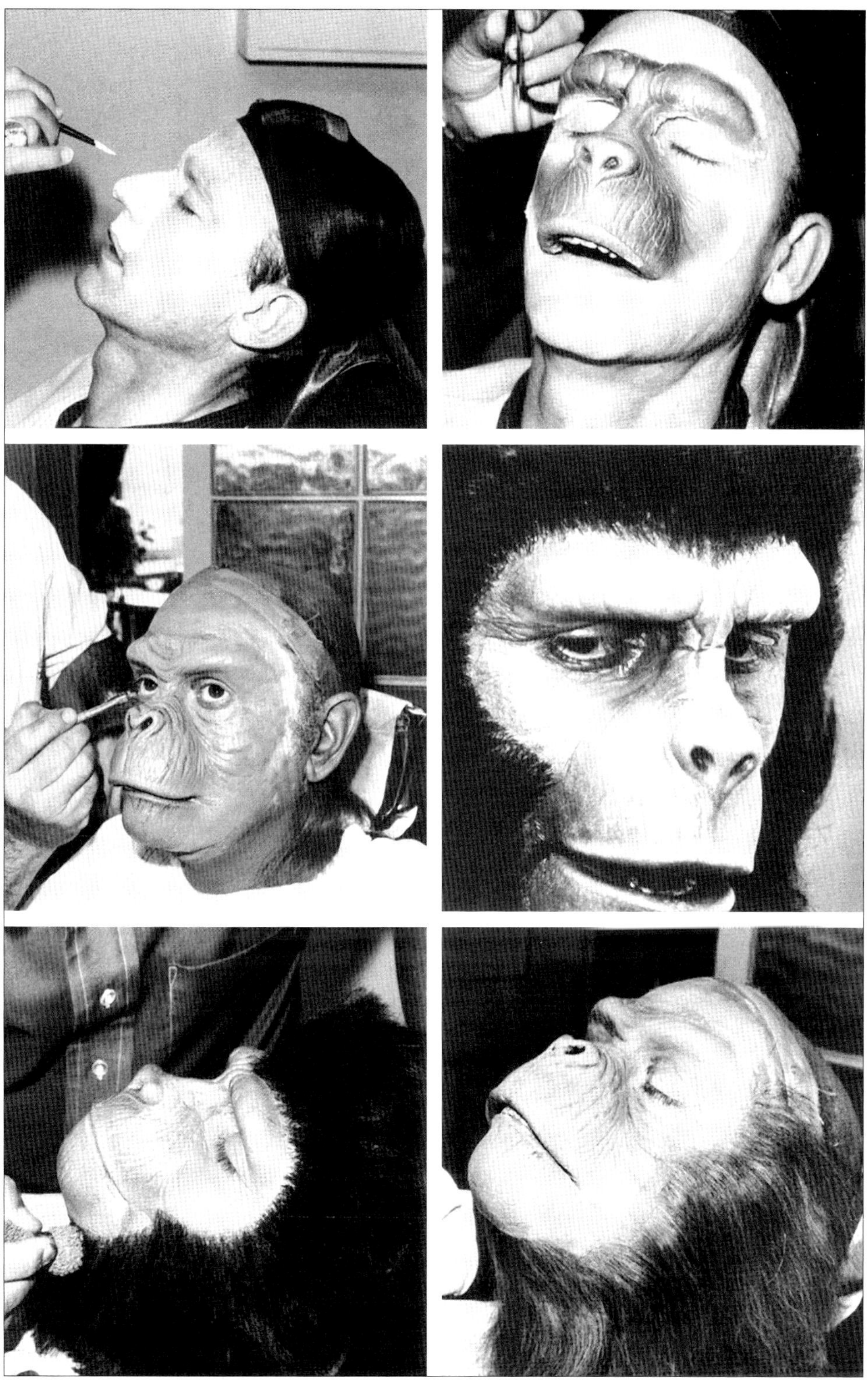

Makeup process with Roddy McDowall as Cornelius,
Planet of the Apes, 20th Century-Fox (1968). *Photos courtesy the Everett Collection.*

Roddy McDowall, director, Ava Gardner, *Tam Lin*, American International Pictures (1971).
Photo courtesy the Everett Collection.

Chris Sarandon, Roddy McDowall, *Fright Night*, Columbia Pictures (1985).
Photo courtesy the Everett Collection.

Goldie Hawn, Roddy McDowall, *Overboard*, MGM (1987).
Photo courtesy the Everett Collection.

Roddy McDowall, Elizabeth Taylor, *Hotel*, ABC Television (1984).
Photo courtesy the Everett Collection.

Left side of Roddy McDowall's powder room, the Hollywood Museum.
Photo courtesy Debbie Moses Ferrari.

Deborah Kerr, Elizabeth Taylor, Roddy McDowall, American Cinema Awards (1985).
Photo by Anne Knudsen, courtesy Herald Examiner Collection, Los Angeles Public Library.

Right side of Roddy McDowall's powder room, the Hollywood Museum.
Photo courtesy Debbie Moses Ferrari.

Roddy McDowall, *Battle for the Planet of the Apes*, 20th Century-Fox (1973).
Photo courtesy the Everett Collection.

geants. Andy Griffith is a hillbilly who gets into the Air Force, but his determination to be transferred to the infantry seems so outlandish that a military shrink and a variety of sergeants, generals, and fellow servicemen are soon on the case. Roddy McDowall is Griffith's best friend and confidant, a redneck from Georgia. Roddy gratefully credits director Morton DaCosta for taking a chance and giving him an opportunity to finally play an American character on Broadway, further distancing him from the image people have of him as an English child actor.

Plot machinations in *No Time for Sergeants* put Andy Griffith and Roddy on a collision course with an atomic explosion in Yucca Flats. The TV exposure helps already strong tickets sales. The scene on *The Ed Sullivan Show* is where the two characters meet and become friends. The palpable affection and good humor between Andy and Roddy make a moment that could seem like a rote narrative device into a meeting that's believable and memorable. Roddy does the show for a year and is bitterly disappointed when he's not offered the role in the film. "It was quite a humiliating experience," he says years later. "I wanted very badly to play Ben [the role]. I asked to do it. And was not very well treated. I hadn't made a picture in a long time. By the time they came around to asking me to do it, I had signed for another play." Warner Bros. contract player Nick Adams ends up with the role.

Monty is a constant in Roddy's life during much of the early 1950s, only leaving for short stretches to make *I Confess*, *Indiscretions of an American Wife*, and *From Here to Eternity.* He remains a part of Virginia's life as well, and for a time, she works as his assistant. They both adore him. But Monty's emotional issues and substance abuse problems are baffling to the siblings. In restaurants, he delights in exhibiting awful table manners, grabbing at other people's food with his bare hands. And Monty can be a mean drunk. When sober or just buzzed, he wants to build people up. When drunk he tears them down, sometimes with long, cutting tirades, other times in a disarmingly sweet voice, using his empathy destructively. His ability to sense what will bring someone joy allows him to sense what will cause them pain, so he goes in for the kill. In his diaries, Christopher Isherwood calls Monty a "dismal kind of degenerate, with ugly, unfunny, aggressive attempts at humor." In *Elizabeth and Monty: The Untold Story of Their Intimate Friendship*, author Charles Casillo writes: "Close friends made allowances for him. Everyone would sit silently staring at their plates while Monty delivered his long, ugly speeches. Then he might pass out, his head in a dish, and Roddy McDowall would lift Monty's head off the plate and lay him down on the carpet."

Roddy struggles to understand, wanting to help, wondering what he can do to help ease Monty's suffering, sometimes worried it's somehow his fault. Virginia's dilemma is more complicated. She falls in love with Monty from the beginning, from the moment he becomes a part of the siblings' life in New York. She does secretarial work for Monty occasionally, and his beauty and passion are unlike anything Virginia has ever experienced. It takes a while for her to realize that Monty isn't going to love her back, that his romantic interest is in Roddy, and that Roddy returns Monty's feelings. She is the isolated third wheel.

It isn't clear whether this is when she understands that her little brother is gay or that knowledge comes sooner. Grappling with her feelings is a struggle. It doesn't help that while Roddy's career soars, Virginia's languishes. She has a small role in a *Hallmark Hall of Fame* drama called "Doctor Serocold," but she books no other acting jobs in New York. Whether this is down to a lack of nerve or talent or just bad luck is unknowable. Adam Kurtzman, her friend later in life, believes the emotional demands of a performing career were just too much for her. "She didn't talk about it much," he says, "but I definitely got the sense that acting wasn't pleasurable for her at all, that she found it a frightening way of life." The details are sketchy, but it appears Virginia has some kind of emotional breakdown at this juncture that requires psychiatric treatment and possibly hospitalization. Eventually she heads back to Los Angeles, where she takes a stenography course and works for Cecil B. DeMille. In New York, Roddy keeps working and keeps cleaning up after Monty when necessary, though not for very much longer. Their split isn't well documented. Common wisdom in biographies of other principal players in this circle posits that Monty leaves Roddy. This might not be the case. There are oblique references in the archives that imply Roddy may decide to distance himself without any official severing of ties. It's impossible to know for sure. That they remain close until Monty's death, however, is abundantly clear.

Monty is in Los Angeles shooting *Raintree County* in May 1956 when he has a terrible car accident coming back from a party at Elizabeth Taylor and her second husband Michael Wilding's house in the hills. Much has been written about how Elizabeth saves his life, digging the broken teeth from his throat where they're choking him, threatening the press that if they publish any pictures of him they'll never get another picture of her, and the terrible aftermath—the painful surgeries to put Monty's once beautiful face back together, the difficult remainder of the *Raintree County* shoot, and the macabre spectacle of crowds turning up to see the film so they can compare which scenes are from before the accident and which are from afterward.

Less is written about that from Roddy's perspective. When he gets the news, he's rehearsing with Kim Stanley for a live broadcast of a program called "In the Days of Our Youth" for *Goodyear Television Playhouse*. He doesn't leave for Los Angeles to be with Monty. It's not possible to say whether that's because of his commitment to the show, discomfort with the idea of showing up at the hospital without a recognized role as a family member, or whether Roddy is just unsure what sort of place he has in Monty's troubled life by this point. Elizabeth doesn't have to justify being by Monty's side. But Roddy would have to provide some sort of justification—to others—but more important, to himself.

Soon after the accident, while Monty is recovering in Los Angeles, Roddy begins psychoanalysis. Virginia is the only family member he tells. He views keeping it from their mother as common sense. If he were forthcoming about it, there would be epic rounds of "What did I do wrong?" dramatics. To what end? An apology? For what exactly? Winefriede's excesses and faults are indistinguishable from the tenacity and willpower that gave him a career in the first place. If she were a "normal" mother, his childhood might have been "better" on some emotional level, but he would likely now be living in London, in university, heading for a life far less interesting and exciting than the life he's leading in New York. So his goal in psychoanalysis isn't to lay blame but to better understand the sources of his own anxieties and thus gain control of them. After a childhood with little sense of his own agency, he now wants to take charge of his own life. Winefriede can no longer have a voice in determining how he wants to live his life. But neither can Monty. He will always hold a place in Roddy's heart, but Roddy is unwilling to go down with the ship that Monty is consciously or subconsciously sinking, seemingly all by himself.

He works with Dr. Cornelia Wilbur. While she's not anti-gay per se, she's one of the many psychoanalysts who advocate ways to "cure" homosexuality. This is still common practice in the 1950s; it begins to wane in the 1960s and is all but disavowed by the mid-1970s. If she tries to "cure" Roddy, it certainly doesn't take, but he credits her with helping him learn how to trust his instincts and decisions.

The one thing he can count on now is his work. Four years earlier, Monty may play a big part in helping Roddy find his feet, but now Roddy is the one doing the hard work, studying, auditioning, working out, resolving to face every situation with as much humility and good humor as he can muster. And he's truly grateful for the life it's giving him. During the rest of the year, he appears in different TV projects opposite the likes of Judith Anderson, Herbert Marshall, Julie Harris, Cyril Ritchard, E. G. Marshall, Anne Jackson, and Maureen O'Sullivan, while also appearing in two Broadway shows. That's how he keeps his own ship afloat.

The first stage show is an adaptation of the nineteenth-century Russian play *The Diary of a Scoundrel*. Roddy is an indolent young rogue intent on succeeding in life but unwilling to earn that success. Instead, he schemes—gleefully conniving his way into the good graces of the Moscow elite by exploiting their narcissism, foolishness, and credulity. When his diaries become public, his acerbic observations about his new circle of friends cause havoc. But the group unexpectedly welcomes him back into the fold, essentially doubling down on their own stupidity. The utter selfishness and venality of the character is such a welcome contrast for Roddy at this moment in his life. This scoundrel is everything Roddy can never be—doesn't *want* to be. But it's cleansing to be inside the skin of someone who doesn't care about others at all, however temporarily. Roddy and costar Margaret Hamilton perform a scene from the play on *The Steve Allen Show*, but tepid-to-terrible notices doom the show. The reviews focus on the ponderousness of the translation and the show's length. The actors aren't faulted. The production closes after just twenty-five performances.

Good as Gold, by John Patrick, the author of *The Teahouse of the August Moon*, is the show that follows, casting Roddy in a broad satire as a scientist who learns how to turn gold into a special kind of dirt that speedily grows giant-sized vegetables. Zero Mostel and Paul Ford become part of the circus in Congress, and with the FBI, as the scientist tries to utilize the formula to feed the world and end hunger, providing the comic engine of the plot. Roddy doesn't need to look hard to find the fun in working opposite Zero Mostel in broad comedy. Most reviewers observe that satire about Washington seems a superfluous sport and complain that the show rapidly loses its energy toward the end of the first act, with two more acts to go. As with *The Diary of a Scoundrel*, though, the critics ascribe the fault to the script, generally praising the actors, including Roddy. It runs only four performances.

The failure of these shows isn't considered as catastrophic in this era as it might be today. Broadway has a very different financial model at the time, where costs are more contained than they are now, and money can be made even if something isn't a big hit. Roddy finds Broadway more creative and daring than Hollywood, attributing that to the fact that no studio heads are in charge. Though he always maintains positive relationships with studio and network executives, as a whole he views them as fundamentally uncreative and focused on following safe formulas that appeal to whatever they imagine the masses want.

One remarkable difference seen through the lens of someone working in theater today is the gargantuan size of Broadway casts in the 1950s. One of Roddy's biggest hits still ahead of him is *Compulsion* with a cast of thirty-eight, including a very young Suzanne Pleshette in a bit part; *No Time for Sergeants* has a cast of twenty-six; another future play, *Handful of Fire*, has a cast of twenty-three. It would be all but unthinkable to try to stage musicals today with casts this large, let alone straight plays, and these casts numbers don't include understudies or standbys. In the 1950s and 1960s, theater is affordable entertainment rather than a business defined by productions being blockbusters or costly disasters. Shows closing quickly is disappointing but not necessarily a blow to one's career.

Roddy is a familiar sight in the theater district, zooming around on a red Lambretta, an Italian scooter in the Vespa mode. He takes pictures of everything, including performers he meets when working. Some begin using his photos as their professional headshots. He also jets back and forth between New York and Los Angeles, starring in four live shows broadcast from California in 1957 alone for *NBC Matinee Theater*, the first daily hour-long dramatic anthology series on TV, featuring original material and literary adaptations. The pressure of the series going live with five different shows five times a week is extraordinary. It's an incredibly demanding process. While one episode of the program is on air, the following day's episode is in final rehearsal. Both are happening at the same time, in the same studio, with a soundproof curtain separating the two shows. Two crews of seventy-five technicians each work on the projects, while four future episodes are in rehearsal in four rehearsal halls in a facility at the corner of Vine and Selma in Los Angeles.

"The Vicarious Years" is based on a novel by John Van Druten. Roddy is a young man searching for the meaning of life as he begins a writing career in England. In "Talk You of Killing?" Roddy is a handsome professor who's a murder suspect; in "Rain in the Morning" he's a husband helping his shy wife prepare a meal to impress his boss; in "The Whiteheaded Boy" he's a med school failure who disappoints his family. The stories are simply told with minimal sets and costumes and aren't that different from doing stage plays in repertory. If an actor isn't prepared, they're sunk. Roddy is something of an anomaly for TV producers. He brings marquee value as someone the viewers consider a star, but he has no star baggage. He makes no unreasonable demands and exhibits no attitude. That's down to a habit developed from his earliest years in the movies. What he wants most of all is to please everyone. He will work as hard as you ask him to if he thinks it means there's a chance of making you happy. But if Roddy is considered a joy to work with, maybe a big part of that is how much joy the work brings him.

He turns thirty in 1958. Sometimes he still plays the confused son who needs parental love. Or he's the graduate, the new hire, the newly married, the naïf. More often, though, particularly in the theater, he's able to carve out very different personas—as he does quite memorably with *Compulsion*, an adaptation of the bestselling Meyer Levin novel, loosely based on the Leopold and Loeb case. Dean Stockwell and Roddy McDowall kidnap and murder a young boy to prove they can get away with the perfect crime. Their psychosexual obsessions are on display as they go on trial, with Roddy as the sadistic mastermind of the plan and Dean as the masochistic follower and true believer.

Creating this character is exciting and terrifying. Who is this monstrous person who plans a murder just to please himself? What horrifying need is he satisfying? What is he covering up with layer upon layer of delusion to enable him to justify his actions? Roddy's first step is to remove any sense of judgment. Words like "monstrous," "horrifying," and "delusion" won't help him connect. What will help is giving himself over to the character's attraction to a godlike sense of power—the size and immensity of that experience—and the freedom of indulging any sexual kink that occurs to him. Roddy connects to the thrill of all that, as he also constructs the character's buried pain and fear. He and Dean Stockwell find camaraderie and a shared sense of commitment, even as the process proves emotionally and professionally complicated.

Compulsion is a high-profile project with a lot of press attention. Meyer Levin writes the script, but the producers Michael Myerberg and Len Gruenberg believe it adheres too closely to his novel and needs big changes and cuts to work onstage. Meyer refuses. The producers bring in Robert Thom, who reportedly writes much of what's presented. A blizzard of lawsuits and countersuits are filed and argued before the show opens. Meyer Levin even sues Roddy McDowall and Dean Stockwell personally, based on hearsay published in an article about Robert Thom, alleging that their negative remarks about Meyer's writing constitutes slander. As rehearsals begin, Dean comes down with a nasty flu strain, another actor has a heart attack, and the legal challenges keep escalating.

The case against Roddy and Dean is dropped. The idea that reacting negatively to a script can be construed as slander is ridiculous. But the other issues remain unresolved even as the show opens and becomes one of the hottest tickets in town. The actors are praised to the skies. Frank Aston, *New York World-Telegram and The Sun*: "Roddy McDowall and Dean Stockwell who played the killers . . . what a beating they took. Their every moment went full tilt. They did so well so often that it was difficult to choose high spots. Mr. Stockwell probably reached his peak of agony in confessing his unnatural passion, and Mr. McDowall reached his in a heart-tearing jail scene with his mother when he sobbed, 'I want my teddy bear.' They're magnificent, these lads." Walter Kerr agrees: "There are scenes that catch hold in their first few moments and seem to explore every nuance of disturbed and disturbing minds. . . . The grinding arrival at self-knowledge is chillingly drawn." And Brooks Atkinson in *The New York Times*: "Roddy McDowall and Dean Stockwell play the two boys brilliantly, Mr. McDowall gay, antic and arrogant; Mr. Stockwell crushed, weak, gloomy." Critics split on the show itself—some feel its homosexual themes, violence, and general ickiness make it too much to bear. Others see in it an attempt to understand the nature of psychological damage and societal hypocrisy.

For Roddy it's as much a relief as it is a triumph. Not that long ago he was in Hollywood being told his career could be over—that he may never work again. Here he is, a Broadway star, with *How Green Was My Valley* and *Lassie Come Home* happy yet distant memories in the minds of the audience. He doesn't need to dispel his childhood persona anymore. A Shakespearean sprite, a redneck soldier, and a murderous gay psychopath, among his many other characters, do that for him. Roddy

McDowall, former star moppet, is being taken seriously as an adult actor. And he's having fun.

His parents and Virginia fly out to see him in *Compulsion*, as they try to do with most of his shows. Virginia watches with pride as Roddy comes into his own, playing roles completely outside of anything he once imagined. It's harder for Thomas and Winefriede to understand. They can point to Roddy's growing success and know it's positive, and they see that he's doing work he loves. They are, however, somewhat mystified by his attraction to something like *Compulsion.* The world is so full of unpleasantness. Why call attention to such depravity? It's like celebrating evil. These are thoughts they share with Virginia. Not with Roddy.

Winefriede keeps herself busy in Los Angeles with a blizzard of correspondence. All of her godchildren and strays over the years stay in touch. She even trades letters with some of the old execs at Fox and MGM. Who knows? That might come in handy one day. Thomas takes to doing odd jobs for extra income when Winefriede overspends. They have some income from one of the properties they held on to, and Thomas gets a pension. Whenever something unexpected comes along, they write Stephen Weinrib, Roddy's business manager, and he wires them "loans" that go on the books as gifts. Virginia also needs help sometimes. Roddy starts giving her and his parents a regular monthly allowance.

During the 1950s, even in times when he isn't earning a lot, he manages to help support his family. Now he can better afford it as his earning power continues rising. He takes a large, nine-room apartment at 300 Central Park West overlooking Central Park. He aims for an English country feeling, chintz mixed with some modern pieces, but show business is really the main decorative theme. His study is lined with books, tapes, and memorabilia, all alphabetized and sorted, and the walls are covered with framed copies of his own photos and old theatrical posters. He displays scrapbooks of autographs he has collected, movie stills of favorite stars like Alice Faye and Rudolph Valentino, movie ads dating back to 1930, and movie magazines dating back to as early as 1912. He buys a film projector and begins collecting copies of films he loves, though he's always careful not to divulge the full contents of the collection as it grows. He never allows the names of the films he acquires to appear in print, worried that a studio will send lawyers around to make trouble. "They don't care about the films, they just care about your right to own them," he tells Rex Reed. "Have you any idea how much nitrate film is disintegrating in vaults? They'd rather see it burn than be enjoyed by people for centuries to come. Hollywood has never preserved its own history. If it were not for private collectors, most of the great masterpieces would be gone forever."

This world he creates reflects his flowering creativity. It's the world where he begins to entertain, a habit that becomes an essential factor in his life. Dinners, parties—he loves being surrounded by his colleagues and friends, by *their* colleagues and friends, and by other friends of friends. Everyone is welcome at least once. Show rudeness to any other guest, however, and you're out. And whereas social events in Hollywood are geared predominantly around the movie business, Roddy's world includes everyone, not only people from film, TV, and theater, but also artists from the worlds of opera, ballet, painting, and sculpture. Roddy is passionate about anything and everything creative, and his circle of friends begins to grow.

Entertaining comes easily. He keeps the best of Winefriede's tutelage, all the many Sunday gatherings and dinner parties, with the effortless feeling of welcome and fun, but leaves aside the idea of everything centering around him, or wanting to control how things progress. His role is to bring people together who might find one another stimulating. If they do, fantastic; if they don't, it's their choice. He's not his mother.

And the food is never the point, a practice that endures.

He and Monty are still close, but Monty isn't a regular at these gatherings, probably by tacit mutual consent. Monty doesn't like being surrounded by too many people, while Roddy isn't interested in unnecessary drama. He wants his guests to feel transported. His home is a place where everyone should be able to feel they look their best, they're clever, talented, and loved. Nothing ugly or dangerous should intrude on that feeling. Having a drunk or high Monty sprawled across the floor isn't the vibe he's going for.

Actress Marian Seldes is a frequent guest. "[Roddy] would invite so many of us working actors to come and to eat and to talk to other people in the theatre and films. I met Myrna Loy there!" she tells writer James Grissom in an unpublished interview. "He would sometimes invite us in smaller groups to watch old films that we thought had disappeared, and he would put them on a projector himself. We had to be perfectly silent! But afterward we would talk and argue. I loved him so much."

Merv Griffin one night brings a friend of his who works in public relations for game shows. Merv is transitioning from singing to TV work and has gotten a job hosting a show called *Play Your Hunch.* The publicist is a very Southern, funny, prone-to-malaprops young woman named Boaty Boatwright, from North Carolina. She and Roddy are like long lost cousins immediately. Boaty goes on to become one of the most important casting directors, studio execs, and agents around, but more important to Roddy, she's loving, funny, and gossipy without ever revealing anything she shouldn't.

Robby and Sherlee Lantz become a permanent part of Roddy's circle, through Monty at first, but the relationship endures. Robby is one of those remarkable characters who seems to know everything and everybody. Physically he's short, often referred to as "gnomish," he wears large glasses and speaks with a thick, German accent. He writes long, garrulous letters, even when they're both in the same city, and he absolutely adores

Roddy. Robby has a habit of inserting nonsense things he finds funny into letters, with no connection to anything. "Have you seen *Flying Down to Rio* yet?" he asks in a 1963 letter mainly about recent dinner parties and client Myrna Loy's television prospects. "A lovely musical. And wait till you see Betty Grable, stunning! I think talkies are here to stay!" For the record, Robby has a mind like a steel trap. He's almost certainly aware that Ginger Rogers and Dolores del Rio are the female stars of *Flying Down to Rio.*

Robby only acts as Roddy's agent for his photography books (the first is in 1966), but his and Roddy's work lives intersect all the time. Robby's other clients include accomplished directors like José Quintero, Michael Blakemore, and Milos Forman; stars like Monty, Myrna Loy; Elizabeth Taylor, Bette Davis, Yul Brynner, and Richard Burton; playwright Peter Shaffer; writers Carson McCullers, James Baldwin, and Lillian Hellman; and lyricist-librettist Alan Jay Lerner.

Some find it tricky being friends with powerful people. Whatever Roddy's private hopes, he never exhibits any sense of entitlement or expectation. Letters between Roddy and Robby refer to occasions when Robby puts his finger on the scale to help push a deal through for Roddy. But it works both ways. In the early 1960s, when Robby becomes aware that Roddy is spending a weekend with Dirk Bogarde in France, where Peter Shaffer will also be a guest, Robby asks Roddy to somehow steer the conversation to agenting so he can say something positive and helpful about Robby that will appeal to Peter. *Without letting Peter know that Roddy knows that Robby is trying to get Peter as a client.* It's a bit of a game, and they're quite playful about helping each other out.

A sense of play also turns up at Roddy's parties, where he loves inventing games. "There's one where you nominate movies, stars, and producers and you meld," he tells Rex Reed. "For example, you meld Olivia de Havilland and Leslie Howard in

Gone With the Wind with Bette Davis and you have *It's Love I'm After*." There is no Google search to back up the answers. Instead, there's Roddy's personal Internet Movie Database of index cards and little filing cabinets, where he has written down the details of every movie he has ever seen or read about in one of his collected magazines.

Roddy doesn't throw parties to move his way up the social and professional ladder, but his gatherings do attract new people into his orbit. Suddenly Lenny Bernstein and Steve Sondheim are part of his life. This is when he becomes close to Kate Hepburn and Lauren Bacall. Sometimes he's surprised by the level of affection people seem to have for him. It's not that he feels undeserving; it's more that it's puzzling. Why him? The answer he comes to is simple: Why not? He keeps entertaining. He keeps snapping pictures. And he keeps working.

When Katharine Cornell asks Roddy to join her in *First Born*, Christopher Fry's retelling of the story of the plagues of Egypt, Roddy feels honored. She is one of his theatrical heroes, right up there with Tallullah Bankhead, and the idea of sharing a stage is too marvelous to pass up. Anthony Quayle directs and also plays Moses, with Katharine as his mother, and Roddy as Ramses. Another friend, Mildred Natwick, is cast, the production is designed by a friend, Boris Aronson, and Leonard Bernstein is composing songs. Roddy does the out-of-town run in Cleveland, Toronto, and Boston, and gets good reviews, but for unknown reasons it's announced he's "amicably" leaving the show before its New York opening. He remains close with everyone involved, so the amicability of his parting seems genuine. The show isn't a success and runs less than a month.

His next Broadway show runs just five days. Directed by his acting coach Bobby Lewis, *Handful of Fire* takes place in a border town. Roddy is a young Mexican man (there's a description you never thought you would see) who journeys from innocence to cynicism and back again in an allegorical exploration of love, purity, and forgiveness. Joan Copeland (playwright Arthur Miller's sister) is the Mexican virgin who turns to prostitution; James Daley is Roddy's corrupt Mexican rival for Joan's affections. The fact that none of the actors is even tangentially Mexican or Latino doesn't seem to bother anyone, because, as is typical of the time, no one thinks to ask an actual Mexican or Latino person how they feel about it.

Roddy's big moment is when his character realizes that his honesty has made him everyone's fool, and he asks his rival to teach him the art of racketeering. If being a good man gets him nowhere, he will try being a bad man. Roddy revels in going as far as he can with the impassioned speech. While taking issue with the play itself, Brooks Atkinson in *The New York Times* approves. "Roddy McDowall, who plays Pepe, pitches into this speech with sardonic fervor and brings the whole play alive. At that moment, *Handful of Fire* looks promising. But it's never again so stimulating, for the basic conflict is never again stated so clearly. . . . Mr. McDowall gives a swift, tense, varied performance that is always in motion and further evidence of his talent."

While *Handful of Fire* is playing out its very short run, Roddy and Noël Coward are trading letters about Noël's failure to launch his most recent play, *Volcano*, a thinly disguised roman à clef about Ian Fleming and the married woman who becomes the inspiration for Pussy Galore. They meet when Roddy is doing *Compulsion* and Noël is starring in his own *Nude with Violin.* Noël becomes a regular at Roddy's gatherings. *Volcano*, with its looming threat of an eruptive explosion and sexy hothouse Caribbean ambiance, is unpalatable to Noël's usual producer Binkie Beaumont, and Noël isn't amenable to looking for someone else. So he's now adapting Georges Feydeau's French farce *Occupe-toi d'Amélie!* ("Take Care of Amélie") with the help of his assistant, Cole Lesley. He's doing the project for Vivien Leigh and Laurence Olivier. But Larry and Viv have scheduling conflicts, so Noël wants to mount the show in New York first.

Would Roddy like to be involved?

Yes. Roddy would very much like to be involved, thanks ever so.

Occupe-toi d'Amélie! becomes *Look After Lulu.* The central character is a madcap courtesan, in love with one man, accused of indiscretions with another, set amid people hiding under beds and in bathrooms, sex-obsessed foreign royals, a fake wedding that turns out to be real, and a happy ending to the love triangle that seems comically doomed. From the start, Coward struggles with the clash of styles, finding Feydeau's physical comedy unfunny and his plot digressions unfathomable. If the situation were reversed, perhaps Feydeau, who died in 1921, would find Coward's lack of physical surprise and reliance on wordplay just as unpalatable. Still, Noël soldiers on.

Cyril Ritchard signs on as the director. Roddy will play the rival to Lulu's professed true love, who will be played by English actor George Baker, thought to be on the verge of film stardom at the time. But who is to be Lulu? Coward's hopes for Shirley MacLaine or Carol Channing don't come to pass. (Imagining those two up for the same role is bizarre in and of itself.) Roddy suggests his friend Tammy Grimes, who has not done a Broadway book show before. Coward sees Tammy's cabaret act and thinks she's perfect. After a tryout in New Haven, the play premieres to poor business and tepid notices with most critics believing Noël Coward and Georges Feydeau are incompatible. *Look After Lulu* closes after thirty-nine performances. Its London run proves more successful, but it never becomes part of the frequently revived canon of Coward works. It does nothing for anybody's career, but most important, it does nothing to damage anyone's friendships. Noël and Roddy remain close, as do Roddy and Tammy Grimes, as do Tammy and Noël.

During thc *Look After Lulu* run, a friend, the agent Dick Clayton, asks Roddy to do a photoshoot with his client Tuesday Weld, who's making a bit of a splash on TV in *The Many Loves of Dobie Gillis.* The photos accompany a *Pageant* magazine feature on Tuesday Weld called "Shooting Star." It's Roddy's first time as a published, professional photographer, and he's every bit as proud of that article as he is of any of his acting jobs.

His next big TV production is for *Sunday Showcase*, "Our American Heritage: Not Without Honor," a dramatization of the last four years of Alexander Hamilton's life, with Ralph Bellamy as Thomas Jefferson, Arthur Kennedy as Hamilton, and Roddy as his son Philip Hamilton. The show culminates with the famous duel with Aaron Burr, but the pivotal moment narratively is a different duel three years earlier, where Philip Hamilton challenges one of Aaron Burr's acolytes who insults his father's honor. Roddy dies in Arthur Kennedy's arms.

Though most of his TV work is shot in New York, Roddy flies to Los Angeles to star in a live *Playhouse 90* reimagining of Joseph Conrad's *Heart of Darkness*. It's a prestigious gig with a lot of promotion. The production itself is very black-box, with no sense of realistic space, and with jerky, on-the-fly camera movements. Inga Swenson plays his "sister," though they are unrelated, Boris Karloff is the lost guru Roddy travels up an African river hoping to find, and Eartha Kitt is a "native woman." The masochistic, tortuous role is at once surreal and very corporeal. "I'm a tattered man. My skin's come loose in places, and I have trouble holding it on," Roddy says, looking like a ghost of himself. "I have to look in corners for the broken pieces of myself. If I find the hand I've lost I pin it to my sleeve so there will be something for people to grasp when they greet me." The production itself is as imponderable to people used to streaming *The White Lotus* on HBO Max as silent movies can be to someone used to Marvel flicks. It's something of a completely different age. Yet the majesty of the performances endures.

It's been almost eight years since Roddy has made a movie. Producer Arthur Freed at MGM is looking for a change of pace. Known primarily for his musicals, from *Babes in Arms* in 1939 to the 1958 Best Picture winner, *Gigi*, Freed wants to turn *The Subterraneans* into a film. Jack Kerouac's follow-up to *On the Road* is a fictionalized story based on his romance with Alene Lee, an African American woman, in Greenwich Village, and is set among Beat Generation characters steeped in bebop jazz. Arthur Freed intends to make the film low budget, black-and-white, and avant-garde, without the glossy sheen of most MGM products. He instructs writer Robert Thom (of the *Compulsion* rewrite) to make the love interest white and to switch the location to San Francisco but to keep the jazz element.

Jack Kerouac's story is largely about the emotional connection a number of Beat characters have with jazz played in basement ("subterranean") clubs, juxtaposed with the emotional disconnection and misconnections they have with one another. The film gives us George Peppard as a devilishly handsome, self-loathing, self-aggrandizing, failing writer who falls in love with the skittish, emotionally damaged, uncommonly beautiful Leslie Caron. Neither one bears much of a resemblance to their character counterparts in the novella.

While the book has eight main characters, the script reduces that to four, including a meaty supporting role that has the new, grown-up Roddy McDowall written all over it. As it happens, at the time Robert Thom owes Roddy $1,500 for a personal loan. It's extremely doubtful that the offer of a job on *The Subterraneans* is related to the debt, but if it is, it's one hell of an upgrade in terms of repayment. Roddy has a great role, the gregarious, boyish yet sexy Yuri Gligoric, one of the more mercurial members of an amorphous group of Beat friends. He's in love with Leslie but doesn't really do anything about it once she chooses George. Janice Rule is the American flipside to Leslie, every bit as volatile, if not more so, but much more direct about it, turning her emotional turmoil into Beat poetry that she performs with genuinely interesting Method-influenced intensity. All of the poetry is howlingly awful.

In the Arthur Freed unit, one of the champions of the project is likely the *Gigi* music supervisor André Previn, who in his spare time performs progressive jazz as a pianist with small combos in clubs. He's the one person in Freed's orbit who has any connection to the Kerouac universe. He appears onscreen, along with Sarah Vaughan and Gerry Mulligan. The music is terrific and feels authentic. The screenplay, however, is pure squaresville, outsiders looking in on a zoo of Beat characters. A mandated happy ending is engineered by last-minute declarations of true love, an averted abortion, and a marriage proposal, completely negating the countercultural life that supposedly defines and feeds the main characters.

It's a difficult reentry to films for Roddy. Not long before the start of production in August 1959, the studio declares the film will be in color and in CinemaScope (which cinematographer Joseph Ruttenberg quips to Roddy is only good for photographing snakes and cathedrals). The director is fired, and filming shuts down for two weeks early in the shoot when Arthur Freed is unhappy with the footage. Roddy feels untethered, like this is his first film. Which in a way it is. This is his first film as an adult, made utilizing new skills, and demonstrating what's essentially a new body. He's still very trim but now is muscular from working out. When he takes off his shirt in a scene at Leslie Caron's apartment, there's a sensual vibe to it that is startlingly different from anything he has shown on film before. He's not a fan of her acting. ("I loathe Leslie Caron," he writes to Dirk Bogarde. "I think she is a totally talentless flake.") But his performance is extremely persuasive and something of a triumphant return to Hollywood, though the film itself isn't highly regarded.

Once *The Subterraneans* wraps, he flies back to New York to immediately start rehearsals for *The Fighting Cock*, a Broadway adaptation of *L'Hurluberlu* by Jean Anouilh, translated and adapted by Lucienne Hill, starring Rex Harrison as a bitter retired general determined to "rid the world of maggots and teach the people honor." Roddy is the cad who jilts his daughter. Rex challenges Roddy to a duel, only to find humiliation and defeat. Director Peter Brook is just the sort of artistic force Roddy finds exciting, schooled and rooted in the classic theater tradition, but unafraid and fascinated by bold ideas. Rex Harrison is universally praised for his performance and Roddy's notices are respectable, but in the afterthought vein of "the other actors are also excellent." So he's quite surprised when he's nominated for a featured actor Tony Award, in a talented field that includes Warren Beatty in *The Subject Was Roses*, Harry Guardino in *One More River*, Rip Torn in *Sweet Bird of Youth*, and Lawrence Winters in *The Long Dream.*

Showbiz columnists seem genuinely delighted by Roddy's nomination—his first major nod for anything since the early 1940s. Louella, Hedda, Radie Harris, Sheila Graham, Walter Winchell—everyone seems delighted for him.

Sadly, no one uses the headline, "Ex Moppet Star Gets Nod for Fighting Cock."

Chapter 5

The Cool Ones

February 1, 1960: *Life* features a TV section article, "*The Tempest*'s New Impact" with the subhead "Shakespearean fantasy shows Roddy McDowall in a long-sought role," about the upcoming color broadcast for *Hallmark Hall of Fame.* The page is dominated by a two-thirds-page photograph of Roddy as Ariel, fully transformed into a magical creature, more elaborate than in the 1955 Stratford production, casting a spell on the impossibly young, beautiful Lee Remick as Miranda. The tone is chummy and insider. Shakespeare is cool. Roddy and Lee are cool. Richard Burton as Caliban and Maurice Evans as Prospero are cool. "I had to like this a lot to play it on TV," says Roddy. "It took four hours to get into costume."

February 3, 1960: *The Tempest* airs to spectacular ratings, with over twenty-one million people watching—the highest numbers ever for a *Hall of Fame* Shakespeare production.

February 8, 1960: Roddy gets a star at 6632 Hollywood Boulevard for his TV work, as part of the official opening of the Hollywood Walk of Fame.

March 23, 1960: He starts shooting *Midnight Lace* for producer Ross Hunter, his first full-fledged, big-budget A picture since *Holiday in Mexico* in 1946.

March 25, 1960: An iconic episode of *The Twilight Zone* airs called "People Are Alike All Over," with Roddy as the lone survivor of a crash-landing on Mars, who's surprised by how generous the Martians are, until he realizes the spiffy new house they build for him is meant to illustrate his natural habitat. He's their newest zoo attraction.

April 24, 1960: Roddy McDowall is named a Tony winner for *The Fighting Cock.* His friend Lauren Bacall and Darren McGavin present the award at the Astor Hotel in New York to an audience of 1,200 people who work in the Broadway community. Robert Stack accepts on Roddy's behalf since Roddy is in Los Angeles shooting *Midnight Lace* with Doris Day and his costar from *The Fighting Cock*, Rex Harrison.

Roddy McDowall is officially a star again, this time as an adult, but he's not particularly interested in whatever his agents might think is the next "smart" move to take advantage of his renewed stardom, because at the moment, there's a book he likes. His friends are adapting it into a stage musical, and Roddy would very much like to play in their sandbox.

Roddy's involvement with *Camelot* happens easily and simply. He loves T. H. White's book *The Once and Future King*, which is the basis for the show, and just about everyone involved is a friend. Director Moss Hart and librettist and lyricist Alan Jay Lerner are regulars at Roddy's parties, along with Moss Hart's wife, actress Kitty Carlisle Hart. Roddy is also friendly, though not close, with composer Frederick Loewe.

The character that captures Roddy's imagination is Mordred, the bastard son of King Arthur and the catalyst for Arthur's downfall. He loves the idea of playing a true villain with no redeeming features, where the stakes are certainly high, but not in the realistic sense of something like *Compulsion.* To Roddy, the good son of all good sons, Mordred's merry betrayal of his own father is deliciously alien. The more he thinks about it, underlining passages in his copy of White's book, the more the notion takes hold.

When he approaches the creative team about it, they're intrigued and excited about what Roddy might bring to the role but concerned that the part is too small for someone of Roddy's stature. Mordred will have maybe ten or fifteen minutes of stage time in total, and perhaps even more important, in the gigantic *Camelot* cast Mordred isn't designated as one of the star parts that will be allocated a star's salary.

They can't afford Roddy.

Roddy doesn't care. He will make whatever concessions he can, so the numbers are workable. He just wants to be part of what he knows will be a magical experience—he sees it so clearly. They have to trust him when he says this is just meant to be. It's the same feeling he had about Ariel in *The Tempest* the first time, and the second time. They shake hands on a deal with no contract and financial terms that make sense to all involved. If it doesn't work out, Roddy can leave the show whenever he wants with no hard feelings. Of course the unspoken flip side of that is if the creative team doesn't feel it's working for some reason, they can replace him. After all, Roddy has never done a Broadway musical before. *Does he even sing?*

Roddy has always been someone who sings, though he doesn't consider himself a *singer*, and he has performed a few times in small revues along the way, but that isn't the same thing as being in a full book musical with an orchestra and professional singers and dancers. In 1960, the stage rights to the MGM classic Judy Garland musical *Meet Me in St. Louis* are released, and a number of regional productions launch for the summer stock season (including a major one in St. Louis). Roddy signs up for the role of John (the Boy Next Door) in a production opening in upstate New York, at the Sacandaga Summer Theatre, and going on to Toronto. The role has two songs and not a lot of stage time. It's a chance to flex his muscles. The engagements go well, and Roddy is confident that he can take on the challenge of *Camelot.*

In between assignments, Leonard Bernstein introduces Roddy to actress Judy Holliday, who's starting rehearsals for a new play about the great theater star Laurette Taylor, famously the first actress to play Amanda in the Tennessee Williams play *The Glass Menagerie.* The central image for the poster is going to be a photograph of Judy, who's nervous about the project. She is known as a comedy actress, and this is a drama. She wants a picture that captures a different side of her personality. Roddy shoots her one afternoon, coaxing and charming her into letting down her guard. The pictures that emerge are soft, vulnerable, and beautiful—quite different from the bright, brassy shots that her publicists typically use. One of Roddy's photos appears on the show's poster and in *Vogue* with the article, "People Are Talking About . . . Judy Holliday." It's his second published work.

When *Camelot* rehearsals begin in August 1960, Alan Jay Lerner marvels that by skill and the sheer force of his personality, Roddy turns Mordred into a star part. And even as the length of the show becomes an intractable problem, they still write a song just for Roddy, "The Seven Deadly Virtues," where he gleefully mocks the Round Table.

You'll never find a virtue unstatusing my quo
Or making my Beelzebubble burst
Let others take the high road, I will take the low
I cannot wait to rush in where angels fear to go

If Roddy becoming a part of *Camelot* is something that happens easily and simply, the show's journey to Broadway is anything but. With Julie Andrews and Richard Burton as the leads, the handsome, talented Robert Goulet ready to emerge as a star in his own right, and the *My Fair Lady* creative team writing the show, odds seem like they should be in their favor, but the first out-of-town tryout in Toronto is disastrous. Depending on whose version of events you believe, the show runs somewhere between three and a half and four and a half hours long, including intermission, leaving audiences dazed and exhausted. Noël Coward is supposed to have cracked that, "the show was longer than the *Götterdämmerung* . . . and not nearly as funny!"

Moss Hart doesn't seem able to do anything about it. Everyone agrees the show needs "trimming." Cutting two hours from a musical isn't trimming, it's major surgery. And no one is ready to scrub in. Roddy is surprised at Hart's unfocused and haphazard approach. "His direction was adorably flirtatious, but aimless," Roddy says in Steven Bach's biography of Moss Hart. "He would say to me, 'Enter from stage left, go to center stage, look around, then exit stage right. Now, enter stage right, go to center stage, look around, and then exit stage left.' Finally, I asked what I was supposed to be looking around for, and Moss said, 'Nothing, Dear Boy, I just like to watch you walk and twinkle your ass.' That was flattering, I suppose. And Moss was a charmer through and through, but it didn't help me much with my character."

Still, Roddy's enthusiasm for the project stays strong, even as there appears to be no clear plan of action, just a series of catastrophes. Alan Jay Lerner is hospitalized with a bleeding ulcer. Moss Hart's father dies. Then Hart is hospitalized with flu and nervous exhaustion. Just as Lerner seems to be improving, Hart has a heart attack. Both are in the hospital. *Camelot* is rudderless but chugging along, opening with mixed-to-respectable reviews. Box office receipts are robust due to the lingering glow of Lerner and Loewe's *My Fair Lady* driving tickets sales, so the crisis atmosphere is tinged with hope.

The show moves to Boston. Hart is still in the hospital. Lerner tries to step in as the director but remains under a doctor's care for his bleeding ulcer. Loewe is very supportive of the cast and the production team. He's also privately adamantly opposed to Lerner directing, believing Lerner needs to concentrate on drastically cutting the book. The Boston run is largely sold out, even as a demoralized cast tries to figure out what to do.

There have been so many changes, cuts, additions, and rearrangements, that getting through scenes without any major mishaps or disasters feels like flying with constant near-miss collisions.

Roddy remembers it as weeks of polar opposite realities. The show is a four-hour disaster, but it's the hottest ticket in town. Lerner is neglecting the book, ostensibly so he can direct, but no actual directing seems to be happening, just listless run-throughs of the existing scenes moved around. Loewe is publicly supportive of his longtime partner but, in reality, is furious that Lerner keeps insisting on ineptly muddling through as director, a role Loewe believes Lerner isn't qualified to fill. Attempts at signing on an emergency replacement as director go nowhere. Lerner and Loewe fear they will be pilloried in New York by the critics and by envious colleagues, happy at seeing them fail.

Richard Burton and Julie Andrews feel a sense of responsibility to the cast and production team, and through many reassuring cups of tea with castmates in Julie's dressing rooms and lots of stronger beverages in Richard's dressing room, they help keep morale as high as is possible, assuring everyone that things will work out, even as they have their own problems with the material. One of Julie Andrews's biggest songs, "I Loved You Once in Silence," goes into the show the night before they open in New York. Still too long. Still unfocused. With sixty-seven actors, singers, and dancers onstage drowning in what feels like a flop. The reviews aren't as gleefully brutal and laced with schadenfreude as Lerner and Loewe dread; some are very complimentary, but all of them complain about the show's length and lack of focus.

Their record-setting $3.5 million in advance ticket sales keep them going.

Moss Hart is still in the hospital. The length of the show and its general aimlessness cause as many as two to three hundred walkouts at intermissions for every performance. Two months into the run, ticket sales start slowing. The show looks unlikely to last much longer. Then, like the mythical tale of *Camelot* itself, a dreamlike series of events turns everything around. Moss Hart's health improves. He returns to work and sits down with Lerner outlining the kinds of cuts the show should have had before Toronto and might have had before New York if it weren't for his heart attack. The true stroke of luck then comes in the form of corporate synergy. CBS is a major investor in the show. *The Ed Sullivan Show*, the crown jewel of CBS's Sunday night schedule, decides to do a tribute to Lerner and Loewe for the fifth anniversary of the opening of *My Fair Lady*, a phenomenon that is still packing them in at the Mark Hellinger Theatre.

Ed Sullivan lets Lerner and Loewe program the show themselves. They immediately decide there will be nothing from *My Fair Lady.* It's all going to be about *Camelot.* Moss Hart's cuts go into effect—a very unusual turn of events for a show that is already running—and the cast performs four numbers on *The Ed Sullivan Show* ("Camelot," "How to Handle a Woman," "If Ever I Would Leave You," and "What Do the Simple Folk Do?"). The audience in the studio and viewers at home love the songs, Julie Andrews and Richard Burton are adorable, and Robert Goulet becomes a star overnight. It's a fairy-tale ending that Roddy feels justifies his initial belief in the show—how he actually *sees* its success from the beginning. He loves this group of people, and he feels proud going out on stage with them at every performance as they create magic together.

Another aspect of his life is also feeling quite magical. Roddy is in a new relationship with an actor named John Valva, who's living with him in the Central Park West apartment. Roddy's archives don't give an indication of when they meet. It might be as early as October 1959, when John is playing a page in John Gielgud's Broadway production of *Much Ado About Nothing.* It's running when Roddy goes into rehearsals for *The Fighting Cock*, and John Gielgud is a friend and frequent dinner guest. Less likely is that it's even earlier, when, in 1958, John Valva has a small role in a Fort Lee, New Jersey, production of *Mr. Roberts* starring Roddy's friend Farley Granger. Or they might meet in any number of other ways. What is clear is that they're living together well before Roddy is scheduled to leave for Rome to shoot *Cleopatra* in late 1961. John becomes Roddy's first live-in long-term partner. Things would be idyllic if Roddy weren't so terribly anxious about Elizabeth Taylor's health.

The month before *Camelot* opens, production on *Cleopatra* in England is shut down when she comes down with pneumonia. Her health seesaws, as she seems to recover, then relapses several times. Just as the retooled version of *Camelot* begins selling out, Elizabeth is rushed to the hospital again, unable to breathe. A tracheotomy saves her life. Roddy wishes he could be by her side, but all that hokum about how the show must go on? It isn't hokum at all. Roddy will never leave *Camelot* in the lurch to rush to Elizabeth's side, however much he might like to. He sends flowers of course and is in touch with her fourth husband, singer Eddie Fisher.

As a matter of policy, Roddy doesn't get involved in Elizabeth Taylor's love life. If asked for an opinion, he might give it—as diplomatically as possible—but he believes he can be the friend she needs, not by judging her decisions but by accepting them and respecting her autonomy as an adult.

This is not to say that Roddy likes Eddie Fisher or vice versa.

Even Elizabeth doesn't seem to like Eddie that much by this point.

Two years earlier, Elizabeth Taylor and Eddie Fisher are an accident waiting to happen when her third husband, Mike Todd, dies in the crash of his private plane "The Liz." (It's only called "The Lucky Liz" by the press, highlighting how unlucky the plane turns out to be, but Mike Todd never calls it that.) Before his death, Mike is best friends with Eddie Fisher. Eddie is married to Debbie Reynolds, both at the height of their popularity, and in fan magazines, they're often referred to as "America's Sweethearts" (along with any number of other good-looking famous couples, like Lucille Ball and Desi Arnaz, Tony Curtis and

Janet Leigh, and Paul Newman and Joanne Woodward). The Todds and the Fishers spend a lot of their leisure time together. Elizabeth Taylor's grief at losing Mike is profound. She converts to Judaism as a way of honoring him, hoping a purposeful sense of religion will assuage her pain, but while it gives her a feeling of closeness to him, it doesn't ease her sorrow. Eddie Fisher is also devastated. He and Elizabeth share a terrible sense of loss, and it brings them together. At some point that intimacy takes a turn. . . .

As rumors of a liaison spread, Hedda Hopper calls Elizabeth and asks if they're true. Elizabeth responds in a relatively truthful fashion, telling Hedda, "I don't go about breaking up marriages. You can't break up a happy marriage. Debbie's and Eddie's never has been." Where she gets herself in trouble is when she quips, "What do you expect me to do? Sleep alone?"

This isn't something nice girls say to the press in the 1950s and 1960s, when double standards are in full force. (That it's still not something nice girls say to the press in the present day, and that double standards are still going strong, is regrettably also true.) The scandal of Elizabeth Taylor "stealing" Eddie Fisher from Debbie Reynolds is Elizabeth Taylor's first go-round with tabloid vilification. It's not the last. All Roddy can do is protect her confidences and offer his love and support.

While Roddy continues performing in *Camelot*, he also shoots three of his more prestigious TV projects back-to-back. The first is an episode of the gritty cop show *Naked City*, "The Fault in Our Stars," guest-starring Roddy as an unemployed actor. Desperate to eat and pay his back rent, he strangles several cab drivers to steal their money. The character is bitter, sarcastic, and gleefully unlikeable. He finally gets cast in a play only to lose the gig when he's arrested for his multiple murders. It's a tour de force, and among his team of agents and publicists, there's a great deal of talk about him possibly getting an Emmy nomination for the performance. A letter from his publicist about such a nomination comes in the mail just as a telegram arrives from the National Academy of Television Arts & Sciences congratulating Roddy about his nomination for a different show. He gets a nod for Outstanding Performance in a Supporting Role by an Actor or Actress in a Single Program for his work from the prior TV season as Philip Hamilton in *Sunday Showcase* "Our American Heritage: Not Without Honor." He's up against Charles Bronson in "Memory in White," on *General Electric Theater*, and Peter Falk in "Cold Turkey," on *The Law and Mr. Jones.* Roddy thinks he has Arthur Kennedy to thank for the nomination. As Roddy's character is dying, Arthur grabs his head so hard that the hair lace on Roddy's wig comes loose. It's a live show. Roddy seems so intense, gripping his father's hand with heartbreaking intensity—because he's trying to hold his wig in place.

Roddy has little time to contemplate the Emmy nomination, however. After *Naked City*, he goes into rehearsals for the barebones Peabody Award–winning series *The Play of the Week*, in a Philip Barry play called *In a Garden.* Roddy plays a wealthy young playwright who decides to retire from writing but is tormented when George Grizzard, a jealous fellow writer, comes to him with a story about having had an assignation with Roddy's wife, Barbara Cook, in a garden, ten years before. The fabulous cast also includes Frances Sternhagen and Christopher Hewitt in small roles.

Camelot is still selling out, so Roddy can't attend the Emmy Awards ceremony at the Moulin Rouge Nightclub in Los Angeles. He writes to a friend that he's "literally" onstage singing "The Seven Deadly Virtues" in New York when his category is announced and he wins the Emmy. (The exact timing of that may not necessarily be true, but the use of the word "literally" is perhaps as imprecise in 1961 as it is today.) It's a pity Roddy can't be there with other friends winning that night, including his *No Time for Sergeants* castmate Don Knotts—*The Andy Griffith Show* wins Best Comedy Series—and his onetime colleague at Fox, the grand moppet herself, Shirley Temple, wins an Emmy for Outstanding Achievement in the Field of Children's Programming.

Then Roddy gets another prize: an offer to join the cast of *Cleopatra* to play Octavian opposite his friends Elizabeth Taylor, Richard Burton, and Rex Harrison. Octavian is another character with father issues. As Julius Caesar's adopted son and heir, he challenges Mark Antony for control of Rome. It means he (along with Richard) will have to leave *Camelot.*

But before he can play Roman, he once again plays Mexican, in his third high-profile TV production of the year, an adaptation of the Graham Greene novel *The Power and the Glory*, with Laurence Olivier as a drunken priest sent to Mexico to preach in the 1930s. The leftist government of that era has outlawed Catholic rituals and sees the church as mortal competition, so they send Roddy McDowall as a kind of Judas figure to assassinate Larry. The storied cast also includes Frank Conroy, Cyril Cusack, Patty Duke, Mildred Dunnock, Martin Gabel, Thomas Gomez, Julie Harris, George C. Scott, Fritz Weaver, and Keenan Wynn. It's CBS's major dramatic production of the year, with a budget that balloons from $500,000 to going almost 50 percent over budget at $746,000, $125,000 of that going for the construction of a Mexican village on two soundstages in New York. It's an immensely troubled production, with production days sometimes as long as twenty hours. Reviews for screenwriter Dale Wasserman's adaptation and for Olivier's work are poor, but Roddy comes out of it smelling like a rose.

This dynamic, pain-in-the-ass production yields praise for Roddy, but is about to become déjà vu all over again, in Yogi Berra speak. As he prepares to head for Rome, Roddy also feels ready to kick up his photography career to the next level. He's joining the cast of the most talked-about movie in the world. There will be photos to take. There will be photos to *sell.* He meets photo agent Lee Gross. She is attracted to the quality of the work itself when she sees his portfolio. That's the most important thing, she assures him. His celebrity and his access to so many famous friends will drive sales at first, but if the work itself isn't wonderful, who really cares? A few jobs won't result in a *career*. And she wants to know Roddy is serious about a *career* as a photographer. It will take just as much commitment and focus as his acting career. Is he ready for that?

Roddy is ready for that.

Lee will be one of his most enthusiastic correspondents for many years, sending multipage, poorly typed letters, signed "LOVE LOVE LOVE leeeeeeeee," or sometimes just "Love, leeeeee," with the number of vowels in her name rising and falling with her mood. They write each other even when they're both in the same city—late-night insomnia-prompted missives that ramble on about their thoughts. She is fiercely protective of his rights, and she also understands and respects his boundaries—particularly the ones that relate to Elizabeth Taylor. He will sell photos he takes of Elizabeth over the years, but only with her enthusiastic approval. He will never try to coax his pal into anything she doesn't want to do, and he will never trade on her friendship. So don't ask him to. And Lee never does.

The CBS interview program *Person to Person* visits Roddy at home. Roddy's career resurgence is the main thrust of the interview, with a heavy emphasis on *Cleopatra*, how he feels about working with Elizabeth Taylor again, and how they have been close since they first worked together on *Lassie Come Home* almost twenty years ago.

Winefriede McDowall is also excited about Roddy going to Rome to shoot such an important project, but she mostly looks at it through the lens of how it affects her. A small property in England has been willed to the McDowalls. Winefriede sends Roddy long, detailed instructions about how he must handle some of the legal arrangements for them while he's in Europe. Thomas needs financial help to pay property taxes. There are also financial issues involved with Roddy's life insurance policies when it emerges that Winefriede has taken out loans against them without telling anyone. Plus, Virginia wants to buy a house.

His parents and Virginia believe she can qualify for a home loan, but can Roddy cosign the loan if for some reason it becomes necessary? For some reason it becomes necessary. "But we don't know when and where the documents will be drawn up, so you must let me know at every minute where you are," Winefriede restates repeatedly in cards and letters. "I must know how to reach you! This is vital!" (Winefriede also writes about auditioning for a local production of Ionesco's play *The Chairs* to play a ninety-five-year-old woman. "And I may get it! I'm not kidding!" She doesn't get it.)

Roddy is anxious about expenses, typing multiple lists, working and reworking the details of what he will make during the six-month anticipated *Cleopatra* shoot and his expenses.

COMPUTED AT	$1,900.00	$7,600.00
	WEEK	MONTH
Family	40.00	160.00
Helen Scott [maid]	53.00	212.00
Federal Tax 30%	475.00	1900.00
Kaplan-Veidt [agents]	190.00	760.00
Weinrib [business manager]	95.00	380.00
Rent		417.00
Phone		20.00
Gas Light		5.00
Insurance		10.00
R McD	500.00	2000.00
	1466.00	5864.00
Chemical Bank	50.00	200.00 [*]
Irwin Franklin [publicist]	100.00	400.00
	1616.00	6464.00
Leaves a profit of	284.00	1136.00

*[unanticipated expenses, mainly to family, paid by Weinrib]

Separately, there are notes pertaining to Roddy's request for a monthly per diem from Fox of L.800,000 (lira), or $1280. This includes $280 for John and $200 for a maid. He wants to make sure he can rent a villa rather than stay at a hotel for such a long time. He grows increasingly concerned that the issue is unresolved, even as he gets on the plane for Europe. It's eventually approved.

Fox provides Roddy and John with first-class tickets to Spain, where they will spend a few days before traveling on to Rome. An interesting series of letters and memos go back and forth between Roddy's people and Fox, when Stephen Weinrib, Roddy's business manager, asks that Roddy and John be reimbursed for extra luggage charges. It emerges that they have exchanged their first-class tickets for tourist class, pocketing the substantial difference. The different seat class lowers their allowed baggage weight. There would be no overages if they used their original seats. Fox politely declines the request for reimbursement, and Stephen politely accepts their decision. What makes the exchange of correspondence interesting is the utter lack of pretense about Roddy and John's relationship. There is no attempt to classify John as a "travel companion" or "assistant," and hotel accommodations are booked with a double bed.

Rome is beautiful. The villa is beautiful. Roddy's friendship with Richard Burton's wife Sybil deepens and also becomes beautiful, as does his friendship with their five-year-old daughter, Katy, now the actress Kate Burton. All beautiful. But intensely boring. It's weeks, months before director Joe Mankiewicz calls Roddy in to work. After his wardrobe fittings and makeup and wig tests (for his blond wig) there's nothing for him to do but shop and have meals with the variety of out-of-town visitors who drop by.

There are whole books written about the making of *Cleopatra* that recount the grisly saga in every detail, down to how many times Elizabeth Taylor is near death, how many sets are built in

England and Italy, how much is allegedly embezzled by Italian members of the production working both ends against the middle, and the shocking amount of waste involved. We won't take that deep a dive, but some backstory is called for.

Principal photography begins on September 28, 1960, at Pinewood Studios, London, under director Rouben Mamoulian (just as Roddy is leaving for Toronto with the *Camelot* company). Production stops and restarts a few times before recommencing at Cinecittà Studios, Rome, under director Joseph Mankiewicz, on September 25, 1961, and finishing principal photography on July 28, 1962. During postproduction in Los Angeles, there are reshoots, firings, and rehirings through the end of May 1963.

But the whole mess really starts in October 1958 when 20th Century-Fox announces a $2 million film about Cleopatra, intended as a modest historical drama to be shot in CinemaScope and color. It's imagined in the vein of the studio's 1934 version of the story with Claudette Colbert—a love story without battle sequences. Fox's 1917 blockbuster version starring Theda Bara is famously lost, so it doesn't narratively contribute to thoughts about a remake, but its enormous success is part of the mystique and lure of launching a new Cleopatra project.

Walter Wanger, an industry veteran with almost seventy films to his credit, including the 1934 *Cleopatra*, is named the producer. He's a resourceful, resilient professional, who even survives a potentially career-destroying prison sentence for shooting the lover of his wife, actress Joan Bennett, Roddy's costar way back in *Man Hunt* and *Confirm or Deny*. (So many connections . . .) No one is thinking big-budget epic for *Cleopatra*. Maybe Fox contract player Joan Collins can play the role, depending on how well her latest film *Rally 'Round the Flag, Boys!* does at the box office. (It tanks.)

Joan (Collins) is never seriously on Walter's mind. He imagines Elizabeth Taylor as Cleopatra from the start. Elizabeth is at the height of her beauty and power. She is widely credited with much of the enormous success of *Cat on a Hot Tin Roof*, released in September 1958 and destined to be third on the list of the year's biggest box-office hits, and she stars in two of the top films of the previous two years, *Giant* in 1956 and *Raintree County* in 1957 (the macabre expectations about audiences wanting to see Monty before and after the crash prove correct). Elizabeth gets her first Oscar nomination for *Raintree County* and her second for *Cat on a Hot Tin Roof*.

Hollywood lore has it that she demands $1 million for *Cleopatra* as an offhand, outlandish request that will make Walter drop the issue, that she has little enthusiasm for the role, and she agrees to do the film against her better judgment. Walter insists until his dying day that it doesn't go down like that at all; that Fox initially agrees, then reneges on its $1 million offer, by which time Elizabeth very much wants to play Cleopatra and agrees to do it for $750,000 if Fox will reconsider. Does Walter deny that Elizabeth eventually earns something like $7 million for doing the film, once overtime and profit participation kick in? No. He just wants to be on the record about that first $250,000, as he writes in his memoir, *My Life with Cleopatra: The Making of a Hollywood Classic*. Duly noted.

Filming begins at Pinewood Studios in England with Rouben Mamoulian in the director's chair, Peter Finch as Caesar, and Stephen Boyd as Mark Antony. Somewhere between $600,000 and $1 million is spent building Alexandria's harbor facades, Roman temples, and palace interiors, and Cleopatra's barge and throne room. No one likes the script, including its latest screenwriter Nunnally Johnson. Shooting is sporadic. The cold, damp British climate causes logistical problems and exacerbates Elizabeth Taylor's mounting respiratory ailments. A month into the shoot she falls seriously ill with pneumonia. At first, it's thought of as a temporary blip and a good time for some rewrites. But her health deteriorates further. All the while, relations between Wanger and the studio on one side, and Rouben

Mamoulian on the other, are deteriorating over script issues and diverging visions of the film. Rouben wants an elegant and intimate story, focusing on character, with poetic dialogue, and a portrayal of Cleopatra that is more tragic political player than sex kitten.

Rouben Mamoulian references Plutarch a lot.

Walter Wanger doesn't give a shit about Plutarch.

He wants something like *The Ten Commandments*, a sprawling, sexy spectacle and box-office phenomenon. By this point Fox is in financial trouble. Go big or go home seems the attitude. Fox head Spyros Skouras believes Wanger's version will turn their fortunes around.

With Elizabeth Taylor in the hospital, Fox fires Rouben Mamoulian; Peter Finch and Stephen Boyd head for other contractual commitments; and Fox shuts down production. The London shoot of the film that starts out with a proposed $2 million budget ends with $7 million in unrecoverable costs flushed down the loo, directly into the Thames.

Trigger warning: The following are fighting words that many will disagree with. *Arguably*, the decision Fox makes next is bizarre, ill-considered, and financially disastrous. They hire writer and director Joseph Mankiewicz, the man Roddy thinks is an "incredible megalomaniacal, sadistic shit," to drive the *Cleopatra* barge. Roddy's opinions notwithstanding, Joe Mankiewicz is an amazing, singularly gifted writer and director. His lengthy credit list up to this point includes *All About Eve*, *A Letter to Three Wives*, *The Barefoot Contessa*, and one of the biggest hits of 1959, Elizabeth Taylor's film *Suddenly, Last Summer*. Fantastic. But not one of those films has so much as a large outdoor crowd scene, let alone an epic battle involving 30,000 principals and extras. He hates Nunnally Johnson's script and plans to rewrite it himself, even though Johnson's script is tonally already exactly in the vein of the stories he likes to tell—stylish, witty indoor narratives where character and subtext rule the day.

He starts rewriting and will continue rewriting every day and every night for the next year, eight months, and seventeen days until the night before *Cleopatra* premieres, because *arguably*, Joe Mankiewicz doesn't actually know how to make a movie like *The Ten Commandments*. "I thought *The Ten Commandments* was the funniest picture I ever saw in my life," he's quoted as saying, according to Hollywood legend. "Every time God came on with another Commandment, I laughed out loud."

Wit is Joseph Mankiewicz's superpower. *Cleopatra* is not witty.

Just before her tracheotomy, when it looks like Elizabeth Taylor might actually die, Fox puts Joan Collins on notice to be ready to replace her if necessary. Elizabeth's near-death experience erases the notoriety of her theft of Eddie Fisher, and she wins her first Oscar for *Butterfield 8*, playing a character she calls an "obscenity" in a movie she loathes, filmed before the aborted *Cleopatra* shoot in London. (Many years later she attends a casual Oscar party and shows up with both of her Oscars. She sets down her award for *Who's Afraid of Virginia Woolf?* next to the TV set, saying, "Here's the Oscar I won." Then she puts the *Butterfield 8* Oscar next to it. "And here's the one my tracheotomy won.")

Production designer John DeCuir spends $2 million rebuilding the abandoned London sets in Rome, including a replica of the Roman Forum, a 35-foot-tall Sphinx, and Cleopatra's two-story barge. The construction is on such a massive scale that it leads to material shortages in Italy, and the production utilizes just about all the available film crew professionals in Rome. (Producer Jerry Wald cancels filming location sequences in Rome for *Adventures of a Young Man*, because *Cleopatra* leaves no one left in Rome to work on any other American productions.)

Costume designers Irene Sharaff, Vittorio Nino Novarese, and Renie Conley create 26,000 costumes at a cost of $500,000 to $1 million, with $200,000 of that going for Elizabeth Taylor's sixty-five costume changes, the most in any film in history at the time. (Depending on how you classify what is or isn't a costume change, Elizabeth's record still stands for an American film. While Madonna has some 85 changes in the 1996 film adaptation of *Evita*, many are repurposed or embellished versions of other costumes. Elizabeth's *Cleopatra* costumes are self-contained ensembles that are never, *ever* reused. Shah Rukh Khan, in the 2007 Bollywood film *Om Shanti Om*, reportedly now holds the world record with over 200 changes.) Included in the $200,000 costume budget are the thirty wigs and hairpieces created under Sydney Guilaroff's supervision, specifically designed to highlight the shifts in Cleopatra's political and romantic status, including the "Nubian" bob supposedly inspired by ancient Egyptian bas-reliefs but looking more like the work of Vidal Sassoon, gold-beaded headdresses made with real gold strands and semiprecious stones, braided ceremonial wigs used in major sequences like Cleopatra's entrance into Rome, high coiled crowns and stylized buns symbolizing royal formality and authority, and loose waves and curls for scenes with Richard Burton. Mostly she looks like she's in a *Vogue* fashion spread, with hairstyles heavily influenced by the towering hair-sprayed confections of the 1960s.

When shooting restarts on *Cleopatra* in Rome, the principals, in the billing order that will appear on posters and in the credits are: Elizabeth Taylor as Cleopatra, Richard Burton as Mark Antony, Rex Harrison as Julius Caesar, and (in alphabetical order) Pamela Brown as High Priestess, George Cole as Flavius, Hume Cronyn as Sosigenes, Cesare Danova as Apollodorus, Kenneth Haigh as Brutus, Andrew Faulds as Canidius, Martin Landau as Rufio, and Roddy McDowall as Octavian. (Roddy's contract grants him costar billing. He's not aware that Fox is in breach until the night of the film's New York premiere. It's not the first or the last mistake Fox makes that negatively impacts on him.)

The shoot is chaotic, behind schedule, and over budget from

the start as the production team struggles to keep control of the thousands of people working in front of and behind the camera on any given day. Joe Mankiewicz frequently directs one scene while rewriting another during setups; he gets regular energy shots on set multiple times a day (a combination of B-12 and amphetamines that aren't uncommon at the time), often writing through the night, propped up by stimulants and sheer will-power. Elizabeth's health continues to be a problem with days off due to fatigue, emotional stress, and sinus and respiratory issues. Once her affair with Richard Burton becomes widely talked about, the shoot becomes a circus, with the two of them on constant display and dozens of Italian and American employees taking surreptitious pictures and selling them along with real or invented stories of the couple's alleged debaucheries. The truth of what's going on behind the scenes is a lot more nuanced and complicated than the public or even some of the principal players know.

But table that for a moment.

Back to Roddy and John's arrival. Elizabeth and Roddy are thrilled to be together again. She has a gold signet ring made for him bearing the McDowall family crest. Roddy wears it every day from the moment she gives it to him, often onscreen as well. The days and nights in Rome seem to pass uneventfully. After a few weeks of sightseeing and dining out, Roddy grows increasingly bored and restless. He gets permission to shoot photos during filming, getting some great shots that are later sold all over the world, but even when he's on set taking photos, delays between takes while technical details are worked out are interminable. The saving grace is Sybil Burton. They have known each other as long as Roddy has known Richard, but this is when they really forge their lifelong friendship. Roddy, John, and Sybil spend many days together, dining and shopping (Roddy will return to America with an amazing new wardrobe), and everywhere he goes, Roddy snaps pictures. He sends ideas to Lee Gross, pitching travel articles featuring his shots of the city. She isn't hopeful. Photographs from *Cleopatra* are what will sell.

In Rome, Eddie and Elizabeth, along with her three children, Michael Wilding Jr., Christopher Wilding, and Liza Todd, spend a good deal of leisure time with the Burtons, their daughter Katy, and with Roddy and John, who move into the Burtons' large villa next door to the villa where Elizabeth and Eddie are staying. (Vis-à-vis Roddy's careful expense calculations, it's unknown whether he picks up part of the rent on the villa from the funds the studio provides him for living expenses or if the Burtons invite them as their guests.)

At the same time *Cleopatra* is in production, Fox is knee-deep in another mega-expensive epic, shooting on location in France, Italy, Germany, and England. Darryl F. Zanuck's *The Longest Day* utilizes a massive ensemble cast to tell the story of D-Day from both Allied and Axis perspectives. Zanuck is an independent producer now, having quit Fox in 1956 to pursue his own projects. Roddy and Richard Burton reach out to Zanuck asking if they might shoot cameos in his film instead of just hanging around Rome. They join a ridiculously long list of stars in the cast, including John Wayne, Henry Fonda, Robert Mitchum, Sean Connery, Paul Anka, Sal Mineo, Red Buttons, Richard Todd, Stuart Whitman, Eddie Albert, Mel Ferrer, Jeffrey Hunter, Richard Beymer, Peter Lawford, Fabian, George Segal, Tommy Sands, Steve Forrest, Robert Ryan, Rod Steiger, Robert Wagner, Curt Jürgens, Hans Christian Blech, Wolfgang Preiss, Wolfgang Büttner, Jean-Louis Barrault, Christian Marquand, and Bourvil. Everyone is famous. It's like a special wartime episode of *Love Boat.*

Roddy plays an anxious, introspective, young American soldier in a scene on a landing craft during the amphibious landing at Utah Beach. His fate is left deliberately ambiguous as he's swept into the larger chaos crashing in around him. It's a welcome distraction. *The Longest Day* may be expensive and beset with weather issues during its many outdoor sequences, but unlike *Cleopatra*, it's run with clockwork precision. At the end of his shoot, Roddy receives a military service bar made up of the U.S. flag, the flag of Free France during World War II, and the Union Jack, along with a certificate: "For meritorious service beyond the call of duty in the production of *The Longest Day* you are hereby awarded the ORDER OF DFZ and Promoted to the Rank of P.F.C. Roddy McDowall."

Back at *Cleopatra*, once Roddy finally gets to work playing Octavian he enjoys himself immensely. He has a number of juicy scenes, including an emotional monologue after Mark Antony's death that veers fascinatingly between contempt and admiration for his vanquished foe. John Valva plays a small part as a Roman soldier. It's now widely speculated that Roddy arranges the role. Perhaps he does. It could also be the idea of Joe Mankiewicz or Richard Burton or Elizabeth Taylor. John is well liked and might be cast without Roddy's direct involvement.

The story of exactly when and how Elizabeth and Richard's affair begins changes according to who's telling the story. Sometimes it changes when the same person is telling it, with no one sticking to a consistent timeline or series of events. By all accounts, Roddy stays well out of it, even as the atmosphere between the two villas turns volatile. Neither Richard nor Elizabeth wants to hurt or humiliate Sybil, who becomes something of a wounded cause célèbre in the media. No one cares much about Eddie Fisher as a victim. Unlike John, he's not particularly well-liked by the cast and crew, or by the media, who seemingly blame him throughout eternity for betraying Debbie Reynolds.

Roddy's voluminous correspondence reflects the growing fascination with the affair and with everything going on surrounding *Cleopatra* and *The Longest Day*. Robert Thom writes: "By this time I imagine you have finished helping Zanuck keep the world safe for democracy and are back helping keep that

Arab broad in her place. I saw a picture of your new leading lady, Mrs. Fisher. She's pretty."

Lily Veidt (one of his agents): "The rumors coming from Rome and especially around Cleopatra herself are gruesome and I wish you would enlighten us, angel boy, you are much too discreet, and we cannot stand that!"

Ross Hunter: "Are you ever returning from Sodom and Gomorrah? Boaty misses you, I miss you, Myrna [Loy] misses you—and Jane Withers, Pearl White, Rin Tin Tin, and Nazimova—all miss you—get back, ya hear?"

Irwin Franklin (his publicist): "I imagine that the headlines must be traumatic all around, and the best thing for all of us to do, is to stay out of it. I can only hope that none of it is true. What always mystifies, however, is that whenever Liz becomes embroiled, it's always the man who winds up the heavy, and she is perennially nature's child who can never do any wrong. But then, she really is just that, isn't she? Still, Burton is currently in Hollywood the heaviest of heavies."

Robby Lantz: "Thanks for your long, totally uninformative, laudably and lamentably discreet letter. Why don't you do a whole photobook of Elizabeth Taylor? People know her, and while she is not beautiful, she does have a certain appeal. Of course, she is no Susan Strasberg, but who can tell in silent photos?"

Bobby Lewis: "How can I comment about 'all that is happening' when you won't spill any dirt at all? Don't you think that's carrying loyalty to your friends too far? I am forced to continue spreading the no-doubt completely erroneous rumors that I get from fourth-hand sources."

And Gladys Cooper, in a far less flippant vein, commiserates: "Rome must have lost its glamour for you by now poor Roddy. It seems to have lost something for everyone, and it will be a long time before anyone dares to play either Shakespeare's or Shaw's Cleopatra. How very beastly it has all been and it has all become boring and ridiculous."

Roddy's publicist, Irwin, is incorrect when he suggests that

Richard Burton is shouldering the "blame" and Elizabeth Taylor can "do no wrong." She is vilified in the press. A report that the pope has damned her for "erotic vagrancy" turns out to be inaccurate. The charge comes not from Pope John XXIII but from a reader's letter to the editor in *L'Osservatore della Domenica*, the Vatican City weekly. However, the world press, and particularly Italian media, prints a steady stream of lascivious conjectures and outraged condemnations. Elizabeth is terrified when they start shooting the grand tableau of Cleopatra's entrance into Rome seated atop a massive golden Sphinx, pulled by hundreds of slaves. Over seven thousand extras are on hand, and she fears they will scream denunciations. Roddy holds her hand and reassures her. "They love you, my darling." He whispers, "And so do I." He's right. The crowds are delirious at the sight of her. Even when the cameras aren't rolling, they cheer, "Baci! Baci!" ("Kisses! Kisses!")

Lee Gross sells one of Roddy's photos of Elizabeth in full *Cleopatra* drag for a cover of *Paris Match* and is in negotiations with *Cosmopolitan*, *Life*, *Glamour*, and *Ladies' Home Journal.* Roddy wants to dictate in his deals that the articles accompanying any of his photos aren't deprecatory of Elizabeth. Lee is forthright about the fact that such a proviso will be impossible to enforce. "How can we expect them to act with decorum," she writes, "when Miss T herself doesn't especially observe it in her own behavior."

Winefriede finds the entire situation unbearable, especially since she has known Elizabeth for so long. "Today's television newscast said the Italian government is going to request Eliz be removed from Rome," she writes. "E. is less than wise. Like a violent force driving herself to destruction. I feel so sorry. It's like a river of lava coming down until it covers everything, and this whole thing seems to just go on and on. I wish they would shut up. The newspapers are a mess. I do not expect any answers. This is only an opinion. You know that Dad sends love. Devoted love—YBTMH [You belong to my heart], Mother."

As if mirroring the conflagration in the press, a fire breaks out in the middle of the night in the dining room of the Burton villa. Sybil and Roddy put it out, but there's extensive damage to the living and dining rooms. The fire service determines the cause is faulty electrical wiring. They all move out, with Roddy and John finding their own apartment. It's just as well. Living with the Burtons has gotten difficult. Roddy has wanted to move out for weeks but fears doing so will look to the press like some sort of comment on the romantic lives of his friends. Now he and John can move out because the place is uninhabitable. (Dirk Bogarde playfully asks if Roddy set the fire himself just so that he can relocate.)

Back to that earlier mention about truth being nuanced and complicated. Richard is apparently not the only one in the Burton villa with tricky romantic feelings. Roddy and John Valva are a confirmed couple. Roddy gets a ring made for him in the same style as the one Elizabeth makes for him. Things seem golden for them, but at some point while staying at the villa, John begins developing feelings for Sybil. Whether these feelings lead to anything at the time is unknown. But it's hard not to look at the *Cleopatra* shoot as a bit of a hothouse environment of heady emotions and rash contemplations. Radie Harris, a longtime Richard Burton supporter, writes in *The Hollywood Reporter* that Sybil is the one who cheats on Richard first, naming John Valva as her lover. Of course, there's no mention of this being a betrayal of Roddy, since publicly he and John aren't a couple. It appears that Radie's reporting of the liaison is not without basis in fact.

The McDowall family's financial peccadillos continue to intrude as well. Roddy arranges for Stephen Weinrib to sign anything that needs to be signed, pay his parents' property taxes, settle the life insurance policy debts, and cosign for Virginia's mortgage. When Virginia cables asking to borrow $500 for a mink coat, Roddy instructs Stephen to send the money. It's important to note that there's no record of Roddy ever complaining about any of this ongoing financial support. Nor does the loving tone of his family correspondence ever change.

And somehow or other, a movie gets made. Actually, several movies. There's enough footage for what Joseph Mankiewicz now envisions as two films, the first focusing on Cleopatra and Caesar, the second on Cleopatra and Mark Antony. Elizabeth Taylor and Richard Burton go public. Roddy and John return to New York in August of 1962 after spending a month vacationing in Europe once *Cleopatra* wraps. Soon Sybil arrives in New York with her daughter, first staying at the Carlyle Hotel for an extended period, then moving into the same building where Roddy and John live.

From Los Angeles, Irwin Franklin writes Roddy a long, strangely esoteric letter that hints at deeper concerns. "Hold to the simple truth—which is indisputable and indestructible—that you live in harmony and anything else is unreal and therefore nonexistent. . . . Always remember that the blessings we seek to heap upon ourselves become the blessings of all men. If you follow this course, you will have nothing to look forward to other than harmony, peace of mind, and tremendous abundance."

The storm of *Cleopatra* notwithstanding, Roddy has other work and other concerns. While still in Rome he actively begins soliciting for a role in yet another historical epic, *The Greatest Story Ever Told*, a retelling of the life, ministry, death, and resurrection of Jesus, directed by George Stevens. With all those disciples, there must be a place for Roddy. He's cast as Matthew. It's an extended shoot on location in Arizona and Utah. John stays in New York much of the time, but they're very much still together before Christmas, when Virginia writes from Los Angeles. In what starts as a very funny letter about baking Roddy some of his favorite treacly treats, her tone turns more serious at the end. "Forgive me for mentioning the following, but if you and John plan on coming to the house for Christmas, could you see your way clear to remove one or both of your rings? Mother will pick it up right away. I did in New York, and she is much quicker than I."

A very different issue arises at the same time with far more public implications about Roddy's sexuality. Author Flora Rheta Schreiber, later famous for the book *Sybil*, which is adapted into the TV movie starring Sally Field, writes an article in *Cosmopolitan* called, "I Was Raising a Homosexual Child." It is loosely based on an anonymized entry in an academic publication, *Homosexuality: A Psychoanalytic Study of Male Homosexuals*, "Case 129," that bears striking similarities to Roddy's childhood stardom and his sexual history.

It is written by Dr. Cornelia Wilbur, Roddy's psychiatrist.

Roddy feels betrayed and horribly exposed, though it's likely that almost no one makes the connection to him, even though the case study describes a family that seems clearly based on the McDowalls. The mother is a frustrated wannabe who pushes her son and daughter into show business at very young ages. The son becomes world famous and is the sole support for the family while the daughter fades into obscurity. The father is away in the Merchant Navy, leaving the family alone for years. The son grows up trying to transition into an adult career and becomes lovers with a drunken, emotionally troubled movie star. The case changes Roddy into a singer, and the family isn't identified as English, but other than that, the similarities are readily apparent.

The case study offers other disturbing elements. The mother's attachment to her son is implicitly if not explicitly sexualized, and she, in essence, procures boys for her son in order to keep him away from girls, while never acknowledging his sexuality, even after finding him in bed naked with other boys his own age, always asserting that homosexuality is wrong and disgusting. The other disturbing piece of the narrative is that when the movie star breaks up with the son, the young singer is so distraught that he attempts suicide. Believing the study is based on Roddy's psychiatric case notes, however, does not require blind acceptance of these two claims.

Homosexuality: A Psychoanalytic Study of Male Homosexuals regards homosexuality as a curable illness and attributes its onset to mothers who are "unnaturally" attached to their sons. That's a key part of its agenda. At least one author of the study later disavows it, believing his research is skewed by biases of the time. The case histories also tend to regard the subjects' emotional responses to their sexual partners as heightened, overemotional, and hysterical. A "suicide attempt" could be an instance where a patient, wondering how they will go on without their lost love, drinks themselves to sleep. That's all it takes to qualify as a "suicide attempt." The "attempted suicide" story gets repeated and anonymized in Patricia Bosworth's biography of Montgomery Clift, where almost all of the interviews are with straight people who attribute Monty's emotional anguish to self-hatred over his sexuality, an idea his closest friends regard as absurd. (He's a mess but not because of his sexuality.) Most of her interviewees seem to regard the emotional lives of gay people with the same conscious or unconscious biases as the authors of *Homosexuality: A Psychoanalytic Study of Male Homosexuals.* Gay men are just drama queens.

Referring back to Roddy's work stats, with his sixty-two TV appearances and twenty stage shows, it's difficult to imagine when he would have the time to attempt suicide. That said, we really don't know. Maybe he did. Other than the case study, though, there's no public behavior or private information in his archives that point to the kind of depression, frailty, confusion, or emotional turmoil we might associate with a suicide attempt. Though Dr. Wilbur's inclusion of Roddy's notes is a gross violation of his privacy, and a case can be made for malpractice, pursuing the matter would require publicly acknowledging he's the subject of "Case 129," which is out of the question, leaving him no recourse. (In *Sybil Exposed*, author Debbie Nathan recounts other equally serious ethical lapses on Dr. Wilbur's part, including "Sybil" having access to Roddy's medical files.)

Virginia's issue about Roddy and John's rings doesn't come up, because Roddy doesn't get enough time off from *The Greatest Story Ever Told* to make it to Los Angeles. The production turns out to be another difficult shoot, and like *Cleopatra*, seems out of control. The "spiritual epic," as George Stevens calls it, is budgeted at $10 million but ends up costing $20 million, with stop-and-start filming for almost two years, from 1962 through to 1964, and extreme weather conditions, ranging from blistering heat and sandstorms to snow. The disappointment for Roddy is that he finds George Stevens an uncommunicative martinet. After looking forward to working with him, believing him to be an "actor's director," he finds his approach sterile and passionless. Everything is about the camera and the panoramic beauty of the locations. Roddy calls the approach "blockbusting dullness." He's lonely and somewhat confused, both by what his next steps will be in his work, and by what's happening at home in New York.

John moves out of Roddy's apartment and moves in with Sybil. He later tells C. David Heymann, one of many who write biographies of Elizabeth Taylor, that he and Sybil both believe wholeheartedly that they're in love. The relationship lasts for a month, and they both conclude it's a mistake. John tries to reconcile with Roddy, but Roddy refuses. Who knows what, when, and where about the sleeping arrangements isn't as important as what the circumstances reveal about Roddy's capacity for compassion, but also about his unwillingness to reconcile and settle for a situation where he feels he's vulnerable to another person's mercurial nature. He isn't about to throw away his friendship with Sybil, nor will he re-create a dynamic with Monty, where he's the one who feels forced to turn a blind eye and offer unconditional acceptance.

John Valva later marries and has a son. Whether this means

he ultimately identifies as straight, gay, or bisexual is unknown. The theater community is tight-knit, and everyone knows everyone else's business. If John isn't exclusively gay before he and Roddy meet, Roddy may know that. If John has come to believe he's actually straight and in love with a woman, it's possible that however sad it makes Roddy, he may think of it as a positive development for John. However open Roddy is with friends and some family about his orientation, he isn't immune from perceptions of the era that being straight isn't just different from being gay, it's *better*. Who wouldn't want to be "normal" and settle down with a wife, home, and family if it's possible? It could be he doesn't begrudge John this chance at a "normal" life. Sybil remains one of Roddy's dearest friends, and Roddy is prepared to accept the events that occur, whatever they are, and move on.

Making sense of it all these years later can seem challenging. Pointing to the time as the era of "Free Love" only goes so far. Tom Hardy is refreshing in his modern take on the fact that actors live their lives open to a wider range of experiences, sexual and otherwise. "I'm an actor for fuck's sake. I'm an artist," he says in remarks widely quoted. "I've played with everything and everyone." Perhaps there's a bit of that sense of experimentation underlying the events going on in those two villas in Rome and the aftermath. Maybe creative people just have a greater willingness to admit what they want and go after it. "There used to be a game, a joke, where you asked people to write the sign that should hang over your head or your life or something," says Elizabeth Taylor in an unpublished 1991 interview with author James Grissom. "Roddy and Tennessee said that my sign should read 'All Hungers Met,' because if there was a hunger for anything, I probably possessed it, and in my house, my company, you'd meet people who were hungry for just about everything. And I feed everyone, as you know. So pull up a chair, a plate, and an obsession. You're with me."

To all outward appearances, Roddy takes the breakup in stride, but it's a huge adjustment. He thought he and John Valva were headed for a lifelong partnership, like Dirk Bogarde and Anthony Forwood, together since the 1940s—not publicly—but anyone who knows them knows them as a couple. Roddy wants to stay occupied. *The Greatest Story Ever Told* provides plenty of downtime. Lee Gross keeps him busy, and he also discovers a new idle passion: TV game shows. His very first TV appearances in the early 1950s include a couple of stints on what we now call competition reality shows, talent contests like *Chance of a Lifetime*, *HI Talent Battle*, and *Battle of the Ages*, but he has never done any that center around an actual game being played. Roddy loves games and becomes a regular player on *Password*, *The Match Game*, *Picture This*, *Stump the Stars*, and *The Celebrity Game*. His favorite will be *Hollywood Squares*. His first appearance isn't until 1968, but through the 1970s and into the 1980s, he appears over three hundred times on the show.

Meanwhile, while Roddy has been finding Jesus in the American southwest and playing games on TV, back at the Fox lot, *Cleopatra* nears the end of a chaotic, expensive, lawsuit-ridden postproduction period that some consider more interesting than anything that ends up on screen. The last chapter actually starts in the final month of *Cleopatra*'s shoot when Darryl F. Zanuck takes back control of Fox and flies to Rome to take over *Cleopatra* before returning to Los Angeles to immediately begin postproduction once some final exterior scenes are shot in Egypt. Then firings and filings begin.

Walter Wanger is fired. He sues Fox, Spyros Skouras, and Darryl F. Zanuck for $2.6 million. Fox and the executives consider libel actions in return.

A theater exhibitor sues Fox for misrepresenting *Cleopatra*'s quality and commercial prospects, seeking $175,000 in actual damages and $500,000 per theater in punitive damages. Elizabeth Taylor sues the exhibitor for defamation and damage to her professional reputation, seeking $1 million.

Joseph Mankiewicz petitions the Writers Guild of America for sole screenplay credit.

Rex Harrison files suit against Fox for failing to provide him with equal billing alongside Richard Burton and for prioritizing Richard in promotional materials to capitalize on the widespread publicity surrounding his affair with Elizabeth.

Mankiewicz is fired after extensive battles with Zanuck over the edit.

Walter Wanger is rehired.

The WGA declares the credits will read: Screenplay by Joseph L. Mankiewicz, Ranald MacDougall, Sidney Buchman, Based Upon Histories by Plutarch, Suetonius, Appian, Other Ancient Sources, and *The Life and Times of Cleopatra* by C. M. Franzero.

Even with a team of editors at his disposal, Zanuck can't organize a coherent version of the film from the 3 to 4 million feet of film that was shot, which is 120–150 hours of footage, or between 650 and 820 miles of film. Mankiewicz is the only person who knows the footage well enough to finish the cut.

Mankiewicz is rehired.

Working day and night, with plenty of energy injections to keep him going, Mankiewicz delivers a four-hour, three-minute cut of the film, set to premiere in New York on June 12, 1963, in Los Angeles on June 19, and in London on July 31. No one hits pause on the lawsuits once the film opens. Fox will sue Elizabeth and Richard for breach of contract, citing unprofessional conduct and damaging publicity from their affair, separately seeking $20 million from Elizabeth and $5 million from Richard, plus $25 million from them jointly for a total of $50 million. And Elizabeth and Richard will sue Fox for an undisclosed amount alleging that Fox's mismanagement and public scapegoating has damaged their reputations and careers. Every lawsuit is either dismissed or settled with a nondisclosure clause.

The bad blood surrounding the film only seems to increase its marquee value. The New York opening draws ten thousand spectators outside the Rivoli Theatre. By then many of the reviews are in, and most are quite positive, many are raves. Elizabeth Taylor has particularly dreaded them, believing she and Richard Burton will be reviewed on their scandal and not their performances, but it doesn't pan out that way at all. *The New York Times* tallies up the critical response and finds that 80 percent of the American reviews are positive, though only 20 percent are positive in Europe. It's true that Elizabeth's notices are sometimes not as glowing as those of her costars, but plenty of them are enormously positive, while Rex Harrison and Roddy McDowall are the actors who get the most effusive praise.

Judith Crist, in the *New York Herald Tribune*, is a definite fan of Roddy. In an otherwise famously scathing review with a headline calling the film a "Monumental Mouse," she writes: "Roddy McDowall does bring to Caesar's heir an underlying shrewdness and strength under an impassive exterior that is fascinating." Alton Cook in the *New York World-Telegram and The Sun*: "Roddy McDowall has the canniest achievement in the picture, making a sly, ironic cynic of Emperor Octavian." *Variety* calls his performance "especially noteworthy," Wanda Hale in the *Daily News* calls him "outstanding," Frank Leyendecker in *Box Office* says, "Roddy McDowall is extraordinarily fine as the effete Octavian who succeeds Caesar."

One review that means a great deal to Roddy is private, in a letter from Noël Coward. "I think you gave, frankly, the only acting performance in *Cleopatra*," Noël writes. "The whole thing was a curious experience. I love you very much." The tinge of sadness in the comment is telling, for *Cleopatra* becomes a bittersweet experience for Roddy in many ways. The

New York premiere is the first time Roddy sees the film, and he's shocked that his costar billing contract terms haven't been followed, and he appears in alphabetical order with seven other actors. He's also sad to see that some of what he feels is his best work has apparently ended up on the cutting room floor.

This is the first time he sees that John Valva, who didn't have much to begin with, has been completely cut out of the film. Some later speculate that Roddy makes this happen out of spite, but that is a ridiculous idea. Roddy has no input in the editing process, and it would be completely out of character for him, especially since it would mean approaching Joseph Mankiewicz to talk about his personal life—unthinkable. It's also quite possible, even probable, that Roddy and John are still together when those scenes are cut out during the marathon editing process.

The whole premiere event is surreal, from arriving with *The Tonight Show Starring Johnny Carson* airing a special live telecast of the red carpet, with Bert Parks interviewing celebrities. Though common now, making this into a televised event is unusual for the time. Roddy also appears that night on Johnny Carson's regular broadcast, showing off eighteen of his photos of Elizabeth Taylor, exhibiting his other line of work to the show's massive audience.

Everyone on the *Tonight Show* appearance and at the premiere event makes a great to-do about Roddy's beard, grown for *The Greatest Story Ever Told*, and since Rex Harrison and Roddy are the two most important stars from the film who attend, they are deluged by fans and photographers. Both Elizabeth Taylor and Richard Burton have valid reasons for not attending, but the truth is that Elizabeth is frightened in the same way she was before shooting Cleopatra's entrance into Rome, convinced that if she attends a mob of angry villagers will be carrying torches, wanting to punish her.

The thing people sometimes forget about big stars, who allegedly don't care what anyone thinks, is that they often care very much. Not enough to stop themselves from doing whatever it is that brings negative public reactions, but they often care. Elizabeth does. Falling in love with Richard Burton isn't something she looked for. In her mind, it's more like an act of God, something stronger than either of them. If that sounds like something from a movie, well, her whole life has been in the movies. What other reference points are there?

That's another part of how bittersweet the premiere is for Roddy. Elizabeth's absence saddens him immeasurably, not just for her, missing out on the adulation and love, but for himself, missing out on sharing this milestone with his friend. Then there's John. If they were still together, he might have been at the premiere too, with a female date. Roddy is there with Marion Marshall Donen, director and choreographer Stanley Donen's wife. If he and John were watching the film together, they would learn at the same time that John's part is cut out. Now John will have to find out on his own.

The *Cleopatra* premiere in Los Angeles a week later is more of the same. Roddy attends with Jane Fonda as his date and forces himself to sit through the film again. In truth, he really doesn't like watching himself, and his missing work bedevils him. He's relentlessly positive about the film to anyone and everyone who asks, refusing to say anything negative other than agreeing that the shoot was difficult and very long.

The four-hour version plays what are called the roadshow houses, the giant big-city venues where audiences are considered more sophisticated and ticket prices tend to be higher. Before its general release, though, Zanuck really does take charge of the edit and supervises fifty-one minutes of cuts, bringing the length down to three hours and twelve minutes. Roddy is devastated. His concerns about his missing work in the earlier cut pale in comparison to the latest version. Some of his best work is in the last thirty minutes of the film, and it's the section with the most cuts. His big speech after Mark Antony's death is a fraction of what it was. He writes an impassioned letter to Zanuck, thoughtfully outlining all the reasons why he thinks the cuts are a mistake. To Zanuck's credit, he responds with a detailed explanation of the further editing process and a well-reasoned explanation of why he believes the cuts are important. He doesn't budge an inch, but he treats Roddy with uncommon respect and courtesy.

Then Fox makes a catastrophic clerical error. While they correctly submit Roddy's *Cleopatra* performance in the Best Supporting Actor category for the Golden Globes, he's accidentally submitted for the Oscars in the Best Actor category, along with Rex Harrison and Richard Burton. The error is discovered while the nominating forms are already at the printer, and the Academy says they can't rectify the mistake and reprint—it might set a bad precedent.

Fox takes out full-page apology ads in *Variety* and *The Hollywood Reporter* once they realize their mistake, but there's no way to correct it. Roddy is nominated for a Golden Globe. As expected, he's not nominated for an Oscar in the Best Actor category and is not eligible to be nominated for Best Supporting Actor. It feels like a very public humiliation. First his billing, now this. It's indicative to him of how little actors are valued, how little *he* is valued. And there's nothing he can say, nowhere to vent his anger except privately to a very, very few friends and family. Messages of condolence from his friends pour in, but he refuses to say anything on the record that might be construed as petty, egotistical, or both. The phrase doesn't exist yet, but in Roddy's eyes, not getting submitted for the correct Oscar nomination is a textbook example of a first-world problem. Roddy has never put a great emphasis on winning prizes and would certainly find the modern ubiquity of "For Your Consideration" ad campaigns a tacky and reductive turn of events, but missing out on this moment hurts dreadfully.

He loses the Golden Globe to John Huston for *The Cardinal*, the director's first major acting performance. Roddy does win a *Film Daily* award as one of the five Best Supporting Actor performances of the year (they give five awards in each category with no single winner). It's an organization that bestows a record nine Filmdom's Famous Five awards to Roddy for his juvenile performances, every year from 1942 to 1950. Rex Harrison is also honored in the Best Actor category, but neither Elizabeth Taylor nor Richard Burton receive citations. It's nice to have some recognition, but getting a scroll from *Film Daily* isn't quite the same as an Oscar or a Golden Globe.

Despite the controversies or perhaps because of them, *Cleopatra* is a worldwide hit right out of the gate. Its stratospheric cost of some $43 million really does come close to bankrupting Fox, but it turns a profit sooner than many people think, probably by the time of its 1966 sale to ABC for $5 million. It is a very flawed film and is remembered today mainly for its excesses and scandals, but at the time of its release it's a marketing and box-office juggernaut—a true blockbuster. And Oscar nomination or no Oscar nomination, Roddy giving one of the most acclaimed performances in a blockbuster has its advantages. Offers start pouring in. Some on his team urge him to concentrate only on film, still thought by many in the business to be more prestigious than TV. Roddy isn't interested in narrowing his options. He believes that diversifying his efforts means that should the offers dry up someday (as he knows full well they can) he hasn't cut off any sources of employment. He wants to do interesting work that nourishes his creative spirit, but he also wants to stay comfortable financially.

He will consider any offer.

The Greatest Story Ever Told finally wraps in late July 1963. When it's finally released in February 1965, audiences and critics find it the long panoramic slog Roddy predicts. His next feature role is one of the leads in *Shock Treatment*, a complicated tale where former mental patient Roddy murders his wealthy employer and allegedly sets fire to $1 million of her cash as a protest against capitalism. Incinerating that much money convinces the court that he's insane, so he's once again hospitalized. Lauren Bacall is a doctor who believes Roddy is lying about burning the money and manipulates anyone and everyone to try to get the cash for herself. Also intent on proving Roddy is lying, Stuart Whitman gets himself bogusly locked up as a patient, where Roddy and Lauren almost convince him he actually *is* crazy. Carol Lynley has the typical movie girlfriend role, where regrettably her only function is to say, "Don't do it," and "Be careful" to Stuart.

"After I was in *Compulsion* on Broadway, I was inundated with opportunities to play nut murderers," Roddy tells Nora Ephron, then writing for the *New York Post.* She notes that Roddy is currently filming *Shock Treatment*, in which he plays, as it happens, an insane murderer. "But he's not really insane," Roddy says. "In many ways, he's so crazy, he's normal." Syndicated columnist Sheilah Graham reports the dubious idea that Roddy spends a week at the Camarillo State Mental Hospital to sop up atmosphere for his psychotic killer role in *Shock Treatment* because "he's mad for his art!"

He plays another murderer on *Arrest and Trial* for the episode "Journey Into Darkness." The show is basically *Law & Order*. The majority of the episodes consist of two segments, catching the bad guys in the first half and then putting them on trial in the second. Roddy plays a delusional would-be writer who murders a pawnbroker to steal the contents of his safe so he can pay his rent. He develops two emotional attachments, the first to a winsome girl he meets in a bar, Anjanette Comer, the second to the investigating officer, Ben Gazzara. It's a genuinely moving exploration of a man living in a state somewhere between narcissism, excitement, and despair. Anjanette plays a character that could be a throwaway—the needy goodtime girl who isn't terribly bright—but she brings a complexity that makes you feel her life is on the line just like Roddy's. She responds to Roddy with the instincts of a child who wants desperately to please, while Roddy sees her as something between a figment of his hopeful imagination, a savior, and a simpleton. His relationship with Ben Gazzara is equally layered. Roddy wants Ben to respect and understand him; he wants to outwit him, but he also wants to confess. Ben is like a father, a pupil, and a lover. This isn't to look for homoeroticism that isn't there—it's about their tenderness and intimacy.

The *Arrest and Trial* episode is also notable for how instructive it is about the difficulty of nailing down facts on the internet. The plot is described in various ways by different reference sources—all of them wrong in an important way. Some entries contend that Roddy tries to hock his typewriter for rent money, the pawnbroker refuses and is abusive and dismissive, so Roddy kills him. Others have it that Roddy is desperate to get his typewriter back after having pawned it, the pawnbroker refuses unless he pays, and Roddy kills him. There will always be discrepancies about small details, but the true narrative is quite different. Roddy commits murder in the first degree for money—it's planned and carried out calmly and cleverly. He's not reacting to something other than needing his rent money. The other thing most sources get wrong is the verdict, saying he's found guilty but insane and sentenced to a mental institution. He's actually found not guilty, but before the verdict is announced, Roddy confesses in open court. The end. What happens afterward is left ambiguous. It is a fascinating legal question whether he can be guilty at this point even with a confession, since it could constitute double jeopardy, but these mistakes are, in evidentiary terms, material facts, not pedantic carping over minor discrepancies.

Roddy gets another Emmy nomination for the performance but loses this time, to Jack Klugman for *The Defenders*. Other nominees are James Earl Jones, Jason Robards, Rod Steiger, and Harold J. Stone—three of whom have Oscars, including Darth Vader.

When Roddy returns to New York, he puts renewed focus on his photography work. His editor at *Life* sends over a clipping from *Popular Photography* magazine that illustrates his growing stature. In an article about veteran *Life* photographer George Hunt, the writer cites Roddy's work as being "on the highest professional photographic level. . . . As a result, live theater sections [in *Life*] have been unbelievably strong and sensitive."

The idea for his first book of photos, *Double Exposure*, percolates slowly. It doesn't start out as what it becomes—a gorgeous coffee table book, featuring ninety-eight photos and essays by famous people about other famous people. The notion of one person in the arts writing about another person in an unrelated artistic field, featuring his own photos, comes to Roddy after he hears about John Gielgud writing a sort of tribute to Ethel Merman for an event. It strikes Roddy how people can be deeply impressed by someone who's their complete opposite. He pitches the idea to magazines with limited success. He feels the idea is special, though, and he decides to try doing it as a book, talking about it to his friends at every opportunity, seeking feedback.

Three people get it immediately—Noël Coward, David Selznick, and Moss Hart. David Selznick is particularly excited. "He was like a child about it," Roddy remembers, "saying, 'Henry Miller has got to write about Jennifer Jones!' and he set it up for me. He also said, 'Get Alfred Hitchcock to write about Shirley Temple,' but unfortunately that didn't happen." For a brief time, Roddy changes directions and asks Noël Coward to do all the texts, but Noël correctly points out that if the essays are meant to be appreciations of all the creative artists in the book, and if he's glowingly appreciative of every single person in the book, it will come across as hopelessly insincere. Roddy arranges shoots with Joan Sutherland, Giulietta Masina, Ethel Merman,

Edward Villella, Leonard Bernstein, Liza Minnelli, and Tammy Grimes. He doesn't need to shoot Elizabeth Taylor again. He has hundreds of unposed shots of her behind the scenes on *Cleopatra.*

He travels to England on assignment for *Life*, to do the photos that will accompany a story about Laurence Olivier. While watching during rehearsal of a difficult scene in *Othello*, he manages to get a photo of the exact moment when Larry finds the flash of insight that makes the scene work. Turning around, Roddy sees the writer Kenneth Tynan, so moved by what he's watching that he bursts into tears. Kenneth later tells Roddy that after seeing Laurence Olivier perform in *Othello* a number of times, he's awed that he's able to repeat that moment in every performance. Roddy remembers his long-ago conversation with Dame May Whitty about Laurence Olivier, before Roddy ever met the man, and how important her advice about always learning has proved to be.

He continues working on what will become *Double Exposure,* in the end reaching out to several hundred people to get the ninety-eight essays that appear in the book. He does all of the footwork himself, sending out the release forms he needs (196 in total, one for each photo, and one for each essay). His friends pitch in with introductions to a wider circle, people outside Roddy's usual circle, like *Peanuts* creator Charles Schulz and caricaturist Al Hirschfeld, along with seemingly anyone and everyone who matters at this moment in the mid-1960s, and some who are somewhat forgotten, like former silent movie star Louise Brooks, who becomes a dear friend.

At the same time as he embarks on the book, the strong reaction to his work in *Cleopatra* transforms his profile for feature films. He shoots six studio feature films, in less than a year, between October 1964 and September 1965. It's like his early days as a kid, with overlapping schedules on *How Green Was My Valley*, *Confirm or Deny*, and *Son of Fury: The Story of*

Benjamin Blake, and shooting *Lassie Come Home* and *The White Cliffs of Dover* at the same time at two different studios. These six films, *The Loved One*, *That Darn Cat*, *The Third Day*, *Inside Daisy Clover*, *The Adventures of Bullwhip Griffin*, and *Lord Love A Duck*, offer him a huge range of roles, playing, respectively, an obnoxious movie studio executive who triggers John Gielgud's suicide, Dorothy Provine's persnickety suitor who hates cats, the greedy and devious nephew of paralyzed Herbert Marshall, a sycophantic enabler of Christopher Plummer's dark designs on Natalie Wood, a prizefighting butler crushing on Suzanne Pleshette in the Old West, and a groovy but murderous high school student obsessed with Tuesday Weld.

As if that's not enough, he actually comes directly from the set of *The Third Day* with costar Elizabeth Ashley so that they can shoot an episode of the special nighttime version of *Password* together, giving host Allen Ludden the inside tea about their movie-star hijinks on the film. In a scene where Elizabeth slaps Roddy, he puts a dozen Chiclets in his mouth and pretends she's knocked out his teeth. Everyone in the TV studio laughs and applauds while Roddy and Elizabeth exchange knowing glances. They're just *so* cool—members of an exclusive club where everyone is famous, witty, and beautiful.

But Roddy is keenly aware that it can be a club where your membership card expires all too easily. Along with supporting MPTF fundraising activities, he personally keeps up with a number of largely forgotten actors who come from the silent era, including Mae Marsh, Blanche Sweet, Esther Ralston, and Bessie Love, along with Louise Brooks. In their day, these stars are every bit as big as Elizabeth Ashley and Tuesday Weld are in 1964, who are every bit as big then as Zendaya and Anya Taylor-Joy are now.

Roddy is a devoted admirer of Louise Brooks, whose influence in films is largely a function of her little-seen silent films being rediscovered in a major way during the "60 Ans de

Cinéma" exhibition at the Cinémathèque française. Its cofounder Henri Langlois prominently features a huge portrait of Louise from her 1929 G. W. Pabst masterpiece *Pandora's Box* at the entrance and famously declares, "There is no Garbo, there is no Dietrich, there is only Louise Brooks!" She becomes a strange presence in the cultural zeitgeist of cinema history—an expert of the silent era even though her time as a star is brief—and destroyed by alcoholism and an alienating, if intelligent, temperament. She's a total pain in the ass, in person and in her letters.

"After World War II she was broke, even panhandling in the streets. I wanted to photograph her, and John [publicist John Springer] arranged it," Roddy tells Gavin Lambert. "By then she was living in Rochester. We became instant friends. One of the most powerful personalities I've ever met—her intelligence, her humor, the sound of her voice, and the aura of melancholia behind it all."

It's not just women of the silent era Roddy McDowall reaches out to: He spends an hour with Richard Barthelmess in Southampton right before Barthelmess's death, holding his hand, talking about how wonderful Richard is in his silent films, and how fortunate it is that he makes the transition to sound, so Bette Davis can tell him, "I'd love to kiss you, but I just washed my hair," in *The Cabin in the Cotton*. Richard Barthelmess dies feeling seen and remembered.

Another death is far more consequential for Roddy. Winefriede dies in May 1965. Morbid obesity, severe diverticulitis, and bowel blockages plague her through the end of 1964 and into 1965, and she spends three and a half months in the hospital, sparking complications from phlebitis. Her doctors actually contemplate an operation that is an early variant of a gastric bypass, but they determine she's too heavy to risk the five-hour surgery and so send her home to lose weight. She isn't successful. Her health issues escalate, and she prepares herself, writing one last letter to Roddy. She tells him that she cannot cover the depth and breadth of her thanks to him with the words "thank you" and urges him to "remember, once I told you, if you can look at yourself in a mirror each day that's it. Keep up the good work of making people happy, as you have made us happy in so many ways. I love you, your devoted and grateful mother."

Her death isn't a surprise, to her or to her family. Roddy gives no major interviews when contacted by the press. In exchanges between him and Thomas and Virginia, there's the obvious sense of loss, but also the acknowledgment of the inevitability of her passing. They announce that remembrances can be made to the Motion Picture Country House and Hospital. Roddy's own feelings stay private. An interesting thing starts happening for Thomas, though. His letters to Roddy increase, and sometimes they get really silly. It's hard to know whether this is a coping mechanism at being on his own for the first time in forty years or if Winefriede's death makes him feel freer in some way.

A couple of months after her death he writes to Roddy, joking that he's "rather depressed because my attempt to beat the Russians to a soft landing on the moon failed. I was arrested on Columbus Day when they found me nude on the steps of City Hall with a rocket strategically, though painfully placed, and wearing nothing but an eight by ten glossy of Norma Talmadge."

This isn't the tone of his earlier letters, and this feeling of jocularity continues for the rest of his life. The same can't be said for Virginia. She works now as an assistant to director Richard Brooks on the Columbia lot. Thomas and Roddy both worry about her mental health as her depressive state deepens following Winefriede's death. "Between you and me, I think Vee has another complex," Thomas writes Roddy. "She hasn't been out of her house for months except to go to work. But don't say anything. Much love. Don't let your own work exhaust you."

Roddy's string of films and endless television appearances keep him almost frantically busy, flying cross country at a moment's notice, sometimes for as little as a couple of days at a time. While he's shooting his six films after *Shock Treatment,* he also appears as a presenter at the Tony Awards and the Emmy Awards on opposite coasts, he does two anthology episodes each for *Alfred Hitchcock Hour* and *Bob Hope Presents the Chrysler Theatre* and anthology appearances for *The Eleventh Hour* and *Kraft Suspense Theatre*; he guest stars on the drama series *Combat!* and *Ben Casey*; he guests on *The Merv Griffin Show* twice and *The Mike Douglas Show* three times; he also appears on eleven episodes of *Password*, five episodes of *The Match Game*, and special episodes of *The Price Is Right*, *The Celebrity Game*, and *Stump the Stars.*

A standout is his appearance on *Kraft Suspense Theatre*'s "The Wine-Dark Sea." It's another of his loner, oddball performances, opening with drunken, homeless Roddy McDowall and John Larkin stealing a pair of shoes and 85 cents from a fellow homeless man lying unconscious (or dead?) in the street. If they can get at least 95 cents for the shoes from a thrift store, they'll have enough money for muscatel to last through the night and into the morning. They are close friends, living in an abandoned funeral home. When Larkin is killed, seemingly in a botched robbery, McDowall is alone and desperate. He drunkenly tries to convince the police that Larkin couldn't have been involved in the robbery. Roddy is so vehement and violent he's arrested. Sober after being in jail for six days, he pulls himself together and proves his friend is innocent. It won't bring him back from the dead, but at least the guilty party will pay. It's another tour de force in miniature—a small story about a character presented as a small man—with Roddy giving him nuance and gravitas.

In the meantime, Roddy continues photo sessions for *Double Exposure*. He's careful not to interfere too much. Part of the beauty of the idea is to have undiluted observations. Yet often the writers take it upon themselves to seek Roddy's opinions for revisions. John Steinbeck submits five drafts of his essay on

Henry Fonda. Roddy dutifully responds to each draft, assuring one of the most famous writers in the world that his work is brilliant and needs no changes. Roddy seeks Robby Lantz's advice about Walter Kerr's dour essay on Tammy Grimes. "Should I send it back to him?" he asks. Even though Robby finds the piece "confusing, dark, insane, senseless," he advises against it. "You are simply a host, and you would not tell your guests how to dress unless they exposed themselves offensively and that depends, of course, on who they are and what they look like." And the last thing Roddy should want to do is piss off a powerful theater critic like Walter Kerr. Roddy engages with over one hundred people, going back and forth about their essays.

The six films are all high profile, though some fare better critically and at the box office than others. The biggest financial and critical disaster is *The Loved One*, which ironically is now regarded by many as a kind of bonkers classic while the others are less well remembered. Tony Richardson helms the movie, fresh from winning two Oscars for producing and directing *Tom Jones*. He's given a great deal of latitude by MGM—a studio struggling to feel relevant in a changing marketplace. The screenplay, by Christopher Isherwood and Terry Southern, based on Evelyn Waugh's cheerfully morbid novel, satirizes Forest Lawn and Hollywood, among other targets.

In a role that in truth might be better played by Roddy, Robert Morse stars as a young, aspiring English poet who arrives in Los Angeles to stay with his uncle, John Gielgud, a longtime scenic artist at Megalopolitan Studios. Roddy plays the studio head's insufferable son who unaccountably fires John, who then commits suicide. Robert Morse meets Anjanette Comer (Roddy's *Arrest and Trial* costar), destined to become "the first lady embalmer of Whispering Glades," when he arranges the funeral. Playing twin brothers, Jonathan Winters becomes the catalyst for a series of hairpin plot turns involving a pet cemetery, a rocket, a religious cult, a lonely hearts column, and a condemned hillside house teetering on the edge of collapse. Along the way we encounter wacked out characters played by Rod Steiger, Dana Andrews, Milton Berle, James Coburn, Tab Hunter, Margaret Leighton, Liberace, Robert Morley, Barbara Nichols, and Lionel Stander. For some it's an abomination, for others a masterpiece. At the time of its release, the public stays away in droves, and across the board critics hate it, calling it, in various reviews, "tasteless," "grotesque," "morbid," "macabre," "clownish," "ghoulish," "offensive," "disastrous," "excessive," "strained," and "scattershot." It's not an "important" film for Roddy, but it's essential viewing.

He breezes through two cameo turns in *That Darn Cat* and *Inside Daisy Clover*, a notorious bomb starring Natalie Wood as a teenaged movie musical sensation driven over the edge by the machinery of Hollywood. His friend Gavin Lambert is the screenwriter, adapting it from his own novel, and he and Natalie have known each other for years. "At that point in my career, I should not really have taken that role," he confesses to author Robert Hofler. "It was too small. But I wanted to be part of the movie."

The Third Day is a breathless drama that has the tone of an international thriller but is actually about an impossibly glamorous family fighting over a chinaware business, of all things. Selling it will put half the town out of a job when the buyers modernize, and Roddy ruthlessly supports the sale. Mona Washburn, speaking of her son Oliver, Roddy's character, turns to George Peppard, suffering memory loss after an accident, and out of the blue says, "Caesarean. I wonder if that accounts for his personality. Oliver's a rat, but he's all I've got." Roddy and Elizabeth Ashley have enormous chemistry as cousins with a vaguely sexual vibe. She slaps him (prompting the Chiclets prank they recount on *Password*) because Roddy brutally undermines her husband, George, who at this point still can't remember who he is. The director and producer is Jack Smight,

Roddy's director on *Arrest and Trial* for "Journey Into Darkness." Roddy brings some of that kind of complexity here. His narrative function is that of a simple antagonist, but he isn't as cut-and-dried with the role as he might be, giving a stock character a sense of humanity.

The Adventures of Bullwhip Griffin gives him a genuine starring role, as a steadfastly loyal butler in 1840s Boston. His supposedly wealthy employer dies, shocking his granddaughter, Suzanne Pleshette, who learns she's penniless. Her fourteen-year-old brother decides to save her from poverty by sneaking aboard a ship bound for California. Roddy follows and Gold Rush adventures ensue, as they win and lose a couple of fortunes and Roddy gets accidentally known as a fearsome fighter, Bullwhip Griffin. Richard Haydn is a florid confidant they pick up along the way, and Karl Malden is the nominal bad guy. Suzanne follows and becomes a saloon singer. This is a Disney movie, but she has some surprisingly sexy scenes with her boss, Harry Guardino. Roddy shows off his toned physique, handles the physical comedy with cool aplomb, and is adorably sweet on Suzanne without ever making a move. The movie is shot in a style meant to evoke silent movies. The device doesn't work, and some of the comic set pieces don't play as well as they might. It does moderately well at the box office and gets respectable reviews when it's released a year and a half later in 1967, but it does nothing to solidify Roddy's career resurgence. But it doesn't do him any harm either, and Disney is a reliable employer, even though he privately refers to his boss as "the friendly fascist of Burbank, Uncle Walt."

Lord Love a Duck isn't as flashy a project as *The Loved One,* but it aims just as high (or low) in satirizing mores of the day. Director, producer, and cowriter George Axelrod is a friend of Roddy's along with his wife, Joan. George conceives *Lord Love a Duck* as a black comedy commentary on the southern California teenager subculture, describing Roddy's character as a cross between Andy Hardy and Dr. Strangelove, and the film itself as "a latent act of revenge against my own teenaged children." By today's standards Roddy's fixation on Tuesday Weld makes him a creepy stalker. By the standards of the mid-1960s, apparently, he's adorably persistent. Everyone is too old to be in high school, so it stops mattering once you get over the initial shock, and though Roddy at thirty-seven is among the oldest, his age isn't distracting.

Roddy creates a character who's both intense yet laid-back—a fascinating balancing act—as he goes through the film like a genie, granting Tuesday Weld's wishes, no matter the cost. "Just ask, I'll get it for you," he tells her. "I don't do bad things with boys," she responds. "You don't have to do anything," he assures her, as he proceeds to give her everything she dreams of—being popular, getting a job, finding a husband, and becoming a movie star. Her husband target is a wealthy and handsome college senior she meets during a sex seminar at a drive-in church. Roddy befriends and moves in with the jock's mother, daffy but straightlaced Ruth Gordon. With no husband in evidence, Roddy asks if she's divorced. She quips, "We don't divorce our husbands, we bury them."

Tuesday and her cocktail waitress mother, Lola Albright, are more like sisters. Lola has a great line: "You know, I never go out with a married man on the first date." She is truly remarkable, all smiles and sex appeal at first, then revealing a surprisingly dark, empty inner life. Ruth is shocked by Lola, disapproving of her son dating the daughter of such a floozie, so Lola clears her daughter's path by killing herself. In the end, after bumping off the jock when he stands in the way of Tuesday's movie star dreams, Roddy is deemed criminally insane, and Tuesday Weld gets to star in *Bikini Widow.* George Axelrod and the film are nominated for awards at the Berlin Film Festival and Lola Albright wins Best Actress, but it bombs at the box office, and most critics regard it as unfunny and unfocused. George Axelrod is pilloried. Roddy gets good reviews, however, and his youthfully appropriate appearance is duly noted. Tuesday Weld tells Rex Reed it's her favorite film, and she gives the best performance of her career. She isn't wrong. She also picks up her first husband, Roddy's then-assistant, aspiring screenwriter Claude Harz.

Not unlike *The Loved One*, *Lord Love a Duck* survives through the years as a fascinating if flawed example of a veteran filmmaker going outside his comfort zone (in today's vernacular) to create something unique and of its moment. Charles Champlin in the *Los Angeles Times* devotes an entire column to discussing it over dinner one night with Roddy McDowall. "It was a peculiar and difficult role in a peculiar and difficult film, and Roddy calls the making of it a fantastic experience, totally joyous. 'The willingness to fail characterized a good deal about *Lord Love a Duck*. . . . If it chose some fairly obvious targets for satire, like the beach films, it also made some subtle observations on the American fear of aging, and on the loneliness of the exceptional mind in a society which admires being homogenized and not much else.' At the end of a long dinner, Roddy said, 'We've spent two hours discussing what the film meant—how many movies make you that involved?' "

Champlin agrees that not many films can trigger such a conversation. He goes on to discuss how not many actors are eager to talk about the script and dialogue rather than their own performances. Roddy is quite unusual in looking at the broader picture rather than merely his own part in it.

The Cool Ones is another send-up of teen counterculture, this time taking aim at the music business in all its supposed vacuity, and framed with terrible rock songs. Roddy plays a flamboyant music executive with too many Freudian tics to count. *The New York Times* carps, "I venture to guess this will disgust even the kids." It's also one of those films where everyone onscreen talks about how wonderful a performance is—think Patty Duke in

Valley of the Dolls. The other characters listen to her sing, hollowly cheering, "Isn't she great?" No. She's dreadful.

While *Lord Love a Duck* is in production, Roddy rents a house in Malibu. Tuesday Weld has a house nearby, as does then-producer Dominick Dunne (later to become a writer). Every Sunday Roddy has people over for a barbecue that extends well into the evening. He experiments with a movie camera for the first time. The footage is fantastic, with everyone mugging for his camera—Lauren Bacall, Rock Hudson, Jane Fonda and director Roger Vadim, Lee Grant, Mike Nichols, Julie Andrews, Kirk Douglas, Natalie Wood, George Hamilton, Suzanne Pleshette, Judy Garland, Anthony Perkins, and Paul Newman, among others, waving, sticking their tongues out, or crossing their eyes.

"That summer the Royal Ballet came to town with Rudolf Nureyev and Dame Margot Fonteyn, and Roddy's beach house was a meeting ground for British dancers and Hollywood stars," Dominick Dunne remembers in his *Vanity Fair* article about Roddy after his death. "Sharman Douglas, the highly publicized madcap daughter of a former ambassador to the Court of St. James, made an entrance each Sunday, one week arriving on the back of an elephant and the next swimming out of the Pacific Ocean onto Roddy's beach in a long evening dress and pearls. Roddy was here, there, everywhere, in the briefest of brief bathing attire, recording it all on film, a social historian with the zeal of a documentarian."

"It was this wonderful, light, fun atmosphere he created, unlike anyone else," remembers Lee Grant. "Everyone was there—old big-time stars but also young people in their twenties. It was invigorating, interesting, a smart group of people. You always felt alive, interested, and interesting. There was such a closeness in that and in the things we talked about."

Roddy is robbed one night. Among the list of the stolen articles he supplies to the Malibu Sheriff's Department are 2 cameras and a camera case, 1 large navy-blue suitcase, 3 bottles of liquor, 4 cartons of Marlboros, food, linens, and $6,500 worth of his Italian clothes, including 40 ties, 53 shirts, 13 sweaters, 11 pairs of slacks, 4 suits, 2 sportscoats, 2 swimsuits, an overcoat, and a raincoat. Robby Lantz suggests he take the bull by the horns. "Get a film job that takes you to Europe. Buy a brand-new wardrobe."

Sybil Burton commiserates about the robbery when she writes from a stay in London with her new husband, singer and actor Jordan Christopher. There is news of Lord Snowden, Princess Margaret, Boaty Boatwright, and the comedy actor Kenneth Williams. "Princess Margaret was a riot. I always make fun of them all but when one is face to face with that Windsor look one has to behave oneself. I curtsied all the time." More important, there are updates on construction of the new venture she and Roddy are forming—a nightclub and discotheque called Arthur on East 54th Street in New York, at the site of the old El Morocco, the exclusive 1930s to 1950s Café Society hot spot known for its zebra-stripe motif.

Sybil is looking for a business opportunity when she and Roddy hit on the idea for Arthur. The aim is to create a club that feels both expansive yet inclusive, chic yet relaxed, wild yet safe. The name is Mike Nichols's idea. She and Roddy are looking for something that's funny, and Mike suggests "Arthur," after a gag in the Beatles movie, *A Hard Day's Night*, when a reporter stares at George Harrison and disapprovingly asks, "What do you call that haircut?" He answers smoothly, "Arthur."

Before the club opens, she starts scouting for local bands and discovers twenty-five-year-old Jordan Christopher singing with a group called the Wild Ones. She hires them as Arthur's house band before the club is even open. She and Jordan impulsively marry almost immediately after they meet. She becomes Sybil Burton Christopher.

From its opening in May 1965, the place is a hit. "Arthur is the ultimate of nightclubs, the 'in-est' of all the 'in' spots, the last word in the discotheque world," gushes Marika Aba in the *Los Angeles Times*, where, apparently, a nightspot opening across the country is big news. "It's the place to watch Rudi Nureyev frug, Julie Christie dine, an occasional Kennedy mix with the international set. In other words, once your ears get used to steady rock and roll and your eyes to the dim lights, it is the greatest show of them all."

Sybil goes on to say, "You won't have to be famous or rich or social to come here and be part of Arthur. All you have to be is aware and young at heart, and that covers all kinds of people. . . . We don't have special tables for the so-called beautiful people. Anyway, what does that mean? It's such a confusing label."

Roddy is involved as much as his schedule allows, while Sybil works there with the help of a hands-on manager. A press release lists a glittering array of celebrity investors, so many it's almost embarrassing, like "overkill" according to Roddy, including (in alphabetical order) Julie Andrews, Lauren Bacall, Leslie Bricusse, Carol Channing, Jackie Cooper, Bobby Darin, Kirk Douglas, James Galanos, Henry Fonda, Buck Henry, Hope Lange, Janet Leigh, Josh and Nedda Logan, Trini Lopez, the Mamas and the Papas, Alan Pakula, Paul Revere and the Raiders, Rosalind Russell, George Segal, Tom Smothers, Ray Stark, Leslie Uggams, and Natalie Wood. Also prominently featured are Roddy McDowall, Sybil Burton Christopher, and Jordan Christopher.

In pitching a story and photo spread on the club to *Harper's Bazaar*, Roddy talks about its "intangible components" that can't be photographed, like the sound design and the wonderful sense of excitement in the air, but he cites the excellent photographic possibilities of the swank interior and the staff. "Sybil insisted that they all be young and alive and attractive, as opposed to other cafes." He thinks they could all be used with fashion models to impressive effect. A TV documentary special is in the works about the property, with its rich history.

In *Me and My Shadows: A Family Memoir*, Judy Garland's daughter, singer and actress Lorna Luft, remembers the club vividly. "The first nightclub I ever went to was Arthur's, the hippest club in New York in the 1960s," she writes. "Mama and Liza [Minnelli] and Joey [Luft] and I went in a limo with Roddy McDowall. . . . We sat at a table in the back with the A list crowd. Everybody in the place was coming and going from our table. We were the center of attention. . . . All I could think of is, I want to stay here for the rest of my life and never go home. I didn't ever want this to end and for a long time it didn't."

Sybil is sometimes imagined in the press as a sort of demi-celebrity with a queenly role at Arthur but little hands-on involvement. Nothing can be further from the truth. In her own sprawling handwriting, she works out the figures for what the club needs to take in to be in profit, calculating salaries, taxes, legal and accounting fees, rent, insurance, and pensions and welfare, projecting 1,800 patrons per week with various average checks, projecting an average intake of $11,970 per week and a weekly profit of $6,481. She estimates they will be able to begin paying back their investors in as little as six months, and she's right.

But that gritty work ethic isn't nearly as much fun to write about. "Sybil Burton was a white tornado dancing the frug, the monkey, the swim," gushes the *Daily News*. "Kissing fellow celebrities and being kissed by them, drinking by turns, scotch and Devonshire tea, and smiling a smile that said there was no other place in the world she would rather be. . . . Every night she's queen of the scene."

Roddy is thrilled about Arthur and his seemingly endless acting jobs, but other worries cast a pall over this time of so much success. Montgomery Clift seems to be on a deadly spiral, fueled by alcohol and drugs, throwing parties surrounded by a dangerous crowd of enablers and sycophants, where he often ends up unconscious, passed out on the floor while the revelry goes on around him. More than once, he's robbed.

"One night, Roddy McDowall was there," writes Maureen Stapleton in her 1995 biography, *A Hell of a Life*, "when Monty went zilch and flopped to the ground. I started crying and told Roddy, 'We've got to do something. This can't go on. We've got to help him.' Roddy, one of the best people in the world, said very simply, and sadly, 'The only thing we can do, Maureen, is hold his hand to the grave.' "

Chapter 6

The Face Is Familiar

As *Double Exposure* nears completion, Robby Lantz becomes Roddy's agent on the book, negotiating his deal with Delacorte Press. (In a very strange coincidence, Delacorte also publishes *Sybil* in 1973.) Roddy's deal is relatively rich, but the advance doesn't come close to covering his expenses, upward of $40,000. For Roddy, the book is a labor of love, with a large portion of any royalties going to the MPTF, as he continues his commitment to helping the fund in their mission. "We take care of our own and that is so important to me," Roddy tells *Beverly Hills 213*. "They respect people's privacy and let them keep their dignity. I can empathize with that. I personally don't think that my private life or my private views are public property. Because we're in the same industry, they understand that."

Delacorte brings *Double Exposure* out in black-and-white coffee table size, with heavy paper and quality photographic printing. The photographs are stunning and revealing. The quality of the essays varies somewhat, but they are all joyful and fitting in a book that celebrates creative artists. Unhappy with his own work, John Steinbeck ends up backing out, leaving director and writer Josh Logan to write the piece on Henry Fonda. Walter Kerr's piece on Tammy Grimes also isn't included. Instead, cabaret impresario Julius Monk pens a pithy tribute next to film strips showing a mercurial Tammy in twenty-four different images taken by Roddy.

Some of the highlights include Anthony Newley's passionate piece on Sammy Davis Jr.'s magnificence and raw vulnerability in live performance, coupled with Roddy's stunning shot of the entertainer, with every conflicting emotion powerfully on display. Frank Sinatra writes an appreciation of "Prince" Michael Romanoff, the storied Los Angeles restauranteur, dismissing the fact that he isn't a prince by calling him a king, printed along with Roddy's shot of him looking every bit the dashing, royal gentleman Sinatra says he is. Barbra Streisand by Jerome Robbins; Laurence Olivier by Noël Coward; Lauren Bacall by Katharine Hepburn; Montgomery Clift by Marcello Mastroianni—the essays and photographs are fascinating. Perhaps the best is the very first one. Roddy's photograph of Simone Signoret catches her mid-gesture, possibly mid-sentence, communicating a hundred moods in one look, with the shortest essay of all, written by Rosalind Russell: "I would rather see her smoke a cigarette than spend a day in a museum. She smokes it with passion, humor, grace, hunger! To watch Simone is a joy—the actress supreme, the complete woman involved in the exciting business of living!"

The book is the distillation of everything that matters to Roddy.

Giants in all walks of the arts pay tribute to one another, with Roddy in his favorite position, showing these remarkable people to us as he sees them. Sometimes his images are somewhat obscured, as if his subjects want to hide even as they unmask. Richard Burton is so cloaked in darkness, he's almost unrecognizable. Other shots are bright and shiny, capturing the steely strength of Julie Andrews, for instance, that lies just beneath the surface of her humor and grace. Tuesday Weld writes about herself in a prose poem where she free-associates about different aspects of her personality and experiences, while Roddy's picture is a profile shot that looks nothing at all like her. This is the way she sees herself, as an alien gulping for air.

Double Exposure is a revelation for anyone who loves Roddy's world in all its glorious bubbledom. For those uninterested in the arts or show business there's nothing here. It's a closed view of the world—open to all who want to live there—but impenetrable to those who can't, don't, or won't embrace its values. Roddy shares only one photograph and essay before the book is published. He shows Monty the piece Marcello Mastroianni writes about him. He wants Monty to read the tribute but doesn't believe Monty will be alive by the time the book comes out.

Before publication, Roddy is in Germany, shooting *The Defector* with a barely functioning Monty. Roddy agrees to play a small role as a favor, hoping to help Monty get through it. It's a French financed and produced spy thriller—junk by Monty and Roddy's estimation—but meant to prove that Monty is in good enough shape to do a bigger film, a Southern drama with gothic sexual overtones called *Reflections in a Golden Eye* opposite Elizabeth Taylor. Even if he gets through *The Defector* shoot with flying colors, he won't be insurable for a studio film, and Elizabeth puts up her own $1 million-plus salary as a personal guarantee. Just after Monty returns from Germany, he dies of a heart attack at age forty-five. *Double Exposure* comes out five months later. Roddy is right. Monty doesn't live to see it published.

"I had a long talk with Elizabeth," Robby Lantz writes Roddy. "She was very dear, very broken up, and very concerned about you. I told her she rendered Monty the greatest service by being loyal and loving him. . . . The sun is shining, and I admit it surprises me. Take care of yourself. We love you very much. Yours ever, Robby."

Bobby Lewis calls Monty's death "the longest suicide in history."

It's a relatively small funeral by movie star standards. Lauren Bacall and Frank Sinatra are there, along with Libby Holman and Nancy Walker. Roddy is in London shooting a film called *It!* opposite Jill Haworth. Elizabeth Taylor is in Rome shooting *The Taming of the Shrew* opposite Richard Burton for director Franco Zeffirelli. Both are heartbroken and send flowers. Both keep working.

Robert Thom writes a long, brutally honest article about Monty for *Esquire*. Though it skirts anything to do with Monty's sexuality, it details his erratic, abusive behavior, his substance addictions, and like Bobby Lewis, Robert Thom views Monty's last decade as a slow, tragic suicide. Many of Roddy's friends are outraged, variously finding the piece "tasteless," "maddening," "malicious," and "insulting," and wondering why on earth he would write it. Roddy doesn't approve—he could never countenance violating Monty's privacy this way—but he understands why Robert writes it: raging grief at the sheer waste of such a man and such a talent. It is impossible to accept. Writing about it honestly is Robert's way of seeking catharsis. Roddy can forgive that.

He returns from London and makes more television appearances. In *Bob Hope Presents the Chrysler Theatre*, "The Fatal Mistake," Roddy is a British accountant visited every month by a "friend," Michael Wilding, who bestows gifts upon his family, then collects a monthly blackmail check from the accountant. Weary of it, Roddy plans a deadly accident for Michael. It's a happy reunion for the old friends. Michael Wilding is one of Roddy's favorites among Elizabeth Taylor's first batch of husbands, before Richard Burton. He's easily the most well read and erudite, and as fellow Brits he and Roddy have an easy camaraderie.

This marks the last of Roddy's traditional 1950s-style anthology show performances, and *Bob Hope Presents the Chrysler Theatre* is the last of its kind. Toward the end, it doesn't even stick to anthology drama, broadening its scope to include music variety and comedy. Other anthology performances do follow, most notably his appearance in the pilot of *Night Gallery*. By then, however, the shooting style makes the programs into short TV movies rather than the scrappier productions of the 1950s, where the episodes often have the excitement of live theater. It's the end of an era, for TV and for Roddy, who always feels he owes his career resurgence in the 1950s to anthology TV.

He also makes an appearance in 1966 on *Batman*, for the double episodes "While Gotham City Burns" and "The Bookworm Turns" as the Bookworm, a villain who commits crimes inspired by literary plots. Like the Riddler, the Bookworm leaves clues to lure the caped crusaders to the scene of his next crime. Roddy looks fabulous, in a trim brown leather suit, wearing a matching fedora topped with a giant library reading light that swings around, and huge glasses. The shoot is also memorable because Prince Philip is in Los Angeles at the time and wants to see the *Batman* set on the Fox lot. Roddy is a perfect host. The studio asks Cesar Romero (the Joker) to come in as well. Roddy and Cesar show Prince Philip around. Just another day in the land of make-believe. This is the Bookworm's only appearance on the television show. Later the character becomes part of the DC *Batman* universe as a much darker villain—a fire-scarred abused child who grows up to be a serial killer—similar to the Joker's evolution from camp goofball to deranged psychopath.

Roddy makes three other films in between series TV and game show appearances, and his work on the *Planet of the Apes* franchise, which dominates his schedule from 1967 to 1975. His supporting roles in *Angel, Angel, Down We Go*, *Midas Run*, and *Hello Down There* are as varied as the projects themselves. *Angel, Angel, Down We Go* is Robert Thom's adaptation of his own play and his only outing as a director. It's a frank, incredibly erotic countercultural mashup of rock music, parachuting, male nudity, body shaming, ritualistic murder, priceless jewelry, and old Hollywood. If that sounds like a lot to pack into one movie, it is.

Jordan Christopher is a pansexual rock star who upends the lives of zaftig debutante Holly Near, her wealthy mother, Jennifer Jones, and her gay father, Charles Aidman—with all of the aforementioned plot elements colliding in a collage of psychedelic kink. It's by turns outrageous and dreadful, sometimes both at once. Roddy and Lou Rawls are part of Jordan's circus. Roddy is nude or shirtless through a lot of the picture, luxuriating in his own body, stroking himself idly. Talking about her strange, privileged childhood, Holly Near murmurs, "I sat on General MacArthur's knee when I was two." Roddy drolly asks, "Did it excite him?" He has a stoned-out monologue during a communionlike ritual and, apropos of nothing, says, "The draft board told me to go home. They asked me if I were homosexual. I said, 'Baby Man I am just sexual. Sometimes I can just stare at a carrot and Baby Man that carrot can turn me on.'" Roddy is always happy to work among friends, and at the time every studio is hoping to make the next *Easy Rider*, a box-office smash that turns countercultural experimentation into cold, hard cash.

Admittedly, a lot of questions run through one's mind watching it. What does Sybil Burton Christopher think of her new younger husband having love scenes with Jennifer Jones, in a kind of funhouse mirroring of their own age difference? (When Sybil and Jordan meet, she's thirty-six and he's twenty-five, a cavernous gulf in the sexual politics of 1966.) How does the bubbly, sexy Holly Near we meet here become the willowy lesbian feminist folk singer of a decade later? Why is the only African American, Lou Rawls, never allowed to show any skin? What exactly does writer and director Robert Thom think he's doing?

Sybil and Jordan see a rough cut and tell Robby Lantz that

they both vomit in the bathroom, they're so upset. They put the blame squarely on Robert Thom's shoulders as the director, calling his camera work old-fashioned, unimaginative, and cheap looking, going on to malign every creative choice he makes. Robby Lantz adds his own commentary: "The sets are bad, Jennifer's clothes are awful, her hair awful, Holly's clothes bad, even the necklace is bad. Jordan is good, sometimes very good, but often uncomfortable. It could have been dazzling." He moves on to Roddy's performance. "You look and perform very well, Rod, under the circumstances, but like Jordan, are very uncomfortable."

Sybil, Jordan, and Robby try to intervene with Robert Thom, telling him he must step in and recut—he must try to fix it. Roddy stays out of it. He thinks the film is beyond saving. When it's sneak-peaked, audiences in New York and Los Angeles loathe it, and Robert is strangely pleased, taking their rejection as a sign that he's successfully challenging and shocking them. It's released under its own title and bombs. The critics are brutal, pillorying Robert Thom's script and his direction in lengthy, specific terms, mourning the desecration of Jennifer Jones, and mildly praising Jordan Christopher, Holly Near, and Roddy. A year later it's rereleased in a shortened, retitled version as *Cult of the Damned*, to run on drive-in on a double bill with *The Vampire Lovers*. Jordan goes on to sporadic film and television appearances and stars in a nighttime soap for CBS in 1980 called *Secrets of Midland Heights*, but his career never hits the heights he and Sybil hope for. The marriage, however, lasts until his death in 1996.

Dirk Bogarde writes from England about *Angel*, wondering what on earth everyone could possibly be thinking, including Roddy. "What made you do it?" he asks, going on to give his no-holds-barred take on all their mutual friends, including Elizabeth Tayor and Richard Burton, in London while Richard is shooting *Where Eagles Dare*. "Elizabeth and Richard are making cunts of themselves as usual, with a vast yacht moored off the Tower for their dogs to live in, and two policemen guarding the thing day and night. Questions being asked in Parliament and the usual piss-ups. They are so silly and getting tackier with every new addition. Richard Harris has been slung off the new Mike Caine picture in Spain [*Play Dirty*], and Nigel Davenport has taken over at a day's notice. It is apparently a War Story. . . . Boaty is swinging about with an executive's voice and is fully in command of UI [Universal International]. She sounds like a cross between Ilse Koch [a Nazi war criminal] and Danny La Rue [a mainstream-famous British drag queen] and I adore every acre of her. She is busy right now with [Joseph] Losey's picture with Elizabeth [*Secret Ceremony*]. Turned down being Elizabeth's husband in it, a lousy part, but it naturally miffed, poor old Joe, who needs a mate about. But I don't think I could handle the lady and her problems. Life is too short."

Midas Run shoots in Milan and Rome, among other Italian and British locations, so it offers Roddy an opportunity to replace all those clothes he loses in the Malibu robbery. That's really the best that can be said about it. He plays a junior intelligence officer in the British Secret Service who realizes his boss, Fred Astaire, is pulling a double-cross on a government mission disguised as a hijacking of a $15 million gold shipment. It's one of a slew of films in the 1960s that are assembled internationally for tax reasons, with star-studded multinational casts largely wasted.

Roddy plays another boy wonder of the record business, albeit one who's far more levelheaded than his character in *The Cool Ones*, in a family comedy called *Hello Down There*. Tony Randall and Janet Leigh move their family into an experimental undersea habitat, along with their teenage children's newly formed rock band, with the possibility of a record contract hanging in the balance with Roddy. Sea creatures, a rival undersea home builder, and the military cause complications, but Roddy is able to launch the band in an undersea taping hosted by Merv Griffin, as the very young Richard Dreyfuss, blond-bewigged Kay Cole (later in the original cast of *A Chorus Line*), Lou Wagner, and Gary Tigerman sing, "Glub, glub love, I'm floating on a sea of love. . . . Glub love bubble, loving you sure ain't no trouble . . ." with live dolphins chirping along to the beat. Roddy and Merv think they're groovy. The film isn't a hit.

One thing that *is* a hit is *Night Gallery*, Rod Serling's TV series of suspense tales illustrated by various paintings. The pilot is legendary for the Joan Crawford segment, directed by Steven Spielberg, where she plays a rich blind woman who buys a man's eyes but still can't see because of a power blackout in New York City and, in a rage, plunges to her death. Roddy's segment may be less famous, but it's equally powerful. He's a black-sheep nephew who murders his rich uncle. Ossie Davis is the butler, Portifoy. Roddy taunts him, memorably bellowing and cooing, "Portifoy" at every turn. But Ossie has diabolical plans of his own, setting up Roddy to be driven mad by fear, using a series of phony haunted paintings depicting his uncle arising from the graveyard bent on revenge. But in a twist of fate, the paintings turn out to have real evil powers, and the spirit of Roddy approaches Ossie, also bent on revenge.

The show is a ratings hit, and while Joan Crawford gets the lion's share of press attention, Roddy gets enthusiastic notices across the board. William Ragsdale, Roddy's costar a number of years later on *Fright Night*, sees the show as a kid and agrees. He always remembers the way Roddy taunts the butler. During the *Fright Night* shoot, William takes to following Roddy around on set calling out, "Portifoy! Portifoy!" It cracks Roddy up every time.

Producer David Merrick brings Roddy back to Broadway, in a new play called *The Astrakhan Coat*, opposite Brian Bedford as a sophisticated, elegant thug who steals and kills for thrills. Roddy is a hapless waiter who hopes to emulate Bedford's panache by buying his beautiful astrakhan coat, made from the fur of newborn karakul lambs. Bedford mockingly agrees to sell his coat on an installment plan as he sets up Roddy to take the fall for his crimes. Murders pile up. But is McDowall actually guilty? The fantastic cast also includes James Coco and Carole Shelley, but Roddy endures the rehearsal process full of despair, blaming a lack of a directorial concept from Donald McWhinnie and David Merrick's state of mind after the enormous failure of his recent musical version of *Breakfast at Tiffany's*, starring Mary Tyler Moore and Richard Chamberlain. "He was in absolute shell-shock," he writes Dirk Bogarde, "which strangely enough, rendered him impotent in relation to our show."

John Chapman in the *Daily News* is a fan, however. "A slick and scary English job. . . . Its ending is a real twister. Roddy McDowall becomes so absorbed in the case against him that he gleefully declares that this is the most interesting thing that has ever happened to him. . . . Ranging from innocent confusion to strutting bravado to cackling despair, his may be the standout performance in a Broadway straight play this season." Despite his enthusiasm, the play closes after five previews and just twenty performances.

Roddy shoots a *Hallmark Hall of Fame* production, "Saint Joan," adapted from George Bernard Shaw's play, playing Charles, the Dauphin, opposite Geneviève Bujold. He becomes the root cause of Joan's execution when he inherits the throne. It's extraordinarily well received, with the *Chicago Tribune* review stating, "It shows how good TV can be," and the *Los Angeles Times* commending it as "absorbing and exciting," emphasizing the strength of the performances and the production's ability to bring Shaw's play to life. Roddy's portrayal of the hesitant and politically cautious heir to the French throne counterbalances Geneviève's visionary Joan. Their onscreen dynamic is wonderful.

Arthur opens a West Coast location in West Hollywood, and

Roddy is on hand, leading Joyce Haber of the *Los Angeles Times* on a tour. "I think there are eighty investors," Roddy tells her. They settle in the "quiet" room, a pub-themed section of the club, which is a near duplicate of its New York counterpart, with one addition: a giant Peanuts drawing on the wall, which features the familiar characters standing by an Arthur marquee. Lucy is saying, "Can Arthur come out and play?" Snoopy is saying, "Arthur!" There's also another sketch, a large reproduction of a *New Yorker* cartoon picturing a man frantically hailing a taxi while his elderly wife is frugging on the sidewalk. "Arthur," the man tells the cab driver, "and hurry!"

Joyce Haber's piece centers on the hubbub among staff and attendees over whether or not Warren Beatty is going to show. She recounts an excruciatingly exhaustive list of fifty-four named celebrity guests ("most of whom seemingly are investors") with detailed descriptions of what most of the women are wearing. She is most impressed by "Mae West in the flesh! Mae West with a long platinum mane, in a flip hairdo. Mae West in folds of white satin, crystal-beaded at the neckline. Mae West with Reggie Lewis, who was Mr. Universe in an unidentified year."

The clubs have a great run, continuing through the rest of the 1960s, returning profits from their first year on to all the investors. Once paid back for their initial stakes, they earn regular dividends. Sybil and Roddy call it a day when business starts to slow and the novelty of being in the nightclub business begins to fade. In an odd postscript, one of their managers, Mickey Deans, meets Judy Garland and after a brief courtship they marry. He's her fifth husband and twelve years younger. He writes of their brief time together and her tragic death in *Weep No More, My Lady*, published several years later.

That Judy's death is later seen as an inciting incident at the Stonewall uprising, the most visible public beginning of decades of civil rights struggles to come for the LGBTQIA+ community, is at once mystifying and gratifying to Roddy. As with most wealthy or middle-class white gay men, Stonewall doesn't register as a particularly momentous event—just a bunch of drag queens in a street brawl with the cops. Nothing new. Judy's death is as inevitable to Roddy as Monty's was a few years earlier. Another long suicide. They're not symbols of anything for Roddy. They are people he loves and loses. Yet he knows Judy would be touched that she means enough to inspire a generation to fight back.

Roddy keeps up his game show appearances in his "spare time," including a stint on one called *The Face Is Familiar.* Contestants are paired with celebrity guests and shown photographs of well-known people divided into horizontal or vertical strips, which are scrambled, and are only revealed one at a time. The trick is to guess the identity of the stars without being able to see their faces clearly. There's a literal and figurative correlation to Roddy's real-life and reel-life experiences. *Double Exposure* is all about obscuring and revealing identities. The next chapter of Roddy's life is defined by masks.

Ask a classic film fan about Roddy McDowall and they'll quickly cite *How Green Was My Valley* or *Lassie Come Home,* maybe *My Friend Flicka.* Ask a devotee of screen epics and *Cleopatra* immediately springs to mind. Disaster film lovers remember *The Poseidon Adventure.* Horror fans the *Fright Night* films. For science fiction and adventure buffs, though, Roddy McDowall's work on six different projects within the *Planet of the Apes* franchise is the most enduring part of his onscreen legacy—and you don't even get to see his face.

Over the course of eight years, he becomes the emotional and intellectual heart of the five films and the live-action TV series. As any *Apes* aficionado will point out, he doesn't play Cornelius in the second film installment, *Beneath the Planet of the Apes*, in 1970. He's in London directing Ava Gardner in his film *Tam Lin* at the time, so another actor named David Watson, whose voice sounds similar, replaces him. Roddy does, however, provide the opening voice-over, so in terms of bragging rights he can technically say he's in all five of the films (though his voice-over is recycled from *Planet of the Apes* and isn't technically recorded during the production of *Beneath the Planet of the Apes*). Such distinctions matter to the fandom.

The *Apes* franchise is an unusual film series in that, debatably, the sequels measure up to the original, except perhaps for the fifth and final film, where everyone seems exhausted. The TV show goes off in an entirely different direction on its own timeline that doesn't correspond with the films, putting one ape and two humans on the lam through each episode, making the narratives about the chase rather than the interactions between apes and humans.

Roddy is fascinated when he's first approached about *Planet of the Apes* and pleased to learn that most of his scenes will be with Kim Hunter, a friend from New York, and Maurice Evans, his long-ago costar from *The Tempest.* But getting fitted into all of the ape paraphernalia is far more arduous than he could ever imagine. The heavy makeup and prosthetics take as long as three or four hours to apply, and another hour to remove. Legendary makeup artist John Chambers bases his technique on procedures he uses creating masklike prosthetics during World War II to give disfigured veterans a normalized appearance. For the actors, the day begins at five o'clock in the morning, starting with painting wax over their eyebrows and sideburns (sort of like the way drag queens use glue on their brows). The inside of the mask for the top half of the face is then coated with adhesive and a makeup artist glues it to the actor's face. Ears are added. Teeth are painted with black enamel and a chin prosthetic is added. A final facial appliance is attached, holding four individually constructed hairpieces formed to each actor's face. Kim Hunter takes a tranquilizer every morning before her makeup is applied, but Roddy doesn't mind it too much. He tries to sleep during some of it when he can.

The result looks fantastic but severely limits facial movement. Roddy experiments with the best ways of working with the prosthetics. He practices at home in front of a mirror watching his own tics, blinks, and assorted facial gestures, testing out what looks the most natural. Generally, what feels normal doesn't look right, so matching nose, eye, and jaw movements to one's emotions isn't straightforward. Roddy goes on to host improvisational basic training sessions, teaching the other actors some of the physical tricks he learns. Also, and possibly more important to the actors playing apes, he teaches them how to smoke, drink, and eat without damaging the makeup. Long cigarette holders and straws accommodate the first two activities, but still require some special techniques, while eating remains a challenge throughout. Liquid meals become the norm.

The first film is shot during the summer in stifling heat, making the ape masks and costumes that much more difficult for the actors to endure. The heat in the desert scenes at the opening of the film proves so intense that many cast and crew members faint, including director Franklin Schaffner. Roddy loses twenty pounds during the first film. He also takes to driving off the lot occasionally in full makeup, shocking other drivers and getting himself in a little trouble with producer Arthur Jacobs, who decrees that no one see the Ape makeup before the film's release.

Planet of the Apes opens with Charlton Heston as an astronaut who crash-lands on a planet where an ape society hunts and enslaves a race of mute primitive humans. One of his two surviving crewmates is killed and the other lobotomized. Charlton is captured and spends the rest of the film half naked in a loincloth—two months of mostly uninterrupted sun exposure in a shoot dominated by exterior sequences. Charlton is studied by chimpanzee psychologist Zira (Kim Hunter) and her archeologist fiancé Cornelius (Roddy McDowall). Once they learn he can speak, read, and write, they're intrigued by the possibility that man may be the missing link in the evolution of the ape. Roddy and Kim are ordered to lobotomize Charlton by their superior, Dr. Zaius (Maurice Evans), a zealously antihuman orangutan, but instead they help him escape to the Forbidden Zone, a desert territory where, in a past dig, Roddy has found a puzzling artifact, a human-shaped doll that says "Mama." With Maurice Evans and other apes in pursuit, the band of renegades perseveres, culminating in the iconic image of them finding the ruins of the Statue of Liberty, revealing that we're on Earth. Whatever has happened to create this terrible future where humans are treated no better than animals, Charlton Heston bitterly realizes humans likely have only themselves to blame.

The film is successful beyond anyone's wildest imaginings, returning some $33 million on a budget of just under $6 million. Even Fox is surprised. It's not just a hit with audiences; critics are lavish in praising the script, the direction, and especially the acting. Roddy's expressive eyes and his ability to communicate emotion through his voice are central to the film's resonance. Kim Hunter brings an equal level of commitment and heart.

"There you are with your bright, attentive eyes, staring out of monkey fur," writes Louise Brooks. "You gave a performance worthy of a first-class play behind your eyes. I always see a mind working, and I wonder, what is this bastard thinking about?"

Roddy is nominated at the 1968 *Photoplay* Gold Medal as Most Popular Male Star, along with Clint Eastwood, Henry Fonda, Peter Fonda, Elvis Presley, Frank Sinatra, Robert Redford, and the winners, Sidney Poitier and Steve McQueen. John Chambers wins an honorary Oscar for makeup (which isn't an Oscar category until 1981). Merchandise related to the film includes toys and collectibles, action figures, picture and story books, trading card sets, books, records, comics, and a series of graphic novels from Marvel Comics.

During the shoot, Roddy meets Paul Anderson, one of the extra makeup assistants. He's young, artistic, and full of a rotating set of plans. He thinks of going to college to study painting, crafting, and photography; or he could go off to Santa Barbara and find a quiet, healthy life; or spend time "communing with the gods of the woods and deserts and prairies and oceans, sharing peace and oneness with Mama Earth." Or maybe he'll be an actor.

They don't become a couple until several years later, but his first steps into Roddy's life come with helping on a behind-the-scenes home movie project on the *Planet of the Apes* set. Roddy cuts together footage Paul shoots of the makeup process with his own footage and edits together a forty-four-minute short. He mainly shows it to his friends on his many movie nights, but clips are also sometimes used during on-air promotional appearances and screenings, as well as the *Planet of the Apes* conventions that begin popping up in the 1970s. It's released as part of the DVD bonus extras in a 2002 box set of the *Planet of the Apes* movies.

The first sequel to *Planet of the Apes* is *Beneath the Planet of the Apes*, rushed into development and production, this time for a winter shoot to avoid the summer heat. The producers settle on a story of apes and humans discovering a hidden underground city inhabited by mutated, telepathic humans who worship a doomsday nuclear device. Charlton Heston isn't eager to repeat his role and only agrees to don his loincloth in the sequel if he's a secondary character and if he gets to detonate the bomb and destroy the planet. He *never* wants to be asked to be in another *Apes* movie. James Franciscus joins up as an astronaut, sent to rescue Charlton, who basically has the same story trajectory as Charlton has in the first film.

It opens with Roddy in voice-over recorded from the first film's trial scene: "Beware the beast Man, for he's the Devil's pawn. Alone among God's primates, he kills for sport or lust or greed. Yea, he will murder his brother to possess his brother's land. Let him not breed in great numbers, for he will make a desert of his home and yours. Shun him. For he's the harbinger of death." It ends with a different actor in voice-over proclaiming, "In one of the countless billions of galaxies in the universe, lies a medium-sized star. And one of its satellites, a green and insignificant planet, is now dead."

That's supposed to be it for these assorted simians, but the movie does so well that another sequel is quickly developed, *Escape from the Planet of the Apes*. Since the Earth is now "dead," producer Arthur Jacobs switches gears, opting for a storyline about Cornelius and Zira escaping in a rocket ship along with scientist Sal Mineo, and going back in time to present-day Earth. In its first half, the tone is starkly different from the earlier films, played mostly as droll comedy, with Roddy and Kim becoming unexpected celebrities. Things turn darker when Sal Mineo is killed by a zoo gorilla, Kim gets pregnant, and government officials and scientists set out to stop the birth, fearing that a race of talking apes can only spell disaster for humankind. Roddy and Kim die in a shoot-out, but kindly circus owner Ricardo Montalban helps them outwit the authorities. They think Roddy and Kim's baby is dead, but Ricardo switches out their baby with an ordinary chimp. Baby Milo (named after Sal Mineo's character) survives. Production schedules Sal Mineo's scenes to be completed as quickly as possible so he can be wrapped from the film. He's completely freaked out about the makeup and prosthetics, feeling severe claustrophobia and panic, only calming down long enough for long takes when Roddy and Kim hold him in a communal hug for several minutes before the camera rolls. Sal feels terribly guilty about potentially embarrassing Roddy, who arranges for Sal to get the job in the first place, so Sal can earn enough to keep his SAG medical insurance in effect. Sal feels like he's letting his friend down.

The saga continues to the next film, but Kim Hunter calls it quits. "I was very glad I got killed on the third one," she tells *The New York Times*. "For me, three was enough, thanks a lot!"

She never wants to put on ape makeup again. *Conquest of the Planet of the Apes* takes place some twenty years or so later. A virus has wiped out the world's dogs and cats, and the apes are now domesticated pets and servants. Ricardo tells Roddy (Milo) of his true heritage, and Roddy takes on the name Caesar to conceal his identity. After Ricardo dies in custody, Roddy is enraged by the brutality and oppression faced by apes. He becomes the leader of an ape uprising, organizing a revolution against their human masters. In the original ending, Roddy shows no mercy, kills the remaining humans in the city, and vows to destroy all humans on the planet. This ending tests so poorly—audiences love the film but hate the ending—that a more pacifist ending is hastily constructed where Roddy reconsiders and orders the apes to lower their weapons, deciding that they can afford to be humane, since the fight is already won and they "have seen the birth of the Planet of the Apes."

With almost all television work other than soap operas now shooting in Los Angeles, Roddy decides that although he loves living in New York and loves his apartment on Central Park West, he's hardly ever there, and it's time to move back to Los Angeles. He finds a house in the foothills of Studio City. While he waits for work to be done, he rents a house from George Cukor, and while he's in London working on *The Legend of Hell House,* the house burns down with many of Roddy's belongings inside, and his fire insurance policy has lapsed. This comes at a time when he and business manager Stephen Weinrib have parted ways. Somehow in the transfer of responsibilities to Roddy's new business manager Lee Winkler, the fire insurance bill goes unpaid. Thankfully, much of Roddy's collection of films is safely in storage, and prior to leaving New York he signs an agreement with Howard Gotlieb at Boston University to house his archives, and most of his collection of Hollywood memorabilia is already there, including a collection of seventy reels of film purchased from the estate of Errol Flynn in 1960.

There's nothing he can do about the situation from London. At least, *The Legend of Hell House* is turning out to be a very pleasant shoot, and one of his costars is Roland Culver, a castmate of his way back in *This England*. The project is sort of a cross between *The Haunting* and *The House on Haunted Hill.* Wealthy Roland Culver promises a small fortune to physicist Clive Revill, who arrives with his wife, Gayle Hunnicutt, psychic medium Pamela Franklin, and parapsychologist Roddy McDowall to investigate survival after death in the notorious Belasco House, a.k.a. Hell House, which legend has it once belonged to the uncredited Michael Gough, who apparently held orgies there and disappeared after a bloodbath some fifty years before, when twenty-seven people died in the house. (Michael only appears in a pivotal scene near the end as an embalmed corpse.) Roddy is the sole survivor of a previous three-day investigation twenty years prior, when the entire team except for him was killed or went insane. Roddy was physically unharmed but is now a clearly damaged soul who refuses to say anything about what happened during the doomed investigation. He's only willing to come back because he needs the money, but he remains withdrawn, afraid of the house, and reluctant to use his psychic abilities again. He's forced to utilize them again, however, once everyone else supernaturally bites the dust and just he and Gayle are left to face the forces unleashed by Michael Gough. The house is supposedly clean by the end . . . but is it? Roddy remembers the experience as a whale of a time and thinks the world of director John Hough. He also enjoys spending time in London, catching up with old friends.

Upon returning to Los Angeles, he sets about creating a new home virtually from scratch. It's a mid-century classic California ranch-style house. "You'd walk in the front door, and it was low and dark," says Adam Kurtzman, a frequent guest in the 1980s and 1990s, who vividly remembers the details of the house. "The walls were glazed in a deep crimson red. I remember almost every wall in the house being red, so the light that bounced around made everybody look gorgeous. It was like a pink gel. When you peeked behind furniture—which I did—you could see there were zip ties around electrical cords running behind everything so there could be lamps everywhere and no overhead light. Very important. Actresses of a certain age look much better without overhead lighting. Most of the furniture was real 1940s and 1950s American stuff, big comfy sofas and chairs everywhere, and tchotchkes like crazy—candy dishes on every surface. It had a little bit of a grandma quality, and a little bit den of iniquity. . . . His powder room is legendary and that was a cool thing for me. He had Laurel and Hardy's bowler hats on the wall, and all of this sort of autographs and memorabilia, and he had a little *Planet of the Apes* trash can in there, which was the same one I had in my bedroom as a kid. That blew my mind. The same trash can!"

The Studio City house becomes Roddy's new setting for staging his parties and movie nights, which begin in earnest as soon as he moves in. George and Joan Axelrod are regulars, along with Gregory and Veronique Peck, Liza Minnelli, and most of the guests from his Malibu house parties in the summer of 1965, with a few additions, like Sal Mineo, Elizabeth Ashley, and in later years, Tim Curry and Doris Roberts. He casts his parties, bringing people together who might find each other interesting, for instance asking Carol Burnett one night especially so she can meet her idol, Bette Davis, who becomes a friend when Roddy helps her find a new apartment in a building he has a small investment in.

"I always sat in a specific chair next to the fireplace and people were all around and telling stories," Burnett tells Robert Osborne on Turner Classic Movies, when she introduces a night of Bette Davis movies. "I observed more than I contributed, you know, but I certainly was a good audience!" Elizabeth Taylor occasionally comes to Roddy's house, but when she's in Los

Angeles she likes hosting large Sunday parties for family and friends at her Bel Air home, where fried chicken is usually the entrée of choice, and Roddy is a regular guest.

Roddy is also a semiregular guest on *Hollywood Squares.* A typical week's lineup of the early to mid-1970s is Paul Lynde, Rose Marie, Roddy McDowall, Robert Blake, Ernest Borgnine, McLean Stevenson, Leslie Uggams, Karen Valentine, and Cliff Arquette as Charley Weaver. Another week it includes Paul Lynde, Roddy McDowall, Nanette Fabray, George Foreman, Rich Little, Juliet Prowse, and Doc Severinsen. The heavy comedy lifting is always done by Paul Lynde and guests who tell jokes for a living. Sometimes the writers give celebrities some possible jokes for the questions that will come their way, but Roddy doesn't try to compete with the comedians. He's charming, witty without being terribly funny, and plays the game for real.

Conquest of the Planet of the Apes does so well that no one can resist doing it all over again and a fifth film is hastily assembled. Roddy is well up for it. He loves playing in the *Apes* sandbox even though the budget is less than a third of the original and it shows. Billed as "The Final Chapter," the production team means it this time, fearing the franchise is running on fumes. *Battle for the Planet of the Apes* starts with an orangutan Lawgiver, in "North America, 2670 A.D." explaining to an unseen audience the key events of apes and humans six hundred years before, and the story of the chimpanzee Caesar in the early twenty-first century, ten years after a worldwide series of ape revolutions and a brutal nuclear war among humans. Roddy (as Caesar) leads a largely peaceful society of apes endeavoring to live in harmony with the few remaining humans. He's forced to come to the rescue of both species—from an insidious human cult and from a militant murderous faction among the apes. Roddy is as soulful as ever, but the film plays like a bunch of random low-rent action sequences pasted together. A détente is reached between apes and humans. The scene returns to the

Lawgiver, saying it has now been over six hundred years since Caesar's death. The Lawgiver sadly notes that their society still longs for a day when their world will no longer need weapons. They "wait with hope." A close-up of a statue of Caesar shows a single tear falling from one eye.

Roddy puts that statue in his backyard rose garden, where he looks out every morning to see birds perched on Caesar's head.

Paul Newman stars in *The Life and Times of Judge Roy Bean* and it's the only time Roddy is in a film with Ava Gardner, though sadly they have no scenes together. Ava appears briefly at the end of the film as Lillie Langtry, a legendary actress Paul Newman, as Judge Roy Bean, idolizes throughout his life. She plays a cameo with no direct interaction with the main cast—"I just did it for the money, Honey," she quips in her memoirs. Roddy is a slick politician averse to Paul's influence.

Then comes the granddaddy of 1970s disaster movies, *The Poseidon Adventure*. The plot is fairly straightforward. On New Year's Eve, a tidal wave hits a cruise ship, flipping it over so that all the internal rooms are upside down. Playing a priest, Gene Hackman tries to safely evacuate a star-studded crew of *initial* survivors (in order of deaths) Roddy McDowall, Shelley Winters, Jack Albertson, Stella Stevens, and Gene himself; and *surviving* survivors (in alphabetical order) Ernest Borgnine, Red Buttons, Carol Lynley, Pamela Sue Martin, and Eric Shea.

The movie opens at the end of 1972 and is a blockbuster right out of the gate. Though we now think and speak of it as schlock, putting it in the same category as later films like *The Towering Inferno* and *Earthquake*, the reviews are almost unanimously positive, and over fifty years later, the film holds up surprisingly well. As much as the special effects are important in the first third of the film, once the band of survivors is on its way, everything is down to the actors to make us believe—and we do. Shelley Winters even gets an Oscar nomination. Roddy is generally reviewed positively in a list with others, and he's described as "stalwart" by *Variety*, "uncomplaining and decent" by *The New York Times*, and "plucky" by *Time* magazine. In an otherwise blisteringly negative review in *The New Yorker*, Pauline Kael goes further. Decrying her lack of concern with who might live or die among the star-studded (but to her, "lackluster") cast, she singles out McDowall. "The only loss I regretted for an instant was Roddy McDowall."

One of the nastiest themes in many if not most of the reviews, even the positive ones, is the often vicious fat-shaming of Shelley Winters. The word "whale" comes up again and again as if her size is as reviewable as her acting. Here's Pauline Kael, being offensive in any number of ways: "She's so enormously fat she goes way beyond the intention to create a warm, sympathetic Jewish character. It's like having a whale tell you that you should love her because she's Jewish."

After all the pretend deaths in *The Poseidon Adventure*, Roddy is blindsided when Noël Coward dies unexpectedly at the age of seventy-three. No more "Dear Evil Boy" letters and no more chances to work with his idol. Roddy actually credits Noël with giving him one of his most effective tools for navigating the perilous reality that your place on the Hollywood food chain is in constant flux. When playwright John Osborne and the so-called angry young men begin dominating British theater in the mid to late 1950s, Noël Coward begins to seem old-fashioned and out of touch to modern critics. Roddy asks Noël how he deals with their dismissiveness. "I can deal with it because I know that they are wrong," Noël replies. It's as simple as that. Your detractors have no power anymore if you remember that they are wrong.

Shortly after the last *Apes* film, CBS announces a series adaptation. In this version Roddy is Galen, a kind and inquisitive chimpanzee who allies himself with two stranded astronauts in a world ruled by apes. Roddy is happy to return to the *Apes* universe and is also happy to be getting star billing and salary. The show is set in a futuristic California after a nuclear war. Though uncredited, Rod Serling writes the original treatment and two proposed scripts for the series, creating the premise of the three fugitives, two astronauts and a chimpanzee, being pursued by agents of the Apes civilization in 3085, a millennia after the events of *Battle for the Planet of the Apes*. James Naughton and Ron Harper are the astronauts from 1980, thrown into the future by a time warp. The ruins of the Forbidden City are what is left of the MGM backlot in 1974, seemingly one street set, decayed perhaps, but certainly not a thousand years old. Many episodes have the same narrative premise—one among the trio is captured, so the other two rescue him.

It's an arduous schedule for Roddy since the makeup adds so much time to every workday, so certain shortcuts are taken to make the process easier for him. In some episodes, for instance, guest stars playing apes have more detailed makeup than Roddy. Sometimes he wears gloves, while other chimpanzees have their hands intricately made-up and covered in "hand toupees." Roddy hates the hand implements, which can be excruciatingly time-consuming and painful to remove.

James Naughton and his wife join Roddy at one of his dinner parties and then he invites them again for the next weekend. "I asked him, 'Why are you inviting me again?' " James tells Chris Sarandon on his podcast. "And then I went, 'Wait, *she's* [Elizabeth Taylor] not going to be there, is she?' And Roddy goes, 'Yeah, she's going to be here.' But we couldn't go! To this day it haunts me!"

The series tends to focus on the action-oriented aspects of the continual fugitive chase, but occasionally the show delves into interesting territory. In one episode, the trio is captured by a village of semiautonomous humans who sacrifice their own people to a god in a temple that turns out to be an ancient ruin with an arsenal of gas bombs and a distillery to produce poisonous gas in ceramic containers. The chief of the village claims the moral right to use these weapons to rid the world of the ape threat. This is shot during Vietnam War protests against Agent Orange, when chemical weapons are a current event, not just a hypothetical.

The show becomes a huge hit in the UK, but it never really catches on in the US, where its ratings are respectable but don't justify the expense. It lasts only one season, but before it's canceled, Roddy "surprises" Carol Burnett when he shows up in full chimpanzee mode on her show, dressed in a tux. She feigns confusion about why he's in his *Apes* makeup, but thinks she figures it out when he asks to do a monologue from his favorite film. Without skipping a beat, he delivers a short speech from *Cleopatra.* The joke lands with the approving studio audience. They banter back and forth before launching into a hysterically funny duet medley, with Carol doing dry takes on the ironies of a woman and a chimpanzee singing together, and Roddy having a whale of a time getting simianly romantic. They sing and dance through "Exactly Like You," "She's Funny That Way," "They Didn't Believe Me," "Tea for Two," "Speak Low," and "So in Love." Carol's look to the audience is priceless when she sings, "Now I know why Mother taught me to be true— She meant me for someone exactly like you. . . ." Friendship, art, and commerce meld into the perfect meta moment. Carol and Roddy are devoted friends, the mash-up of Roddy as a chimp on a TV variety show is irresistible, and CBS is the network of both *The Carol Burnett Show* and *Planet of the Apes,* so a cross-over moment between the two shows is good business.

Louise Brooks writes a fascinating letter about watching the broadcast. "If anyone told me that a man in an ape face could be adorable, I should strike him. If anyone told me that anyone, you, anyone could dominate Burnett, I should strike him. But there you were with your lovely eighteenth-century legs and charming attention making Burnett quite lovely and charming."

Roddy loves old Hollywood and sees it as his own history, as if he's part of it in its very beginnings, some twenty years before he's even born. He feels as though his own identity has been created and shaped by those who come before and after him. A long-ago crush on the beautiful woman who signs her autograph to a young boy as Mrs. Mickey Rooney becomes the impetus for his turn as a director when he conceives *Tam Lin* as a love letter to Ava Gardner. He shoots the film some five years before his appearance with Carol Burnett, but it remains vital in Louise Brooks's mind. She truly believes directing is the path not taken for Roddy, his true vocation.

Roddy gets his chance when his friend Alan Ladd Jr. brings him a project he's doing with London-based producer Commonwealth United. It was adapted from a Robert Burns version of *Tam Lin,* a sixteenth-century Scottish ballad about a bitch goddess who walks the earth in perpetuity, refurbishing her godhead with the sacrifices of the young. She's a magnet—drawing people in and destroying their lives, sucking them dry. And the ultimate triumph of the piece is that a young man is saved by the true love of a pure young girl.

Roddy's *Tam Lin* centers around Ava Gardner as a wealthy, mysterious, ageless woman in swinging London. She surrounds herself with a revolving group of attractive, decadent young people, including a jejune Joanna Lumley. A particular favorite is her lover, Ian McShane. When he falls for Stephanie Beacham, an innocent vicar's daughter, Ava vows revenge. In the original story, Ava's character is a magical fairy queen, so her punishments are supernatural. Here, her power is ambiguous. She controls her young friends like an alpha dog in charge of a wild pack, and they're ultimately the threat Ian McShane must face down, but a tinge of the otherworldly remains.

There are folders and scripts full of the notes Roddy makes before shooting. He's meticulous with laying out the shots and what he means to convey through various setups. He writes Stephen Weinrib in New York: "I said, action and cut for the first time in my life, and between the two words, managed to direct a scene. I neither threw up nor fainted. I must admit, I sort of enjoyed the whole thing. How about that?" The production is on schedule and on budget. Roddy's ability to understand and communicate with the actors isn't unexpected. Roddy gets extraordinary performances from Ian McShane and Stephanie Beacham. Their love affair emerges as so much more than a narrative trope, with the sharp impact of Ian's pain at the possibility of giving her up, and Stephanie's fear of Ian being killed. Ava Gardner holds the screen as powerfully as ever, part queen and part peasant, with gowns by Balmain, carefully and beautifully lit in every shot. She is every inch a movie star, but she's also much more than that.

"There was one time when she had to take a dagger, stick it into a desk and say something like, 'I will not die,'" Roddy writes in an afterword for her memoir. "And when she said it, her eyes in that moment just filled with blood. It was incredible. She didn't have acting craft, but she had this immediate instinct. So in the sense perhaps the toll was larger for her than somebody who had craft at their fingertips, because she had to really completely do it in that moment."

Roddy finishes overseeing the final cut and looks forward to the film's opening. Unfortunately, Commonwealth United goes into bankruptcy proceedings and *Tam Lin* falls into limbo. After many months of legal and financial wrangling, AIP, the same company that releases *Angel, Angel, Down We Go*, acquires the project. They recut it to their idea of how it will fit in the marketplace, emphasizing its horror elements and violence. It is unrecognizable to Roddy. He writes Alan Ladd Jr. and the other producers an impassioned four-page, single-spaced letter, detailing every reason why he hates every cut. It is released in the UK as *Games and Toys*, and in the United States as *The Devil's Widow*. The poster copy reads, "She drained them of their manhood . . . and then of their LIVES!"

It is the bitterest of disappointments. He holds on to a copy of his print, adding it to his private collection, growing now by leaps and bounds. In the late 1980s, his friendship with director Martin Scorsese proves instrumental in reassembling a new cut that is released in the 1990s. Roddy's new cut is definitely of its moment. The swinging 1960s vibe and some of the photographic effects and camera angles don't age well. Yet you can see where he's going with the piece, and his affection for Ava Gardner isn't just about preserving her beauty through clever lighting and camera angles. He lingers on her face, allowing her movie star mask to slip away, revealing a weariness and confusion in her way of life. Sometimes she looks at these young people as if seeing them for the first time, disgusted with them and with herself. Other times she's pure hedonism, delighted by the next toy, the next game, the next lover.

There is also a bittersweet sense of loss on a personal level. During the *Tam Lin* shoot, Roddy becomes involved with someone named Howard, identified in quite emotional letters only by his first name. They are together for several rather intense, somewhat volatile months. After wrapping, but before returning to the US, Roddy falls ill with a serious and painful infection that is further exacerbated by an allergy to the morphine they give him in the hospital. Howard apparently makes things worse.

"I just know that I can and do love, but that I'm not able yet to show it in the only ways that you need it shown . . ." Howard writes in saying goodbye. "Try to understand my pain in writing this—it is unbearable. . . . But now rest, and work with as untroubled a mind as I can wish for you and be with people whose love helps you and means something." Howard goes on to decry how wrong his letter seems when he reads it back to himself. He begs for forgiveness and signs it with the letter H in the middle of a heart. There is no copy of a response in the archives from Roddy, but he apparently tells Sybil all about it. She writes: "Dear Rod, I saw in Henri Bendel's the perfect Christmas gift for you to give to Howard. It's a gaily painted, old fashioned fruit basket, and it's packed with individually wrapped jumbo pretzels. On the card I suggest you write, 'Choke yourself. Signed Rod.' Okay? Love, Sybil."

Roddy arrives home to a cancer scare for Thomas that turns out to be a false alarm, good news about Virginia's latest bout of depression (she's working at a new job), and financial problems from them both—with incredibly long, complex letters about taxes, Virginia's benefits for psychological care, and whose name particular assets can or can't be in while satisfying the requirements of Virginia's government mental health benefits. Roddy avoids personal discussions, even when Virginia asks, preferring to link his downbeat feelings to work. He hopes to direct again but regards the scripts being sent to him as dreadful: "None of which need a director as much as they need a frontal lobotomy."

Between *Apes* projects and postproduction on *Tam Lin*, there are other jobs, including a small role in the smash-hit Disney comedy *Bedknobs and Broomsticks*, and constant episodic appearances—on *Columbo*, *Medical Center*, *The Name of the Game*, *Ironside*, *Love, American Style*, *McCloud*, *Mission: Impossible*, *The Rookies*, *Barnaby Jones*, *McMillan & Wife*, and *The Snoop Sisters.* Often, he works with friends. Peter Falk of *Columbo* is an old buddy from their New York TV days (Roddy beats Peter for the Emmy the year he wins), Roddy has known Robert Stack of *The Name of the Game* for years (as it happens, Robert accepted that Emmy for Roddy), and Rock Hudson of *McMillan & Wife* is a longtime pal. In series dramas, Roddy tends toward playing doctors and professors. Sometimes he's the doctor or professor who helps solve the crime. Often, he's the doctor or professor who *commits* the crime, which is much more fun.

The main thing is to keep working.

There is a constant drumbeat in Roddy's head that if he stops—if he isn't in a whirl of motion and activity—his career might disappear again. Of course, the truth is, it never has gone away. In the late 1940s, he may have been doing work he doesn't like in the transition between his child and adult roles, and he certainly achieves an amazing renaissance when he moves to New York, but he always has employment; from the time he's eight years old, he works nonstop. The fear of it slipping away just never really leaves him. It's like he's a shark—if he doesn't keep moving forward, he'll drown. So he works as much as he can, knowing that things can change rapidly, and there's no security in show business. "My whole life I've been trying to prove I'm not just yesterday," he tells Michael Buckley.

He begins seeing Paul Anderson seriously now, and within a few months after Roddy's return from England, Paul moves into his Studio City house. Paul works only occasionally as an actor, most notably in a 1976 production of Harold Pinter's *The Homecoming* at an Inglewood semiprofessional theater, and as one of the costars of Roddy's tour of *Charley's Aunt* in 1975 to 1976. Paul and Sal Mineo start writing a play together at some point in the 1970s. What happens with the project is unknown. Sal Mineo is murdered in February 1976 while Roddy and Paul are on tour. It's a shocking, senseless act—a robbery that escalates to a knifing right on the streets of West Hollywood in front of Sal's apartment.

Rumors develop over time that Sal Mineo's death has something to do with his sexuality. This isn't the case. It's possible that his death is conflated with that of silent star Ramon Novarro, who is murdered by two men he hires for sex because they erroneously believe he has a hidden cache of money. There is still a stigma about homosexuality—a subject Roddy never discusses publicly. Writer Robert Hofler remembers how circumspect Roddy could be. "Whenever I would ask if an actor were gay, he would say, 'Oh? I never heard that,' and just smile innocently. He never said a word about anyone." Actress Illeana Douglas, though, remembers him loosening up a little by the

1990s. "My favorite phrase of all time," she says, "is you would mention, you know, a certain male actor, and Roddy might say, 'Oh, he's a soft gay.' What that meant was, you know, he's married, but he's gay. I loved that."

Before Stonewall in 1969, there is the Mattachine Society, formed in 1950 by Harry Hay, to seek decriminalization of consensual sexual activity between adults and the end of discrimination against homosexuals in employment and housing. Roddy is aware of the movement and sometimes offers financial support when asked by Gore Vidal, one of the early board members of Mattachine, but Roddy has no public profile on gay issues.

The one part of his sexual identity that does go somewhat public is a very funny, lurid article in a men's magazine called *Vice-Roi* spreading the news about Roddy's biggest "hidden asset," in "The Biggest Tool in Show-Biz: Do You Feel Inferior?" Agent and producer Guy McElwaine, George Cukor, Robby Lantz, Dirk Bogarde, and many other of Roddy's friends find the article hysterically funny and can't resist teasing him. Roddy takes to answering them back, signing his notes Long Dong Silver, after a British porn star (the name comes into popular usage twenty years later when Anita Hill references it during the Clarence Thomas hearings).

"I don't push myself down people's throats if you know what I mean," Roddy is falsely quoted as saying "I just sort of lie back and let it all come to me," while the "interviewer" gives details about his orgies—strictly hetero—and his custom underwear that costs $20 per pair that he must have made because nothing else will support his prized possession. The notion of Frank Sinatra, Robert Mitchum, Sammy Davis Jr., Dean Martin, Peter O'Toole, Paul Newman, and John Wayne all pulling out their junk to compare sizes, with Roddy winning by a head (as it were) is dumb and risible, and few headlines emerge in the wider press, which isn't yet in the habit of commenting on the genitalia of celebrities.

But a very real public scandal arises that can't be laughed away.

On an early morning in September 1974, the FBI raids Roddy's house while he and Paul are still in bed. It's part of a broader investigation into pirated film prints and the illegal collecting of copyrighted motion pictures. Roddy's collection of some 160 films and 340 tapes is confiscated. Many of the films are studio prints not authorized for private ownership. Federal agents also seize projectors, video recording equipment (including early Betamax/VHS prototypes), and still photographs.

The FBI values Roddy's collection at $5 million, though Roddy's records indicate he has paid in the low five figures for everything.

News reports are generally respectful, emphasizing Roddy's full cooperation with authorities, and carefully explaining that his goal is preservation, not profit. Roddy's straight friends are appropriately horrified and offer their support. His gay friends look at it through a lens reflecting a different level of concern. Homosexual acts are still illegal in California in 1974. A sweep of gay people by law enforcement may be relatively rare by the mid-1970s, but it isn't unheard of. When men with guns come banging at the door, Roddy and Paul might not immediately make the distinction that if the raid were about their private life together, the men would be from the LAPD rather than the FBI.

The home video revolution is just beginning, and it's yet to be definitively determined whether recording to tape directly from a television broadcast is actually legal. At the moment, some TV networks and film studios are arguing that it's not. Roddy never thinks about the legality of buying film prints since he's not exhibiting or selling films to make a profit. Some of the people he buys from, however, *are* selling films at a profit, and they're the prime targets.

The FBI inventories an astonishing collection of film prints, and it takes several trucks to haul everything away. (Each feature film can comprise anywhere from ten to fifteen reels of film.) Classic films include *Gone With the Wind*, *Dinner at Eight*, *Alice Adams*, *Dial M for Murder*, *The Best of Everything*, *Wild River*, *That Hamilton Woman*, *Libeled Lady*, *Too Much Too Soon*, *The Great Waltz*, *Showboat*, *The Magnificent Ambersons*, *Camille*, *She Done Him Wrong*, and *The Valley of Decision.* Some are gifts, like *Giant* from Rock Hudson and *A Double Life* from Ruth Gordon and Garson Kanin, as well as *Breakfast at Tiffany's* from its producer Richard Shepherd. He also has a significant collection of his own films and television performances, including *Just William*, *Saloon Bar*, *How Green Was My Valley*, *The White Cliffs of Dover*, *The Pied Piper*, *On the Sunny Side*, *Lassie Come Home*, *Black Midnight*, *Tam Lin*, *Planet of the Apes*, *Escape from the Planet of the Apes*, and from TV, *The Wine-Dark Sea*, *The Twilight Zone*, *Combat*, and *Heart of Darkness.* Silent films include *Broken Blossoms*, *The Passion of Joan of Arc*, *The Dawn Patrol*, *Tol'able David*, *The Spanish Dancer*, *Manhandled*, *Orphans of the Storm*, *Metropolis*, and *Intolerance.*

In an interview in *Penthouse* magazine of all places, MPAA president Jack Valenti says, "We have no desire to infringe upon the rights of legitimate collectors, although we would like to compile a good inventory of what is owned."

And yet the film studios are egregiously negligent and indifferent to preservation and restoration, with many films left to rot in their own nitrate content in storerooms without temperature regulation. Jack Warner once burns a storehouse of irreplaceable film prints (including some excised footage from the Judy Garland version of *A Star Is Born*) because he wants the storage space. Several months prior to the raid on Roddy, Technicolor sells off some now obsolete machines and, as part of the process, stacks up hundreds of films in an outdoor lot to await destruction. Despite pleas from collectors, historians, and the American Film Institute, all of whom offer to pick up and preserve the films, Technicolor can't sell or donate them because of copyright issues. A few collectors even plan a break-in but find the films are guarded by FBI agents. All are destroyed with no record of the titles involved.

Roddy takes no chances. After two lengthy interviews with FBI agents, he and his attorneys deliver a list to the FBI and to Justice Department prosecutors of two hundred entertainment industry professionals and major society figures who are ready, willing, and able to testify on his behalf as character witnesses, including some of the figures ostensibly on the other side of the case, like Lew Wasserman, Jack Valenti, and Daryll F. Zanuck.

It takes ten months to sort out the FBI's case, during which time Roddy doesn't know if he will be charged, whether he will have to testify against people he has purchased films from, and whether his property will be returned. Everything goes Roddy's way. In July 1975, the Justice Department announces sixteen felony indictments, the FBI announces there will be no charges, he won't be called to testify, and his property will be returned.

When the Justice Department makes the announcement exonerating Roddy, he's busy shooting a *Police Woman* episode called "Pawns of Power." Angie Dickinson is investigating a mysterious string of blackmail and extortion cases. Is Roddy the cool, charming brains behind the operation, manipulating powerful men into compromising situations? And is his old *Camelot* costar Robert Goulet his accomplice or his pawn?

If Angie can't figure it out, maybe someone should call the FBI.

Chapter 7

The Fantastic Journey

Thomas Andrew McDowall outlives his late wife, Winefriede, by thirteen years, dying of cancer in July 1978, just two weeks shy of his eighty-second birthday. In the final months of his life, Roddy spends time with him daily. He isn't doing a film or a play, and most series are on hiatus from late May to late August, so there isn't a lot of episodic work. Thomas keeps a lot to himself, and his children learn that he has been ill longer than they know. Once they're aware of his illness, he downplays symptoms and prognoses, minimizing his suffering, eager for them to get on with their lives. He's the opposite of Winefriede, seeking no sympathy, wanting no fuss.

Roddy's feelings about his father are somewhat complicated by memories of his mother's outsized presence and overweening need for control. During Roddy's childhood, Thomas is completely at ease exercising authority over others in his roles in the military and in business—he just won't go against Winefriede, always accepting her behavior and decisions. Yet after her death, Thomas is the parent able to accept and acknowledge Roddy's romantic partners. Thomas faces up to Virginia's emotional struggles in a way that Winefriede would never permit herself, and Thomas is the one who trusts Roddy to make his own decisions. (Thomas takes a more active role trying to advise Virginia because of his concern about her frequent depressions.)

To some extent Roddy and Virginia feel like orphans at the ages of forty-nine and fifty respectively, with no other close family. Neither will have children. They will be the end of this branch of the McDowall line—a self-enclosed side of the family that has little interaction with relatives outside their immediate circle. Winefriede sets it up that way and that's how it stays. Roddy sends Thomas's and Winefriede's letters and memorabilia to the Boston University archives, for curious writers to discover years later. It also saves him and Virginia the difficulty of sorting through everything and deciding what to throw away. They throw away nothing.

Roddy quickly gets back to work.

He is a series regular on three more shows over ten years: *The Fantastic Journey* in 1977, *Tales of the Gold Monkey* from 1982 to 1983, and *Bridges to Cross* in 1986.

The Fantastic Journey finishes production about six months before Thomas is diagnosed with cancer. It's a *Lost in Space* concept, but instead of a ship going off course in outer space, a boat goes off course in the Bermuda Triangle. A scientific expedition gets transported through a portal to another dimension, trapped with beings from the future and from other worlds. Characters from different times and places come together as a group, including Jared Martin, a man from the twenty-third century with undefined special powers, Carl Franklin, a new doctor from 1977 who arrives with thirteen-year-old Ike Eisenmann, orphaned in the first episode, Katie Saylor, the daughter of a mother from Atlantis and an extraterrestrial father, and Roddy, a brilliant but eccentric scientist with a shifting sense of morals from the 1960s.

Roddy doesn't join the cast until the third episode, as what seems to be a guest character. He's an evil scientist with an army of hot, hunky androids, who apparently either don't wear much underwear or perhaps belong in that *Vice-Roi* article—the camera lingers somewhat embarrassingly. After threatening to kill most of the series regulars, Roddy goes from antagonist to protagonist in a scene at the end and joins the travelers, embarking on his own journey of rediscovering his sense of humanity. Offscreen, Roddy becomes something of a friend and mentor to Ike Eisenmann, then in high demand as a child actor but heading into puberty and a major career disruption, eventually carving out a career as a director and producer.

Like the *Planet of the Apes* series, *The Fantastic Journey* is a show where the characters are constantly on the run to new places, interacting with guest actors like a pre-*Dynasty* Joan Collins, Mary Ann Mobley, John Saxon, Christina Hart, and Gary Collins. Though it's reportedly a show with a healthy budget, the overall impression is of haphazard production quality. During an earthshaking volcano and avalanche, for instance, the camera lurches this way and that, but the actors forget to follow along, just standing there while the picture moves around. Special effects are generally low-tech, not much above the early *Dr. Who* episodes, before the twenty-first-century reboot, back when part of the fun is the cheesiness of the creatures and the inexpensive visual embellishments when characters teleport or get laser-zapped. Despite lackluster ratings and lasting only one season, the show does extremely well outside of the US, proving popular in territories throughout Europe, Asia, Australia, New Zealand, and South Africa—giving Roddy's international profile a boost.

He makes three features next. *Charlie Chan and the Curse of the Dragon Queen*, *Class of 1984*, and *Evil Under the Sun.* Two are pastiches in the cozy crime genre, offering familiar takes on Charlie Chan and Hercule Poirot (both played by Peter Ustinov) while the other is more of a walk on the wild side.

In *Charlie Chan and the Curse of the Dragon Queen*, Roddy has a perfectly fabulous time playing a dementedly disgruntled butler who serves meals perched in a supercharged wheelchair, tossing plates with reckless abandon. Peter Ustinov is retired detective Charlie Chan, summoned to San Francisco to investigate a series of bizarre killings. At first it seems Angie Dickinson as the mysterious Dragon Queen is behind the murders. Or it could be Lee Grant, a daft widow who talks to her departed husband's ashes in an urn and tolerates the eccentricities of her rude butler and her paranoid maid, Rachel Roberts in her final performance.

Director Clive Donner and producer Jerry Sherlock aren't yet conscious of the perils of non-Asians playing in "yellow face," but Asian activists make their voices heard with effective protests that engender much positive publicity for their point of view and quite negative press for the film. It's hard to know whether their outcry or the film's general mediocrity is responsible for its failure commercially and critically. Roddy and Lee Grant certainly make the most of it. "Here we were, these really elegant folks," Lee Grant says with a laugh. "We were doing this terrible movie, but it was so wonderful to be with Roddy again. We hadn't really seen each other all that much since that summer in Malibu in 1965."

The run of big-budget, star-filled Agatha Christie films of the 1970s and 1980s from producers John Brabourne and Richard Goodwin starts with a bang as *Murder on the Orient Express* opens to huge box office and an Oscar for Ingrid Bergman in 1974. *Death on the Nile* is another hit in 1978. *The Mirror Crack'd*, in 1980, isn't as solid. Despite its movie star lineup of Elizabeth Taylor, Rock Hudson, Kim Novak, and Tony Curtis, and Angela Lansbury as Miss Marple, it isn't particularly successful, and they wonder if Miss Marple isn't as much of a draw as Hercule Poirot. So they return with another Poirot mystery, *Evil Under the Sun.*

Roddy, Peter Ustinov as Hercule Poirot, Maggie Smith, Diana Rigg, Jane Birkin, Sylvia Miles, and James Mason are on hand at a sundrenched resort where actors, former actors, a long-ago murder, a fake diamond, and mistaken identities create the puzzle that Poirot ultimately solves. Roddy is a gossip columnist and unauthorized celebrity biographer of infamous actress Diana Rigg, who's furious with him for publishing personal details about her. Their mutual animosity makes Roddy a suspect when Diana is murdered. His character is a woman in Agatha Christie's original novel, but the gender is switched specifically to give Roddy a juicy comic role where he gleefully patterns his vocal inflections, syllable for syllable, after Tallulah Bankhead.

Class of 1984 is in an entirely different universe from the musty nostalgia of a Poirot or a Charlie Chan movie. Perry King is a new teacher at a troubled inner-city high school where violent punk students terrorize anyone and everyone. Roddy is a science teacher on the verge of nervous collapse who carries a loaded gun to school every day—based on a true report of a teacher brandishing a pistol and threatening his students, according to writer and director Mark Lester. The violence is startling and visceral. Roddy's breakdown is epic, starting with him pulling his gun on his students, then later culminating in him trying to run their ringleader down with his car, flipping, and dying in the fiery crash. He's the oddball who can't and won't fit in, a character reminiscent of some of Roddy's TV anthology work in the 1950s.

His third series-regular project, *Tales of the Gold Monkey*, is from *Magnum, P.I.*, *Quantum Leap*, and *JAG* creator Donald P. Bellisario. Set in 1938, just before World War II, the pulp-adventure-style series follows Stephen Collins as an ex–Flying Tigers pilot with a cargo plane for hire in the South Pacific, and a home base on the fictional island of Boragora. He gets caught up in espionage, smuggling, ancient treasures, and morally ambiguous adventures. Roddy is "Bon Chance" Louie, the French magistrate and authority figure on the island, who also serves as the bartender of the Monkey Bar, where a statue of a gold monkey gives the show its title. Roddy is witty and wily, with a roguish air and a mysterious past. He's respected by all factions—the locals, military, and even spies—maneuvering his way through

Stephen's adventures with a *Casablanca*-style neutrality, but with hidden motives. It is a happy reunion. Roddy and Stephen know each other from the 1977 miniseries adaptation of Robert Ludlum's *The Rhinemann Exchange*, where Stephen is an American intelligence officer during World War II and Roddy is a shadowy double agent. As a Frenchman in *Tales of the Gold Monkey*, Roddy speaks English with a refreshingly believable French accent, often ad-libbing in actual French, a language he knows relatively well. (In terms of accent authenticity, early 1980s TV is about at the level of Hollywood films in the 1930s and 1940s, which is to say often rather lazy and nonspecific.)

Writer and producer Tom Greene remembers Roddy with a great deal of fondness. "The guy carried with him the whole history of Hollywood, yet you couldn't meet a more real, genuine, lovely person. No ego, no pretense—he would walk around the lot with his ever-ready camera clicking pictures away as if he was a tourist from Missouri." Tom writes the episode "Last Chance Louie," centered on Roddy, enigmatically filling in his backstory. He shoots a visitor to the island point-blank in front of dozens of witnesses, grazing the man's ear. As magistrate, he immediately closes the case, letting himself off the hook. But when the man turns up dead, Roddy narrowly avoids the guillotine—he's unable to exonerate himself of such a serious crime.

There's a sequence where Roddy is on the balcony of the Monkey Bar telling Stephen Collins why he shot the man, an old adversary. He has a two-page speech, almost unheard of in episodic TV. It's a crying scene, and Roddy records it over and over, as camera issues and flubs necessitate shooting the scene multiple times. Roddy nails it on every take, with tears flowing just when they're supposed to, but each time seeming fresh, real, and spontaneous.

Tom Greene also vividly remembers an incident of kindness. On his first day on set as a writer and producer, there are problems with a scene where a man is killed and discovered the next morning. Roddy has a scene with Stephen Collins giving a eulogy. Tom goes on the backlot to bring over new pages. A group of suits from Universal and ABC are watching. Roddy does the scene where he eulogizes the man and then while the cameras are still rolling, he looks up and says, "Who wrote these new lines? This is wonderful stuff!" Tom is introduced as the new writer and producer in a decidedly positive way. "It was obvious that Roddy had seen me running back and forth with pages, and he could also sense my concern if I was pulling it off," says Tom. "He had the class to make a big deal about it while the cameras were rolling. He knew it was a time when everyone would be silent and all eyes and ears would be on him, so it would have the most potent effect to compliment me. I shall never, ever forget him for that magnanimous gesture."

Ratings are much better than for *The Fantastic Journey*, but the high production costs keep the network from renewing the show for a second season. It takes on a rich afterlife, though, with podcasts and live events for fans with surviving cast and crew doing Q and A panels and meet and greets.

Bridges to Cross in 1986 aims for a Spencer Tracy and Katharine Hepburn vibe. Journalists Suzanne Pleshette and Nicolas Surovy are a divorced couple, named Tracy Bridges and Peter Cross (hence the title), who compete with each other for stories. Suzanne swans around in 1980s versions of the kinds of outfits Joan Crawford wears in the 1940s. You live for her wafting into the airport in a gold lamé ballgown with matching cape, throwing her weight around and making everyone bow to her will. "You better go buy some snorkeling equipment," she growls, "because you're in real deep." Roddy is the executive assistant and majordomo to Suzanne's posh neighbor, Eva Gabor, who also wears ball gowns whenever possible, and José Ferrer is Suzanne's acerbic editor-in-chief. It should work, but while the show is written in the vein of *Adam's Rib* (though not perhaps with the brilliant wit of its writers, Ruth Gordon and Garson

Kanin), the directors and editors seem to have no sense of comic rhythm, treating the whole thing very seriously indeed, and the show only lasts six episodes.

Roddy is a perennial favorite hire for pilot episodes going back to *Night Gallery*, and subsequently appears in the pilots for the hits *Hart to Hart*, *Trapper John, M.D.*, *Buck Rogers in the 25th Century*, and *A Man Called Sloane*. He's a key character in each of them. *Hart to Hart* stars two longtime friends of Roddy's, Robert Wagner and Stefanie Powers, as a fabulously wealthy, glamorous couple, a bit like William Powell and Myrna Loy from the *Thin Man* film series. Each episode is introduced by Lionel Stander, their loyal, gravel-voiced butler, cook, and chauffeur. He pithily describes their life, and then before the theme music soars, he quips, ". . . because when they met, it was murder!" In the pilot, Roddy McDowall and Stella Stevens are doctors at a health farm where a friend of Robert Wagner's dies under suspicious circumstances. Here they get to be the villains, a much more colorful state of affairs than dying early in *The Poseidon Adventure* a decade earlier.

Trapper John, M.D. is a medical drama procedural spin-off from the film version of *M*A*S*H*. (For profit participation accounting, a long, complicated court case is required to prove that it is indeed a spin-off from the film, not the TV series, even though actors from the TV show are shown in framed photographs in the main character's office. So there.) Pernell Roberts of *Bonanza* fame plays Trapper John. In the pilot, Roddy is a revivalist minister and con man who's too parsimonious to donate his blood to the critically ill Jack Gilford (Roddy's costar in *Look After Lulu*), even though he's the only donor who has the same rare blood type, and the hospital has none in store. Pernell tricks Roddy into donating the blood, and Jack lives to eat another box of crackerjacks.

Roddy plays an evil overlord who uses slave labor on an alien planet in the feature film version of *Buck Rogers in the 25th*

Century that serves as the series pilot and an international launching pad for the show. Roddy shows up again in a later episode as a different character, an effete android who functions as a historian and entertainer on a planet of Amazons—the campy comic relief.

In *A Man Called Sloane*, Robert Conrad is a freelance spy whose wing man is Ji-Tu Cumbuka, a man with a detachable hand that can be replaced by a variety of implements like drills, guns, and other weaponry. Although Robert doesn't work for the government, he frequently accepts assignments from Dan O'Herlihy, the head of a secret government agency. In the pilot, Roddy is a mad scientist powering sexy female androids with plutonium. As you do.

Of course, many of the pilots Roddy makes (some as a series regular, others as a guest star) don't go to series, including such shows as *Topper Returns*, *The Million Dollar Face*, *Judgment Day*, *Small & Frye*, *This Girl For Hire*, *London and Davis in New York*, and *Remo Williams: The Prophecy*—where he plays (respectively) a man living with 1940s ghosts Stefanie Powers and John Fink; a power-hungry cosmetic executive battling against Tony Curtis; a lawyer representing Hell in a cosmic courtroom, opposite Victor Buono; a shrinking private detective who can fit in Darren McGavin's pocket; a mystery writer who helps solve real crimes; aide-de-camp to photojournalist Richard Crenna; and a Korean martial arts master. If Roddy can play Mexican, why not Korean?

The best pilot doesn't even air and can be quite hard to find, appearing and disappearing on YouTube and various other sites. It's a 1994 HBO pilot, called *Galaxy Beat*, about a ragtag team of "Galactic Peacekeepers." Roddy is a fish-man navigator, Corporal Cod. Though very fit, Roddy is sixty-six years old by the time he makes *Galaxy Beat*, so he does the voice with another actor in a mask gymnastically physicalizing the cod, hopping up and down the halls nonsensically like a frog, leaving puddles of water everywhere he goes. The team includes a fearless leader, the handsome, egocentric Gregory Harrison; Tracy Scoggins as a traditionally feminine beauty with a startlingly masculine manner; and Alex Désert as Gregory's sidekick, a 5,449-year-old "anomaly" with a bro-crush. When Gregory doesn't like an assignment, he asks Michael Dorn as Chief, the computer in charge of personnel assignments, "Are you joking?" And Dorn responds, "I'm incapable of joking. I was programmed by Gentiles." The show is hysterically funny and you can imagine it streaming right now.

Roddy works a lot for Aaron Spelling. *Hart to Hart* is a Spelling show, as is *Fantasy Island*, where Roddy plays Mephistopheles twice, a slave hunter in the old South in a third episode, and then an alcoholic ex-circus performer with a career-ending injury in a fourth. On *Love Boat*, Roddy thinks Tammy Grimes is pressuring him into marriage too soon. It's a happy reunion with his friend and former *Look After Lulu* costar. And in *Hotel*, he gets to star opposite Elizabeth Taylor. She doesn't make a lot of episodic TV appearances, and her appearance on *Hotel* with Roddy is big news and a ratings bonanza. The storyline trades heavily on their real lives. Elizabeth is a former movie star who fires longtime assistant Roddy in a dramatic confrontation. Then she must make amends to allow for a tearful reconciliation.

In the 1970s and 1980s, Roddy remains close with people he has known from earlier years, but he also develops new friendships. Joan Rivers becomes a dear friend, and Roddy is Joan's daughter Melissa's godparent. When he and Joan meet, she's not yet in her Elizabeth Taylor fat jokes period and Elizabeth isn't yet heavy. As Roddy likes to do with friends, though, before long, he and Joan are working together, on her writing and directing debut, *Rabbit Test.* The film is a comedy about the world's first pregnant man, Billy Crystal. Roddy plays a Romany grandmother (a "gypsy" in the parlance of the time) as well as a medical professional named Dr. D&C Fishbine. There are many people in his circle involved, including actress Doris Roberts, *Hollywood Squares* chums Paul Lynde and Peter Marshall, and the famed "female illusionist" Charles Pierce as the Queen of England. Teaser newspaper ads for the film are fake ads for parodies of popular movies with a rabbit twist—*Paws* (instead of *Jaws*), *Hare Wars* (instead of *Star Wars*). Joan remortgages her home, convinces her father to take out a second mortgage, hosts fundraising dinners across the country, and takes out loans against her future Las Vegas earnings. It's the kind of hard work and perseverance Roddy relates to and admires.

When Elizabeth Taylor gets heavy in the late 1970s, Joan creates something of a cottage industry out of telling fat jokes about her. ("She puts mayonnaise on an aspirin. . . . She stepped on a scale, and it said, 'Come back when you're alone.' . . . She told me she ate something that disagreed with her: Kansas.") When Joan moves into her very grand home in Bel Air, she decorates in a style that's by turns extravagantly baroque, rococo, and neoclassical. She loves giving very formal dinners. One night she invites columnist Liz Smith, George Hamilton, and Roddy McDowall, among others. Roddy mentions the upcoming dinner to Elizabeth Taylor, who decides she wants to show up as a surprise. This is the mid to late 1980s, and Elizabeth is in great shape again—perfectly ravishing. Roddy sets it up for Elizabeth to go as George Hamilton's date. It's formal, with place cards, so when Joan asks for George's date's name, he gives it as Leslie Benedict, her character from *Giant*.

No one says a word to Joan Rivers about Elizabeth coming. "I loved being part of this prank," Liz Smith is quoted as saying in Leslie Bennetts's book on Joan Rivers, *Last Girl Before Freeway*. "And Elizabeth had confidence in herself to do it with humor. Never maliciously." George Hamilton is the last guest to arrive. The doorbell rings and Joan's husband, Edgar Rosenberg, answers the door. He calls frantically for Joan. Standing at the front door with George is Elizabeth Taylor. They step in and George introduces Elizabeth, who says simply, "It's so wonderful for you to invite me." Roddy and George love playing the joke on Joan, who really does become surprisingly flustered. Roddy never likes the jokes about Elizabeth, but he can forgive them because they never hit where Elizabeth lives. She knows she's heavy when she's heavy. And she knows she's fantastic looking when she pulls it all together.

The tour of *Charley's Aunt* is an opportunity to work with Vincent Price and Coral Browne, along with Joanna Gleason and Annie Potts, and Roddy's own partner, Paul Anderson. Although there's no definitive account of how that casting comes about, Paul is an unknown, so it's reasonable to assume that Roddy pulls strings for him to be cast in a major role. Roddy and Paul are extremely discreet about their relationship while on tour. Old friends Vincent and Coral know them as a couple but make no hint or reference to it in rehearsals or backstage during performances. Though such circumspection is "normal" and goes unremarked upon at the time by Roddy and his friends and colleagues, it's curious to wonder if going from the relative openness of their life together in California to several months of furtivity contributes to their breakup after the tour. It probably doesn't help that while Roddy, Vincent, and Coral receive uniformly positive reviews, Paul does not. He's generally considered in over his head.

Roddy gets an offer to play the lead in the first Broadway production of *Otherwise Engaged*, written by Simon Gray and directed by Harold Pinter. The main character is a suave, intelligent, yet emotionally guarded literary editor who craves solitude and control. The action is confined to a Saturday afternoon when he plans to listen to *Parsifal*, but his sacred alone time is repeatedly and maddeningly interrupted by a stream of visitors. It's a tour de force of tragicomedy, and Roddy would very much like to do it. Unfortunately, rehearsals start during production of *The Fantastic Journey* and Roddy is unavailable. Tom Courtenay plays the role to great acclaim. While not quite the heights of Broadway, Roddy does get the opportunity to play it regionally at the Parker Playhouse in Fort Lauderdale, Florida, for a three-week run that sells out and is extended to four weeks.

A few years later, Roddy embarks on a tour of *Harvey*, playing Elwood P. Dowd, the gentle eccentric whose best friend is an invisible six-foot-tall rabbit. Famously originated by Frank Fay on Broadway in 1944 and immortalized by James Stewart in the 1950 film, it's a role that walks a tricky balance between pathos and comedy. Venues include Dallas Summer Musicals, Music Hall at Fair Park, Fort Worth's Casa Mañana, Oklahoma City Civic Center Music Hall, Fiesta Dinner Playhouse in San Antonio, and the Beverly Dinner Playhouse in New Orleans, where the audience one night gets an extra treat. Elizabeth Taylor shows up unannounced at one performance, creating major buzz in the local media. They can't resist remarking on the fact that the screen legend ignores the venue's no-smoking policy. Roddy's reviews are positive across the board, with critics praising his work as "appealingly gentle," "introspective," "wistful," "ethereal," and "delightful." For her part, Elizabeth Taylor writes him that "[it] felt like watching Elwood float through a dream—you brought something magical to the part that I've never seen before."

Back in Los Angeles, he makes a strangely prophetic 1980 TV movie called *The Memory of Eva Ryker* with his close friend Natalie Wood. She plays both mother and daughter, the latter having been killed on a cruise ship during World War II; her daughter then finds herself investigating her mother's death. Roddy plays a character similar to his role in *The Poseidon Adventure*, but thankfully, he doesn't die this time. The eerie thing considering the events that follow is that there's a sequence of Natalie Wood floating face down in a flooded stateroom.

That image is relatively fresh in Roddy's mind when Natalie Wood dies in an accidental drowning not long afterward, during an evening relaxing on the yacht *Splendour* with husband Robert Wagner and the actor Christopher Walken. Perhaps Roddy isn't quite as close to Natalie as he is to Elizabeth Taylor, but their dynamic is similar. They meet as children and are part of each other's lives from then on. And this isn't a death that could be anticipated and prepared for like Montgomery Clift's or Judy Garland's. Natalie Wood is in the prime of her life and her talent—with a new movie coming out soon and rehearsals scheduled to start just weeks later for a stage appearance in *Anastasia* at the Ahmanson Theatre in Los Angeles. Her death is a horrible shock.

At a private service in Westwood, with Russian music playing in the background, Roddy delivers a eulogy. Seemingly everyone is famous, but the grief is so overwhelming that the mourners no longer appear as celebrities but as broken people beyond solace. In Robert Wagner and Natalie Wood's living room, many of them gather after the service. A framed poster for *Anastasia* rests against a wall in the den. Roddy sits with Christopher Walken, both of them staring off into space. Elizabeth Taylor sits with Robert Wagner. There's nothing for anyone to say. Stefanie Powers, ashen and red-eyed, weeps openly. A week earlier, Natalie and Robert Wagner are consoling Stefanie on the death of her beloved William Holden. As nightmarish as it is for Roddy, the aftermath in the weeks following her death is almost as emotionally devastating as the death itself. He believes the conspiracy theories that arise blaming Robert Wagner and Christopher Walken are disgusting and libelous. He doesn't entertain any other notion than her death being an accident. Robert is in pieces. Natalie is gone. What possible reason can there be to persecute the man who loved her most? Roddy's own grief remains private. Three major losses happen so close to together—

his relationship ending with Paul, his father's death, and Natalie's drowning. He responds the only way he knows how. By working. There is always the next job, the next group of cast and crew that becomes "like family," and the next character. He can lose himself.

The TV biopic *Mae West* provides a welcome relief. Roddy is happy that the legendary actress is having a moment—he writes the Academy every year proposing a special posthumous Oscar for Mae West, with his suggestion falling on deaf ears. She is just the sort of Hollywood icon Roddy feels should be enshrined in the collective memory of our culture. Opposite Ann Jillian as West, Roddy plays a fellow performer, based on real-life 1920s drag queen Bert Savoy. (Ann is also a former child actor, most notably costarring as Dainty June in the 1962 film version of *Gypsy,* with Natalie Wood as Gypsy Rose Lee and Rosalind Russell as Rose.) In *Mae West*, Roddy helps Ann develop her signature style when they meet in vaudeville. Piper Laurie is the stage mother who makes it all happen, and James Brolin is Mae West's romantic partner, personal manager, and legal advisor Jim Timony, promoted from Early Supporter in real life to the Love of Her Life onscreen because of what the producers see as the narrative demands of the project. Ann Jillian's work is mostly well received. She bears little physical resemblance to the buxom Miss West, and her dancing is far more graceful and energetic, but she manages to find the essence of the performing rhythm without making it seem like parody or impersonation. Curiously, however, the film tells the story of Mae West, a woman famously known as the architect of her own destiny, with a narrative that, while claiming her as an iconoclast, actually defines her by the men in her life. Roddy is circumspect about the project, saying nothing but good things publicly and nothing at all privately, but as a friend and onetime photographer of Mae West, it must be odd seeing her portrayed as a character who's generally reactive rather than proactive. When she quarrels with James Brolin and is on her own again, Roddy unaccountably goes from fellow performer to personal assistant and gay BFF with no explanation as to his changed career. It's the same trajectory he has in Barbra Streisand's follow-up to *Funny Girl*, when he's a performer who becomes *her* personal assistant and gay BFF in *Funny Lady* back in 1975. At least in *Mae West* he isn't subjected to a homophobic onslaught of insults as he is in *Funny Lady*—from James Caan as Billy Rose.

In the time of the *Mae West* project, the big three broadcast networks are in an era of the big-budget, star-studded TV miniseries. (Fox isn't yet a true competitor until the end of the 1980s.) The miniseries genre is popular from the end of the 1970s through the 1980s, having its own golden age not unlike anthology TV in the 1950s. *The Martian Chronicles*, starring Rock Hudson, is a high-profile adaptation of the Ray Bradbury novel, penned by Ray and screenwriter Richard Matheson. Set in the twenty-first century, as Earth begins colonizing Mars, Roddy and Fritz Weaver play priests who discover a trio of glowing spheres, first believing they are gods, but coming to understand they are each the consciousness of an ancient Martian, and don't want to be worshipped. Ray Bradbury himself calls the miniseries "boring," and the reviews are decidedly mixed, although Roddy and Fritz, along with other cast members Barry Morse, Bernadette Peters, and Darren McGavin are all praised.

Hollywood Wives in 1985 is one of the most iconic of the glossy miniseries adapted from the soapy, sensational novels of writers like Jackie Collins and Judith Krantz (an update of Jacqueline Susann's *Valley of the Dolls* is on offer as well). Candice Bergen, Joanna Cassidy, Mary Crosby, and Angie Dickinson are the wealthy, attractive, snobbish "wives" caught up in the scandals and excesses of Tinseltown. Roddy is a *pimp*! He aims to get the object of everyone's affection, Andrew Stevens, back on his books (to service ladies, *natch*, not gents), but Andrew decides to become a star instead. Choices. Andrew's evil twin who's bent on murder crashes the party, threatening to spoil everything. It's great fun and a ratings smash.

Right on the tails of *Hollywood Wives*, Roddy is cast as the March Hare in a mega, star-laden, heavily hyped adaptation of *Alice in Wonderland* and *Through the Looking-Glass*. Alice is played by newcomer Natalie Gregory, but everyone else belongs to a who's who of Hollywood royalty past and present. Even the trees and flowers are famous. The exhaustive (some might say exhausting) cast includes Red Buttons as the White Rabbit, Anthony Newley as the Mad Hatter, Arte Johnson as the Dormouse, Jayne Meadows as the Queen of Diamonds, Selma Archerd as the Queen of Hearts, Robert Morley as the King of Hearts, Martha Raye as the Duchess, Telly Savalas as the Cheshire Cat, Lloyd Bridges as the White Knight, Ringo Starr as the Mock Turtle, Ann Jillian as the Red Queen, Carol Channing as the White Queen, Harvey Korman as the White King, Jack Warden as the Owl, Eydie Gormé as Tweedledee, Steve Lawrence as Tweedledum, Karl Malden as the Walrus, Louis Nye as the Carpenter, Jonathan Winters as Humpty Dumpty, Anthony Zerbe as the Wasp in the Wig, Steve Railsback as the Jabberwocky, and John Stockwell as the Unicorn. A huge collection of stars even play smaller characters, including inanimate objects, insects, animals, and flowers, including Sherman Hemsley, Donald O'Connor, Sally Struthers, Donna Mills, Shelley Winters, Scott Baio, Sammy Davis Jr., Pat Morita, Imogene Coca, Sid Caesar, John Stamos, Ernest Borgnine, Beau Bridges, Merv Griffin, Patrick Duffy, Steve Allen, Zsa Zsa Gabor, Donna Pescow, Howard Morris, Rob Paulsen, and George Gobel; with music by John Sebastian, Steve Allen, and Leslie Bricusse.

The miniseries is a ratings hit, loved by viewers for its cast, but it's met with mixed critical responses. Many carp about its heavy-handed moralizing, spectacle, and slow pace. They're not wrong. Anthony Newley as the Mad Hatter seems a poor man's Willy Wonka at first, singing a lackluster solo. But once Roddy and Arte Johnson start riffing with him, the sequence catches fire. The trio creates their own babbly, bubbly comic universe.

Back during the 1985 *Alice in Wonderland* shoot, Roddy actually has other things on his mind than his Mad Hatter tea party. Once his sequence is finished, he spends most of his time at "The Castle," Rock Hudson's secluded hilltop estate, sitting by his friend's bedside as Rock is dying of AIDS. Elizabeth Taylor becomes the public face of Rock's illness, particularly after his death, but Roddy is behind the scenes the entire time, helping to coordinate private home care and doing his best to shield Rock from the media during his final days. He's one of the executors of Rock's estate, and he burns some of his most private papers, shielding them from any public scrutiny. Rock's death follows the passings of George Cukor and Richard Burton, two men who are also intrinsic parts of Roddy's history.

Rock is the first major Hollywood star to publicly acknowledge having AIDS, and his death is a seismic cultural event throughout the world. Roddy and Elizabeth both mourn Rock in their own ways, each supporting the other as he remains the protective, behind-the-scenes facilitator and she becomes the most prominent celebrity AIDS activist on the planet. Enraged by her dear friend's suffering, she declares that nobody should die alone, ashamed, or ignored. She cofounds the American Foundation for AIDS Research in 1985 and founds the Elizabeth Taylor AIDS Foundation in 1991, funneling millions of dollars of her own money into research, treatment, and care, as well as raising hundreds of millions in funds from all over the world. She demands attention from the rich and powerful, leaving behind a legacy of humanitarianism that rivals her legacy as an actress. Roddy is often at her side, not just at gala fundraising events, but as a connector, quietly bringing people into Elizabeth's orbit who can help her reach her goals.

Just a month after Rock's death, Elizabeth presents Roddy with the American Cinema Foundation Career Achievement Award. He's a cohonoree with Deborah Kerr. His first words as he steps to the stage are, "Lassie and Flicka would never believe it!" The evening is tinged with the sadness of Rock's recent passing, and Roddy is both emotionally overwhelmed and sort of embarrassed. Thinking back to Virginia's long-ago assessment of Roddy as someone who outwardly greatly needs to be loved, the occasion hits with a wave of such affection and approval that it's gratifying beyond words, but Roddy isn't entirely comfortable being the center of attention in such a setting, as himself, without a character to play. Robert Wagner hosts the show with Elizabeth, and friends like Anna Lee, Maureen O'Hara, Jane Powell, Joan Rivers, and Carol Burnett, along with former *Camelot* costar Robert Goulet, all pay tribute.

The audience seems to Roddy to be everyone he has ever met in his entire life, or at least everyone who's still alive, including some of the silent stars he visits with as much as he can, like Vilma Bánky, Viola Dana, Billie Dove, and Laura La Plante, as well as friends, costars, and colleagues like Suzanne Pleshette, Lee Remick, Nancy Walker, Jill St. John, Lionel Stander, Judith Anderson, and Karl Malden, along with June Allyson, Eve Arden, Joseph Bologna and Renée Taylor, Mae Clarke, Joseph Cotten, Yvonne De Carlo, Kathryn Grayson, June Haver, Paul Henreid, Anne Jeffreys, Howard Keel, Ruby Keeler, John Kerr, Janet Leigh, Fred MacMurray, Walter Matthau, Virginia Mayo, Joel McCrea, Dorothy McGuire, Robert Mitchum, Sidney Poitier, Robert Preston, Cesar Romero, Ann Rutherford, Lizabeth Scott, Martha Scott, Jane Seymour, Dinah Shore, Alexis Smith, James Stewart, Ruth Warrick, Cornel Wilde, and Jane Wyman.

The focus is of course his film work, but organizers of the award also cite Roddy's philanthropic activities, including his contributions to the photo collection library at the Academy, where he's instrumental in the curating, cataloging, and preservation of the photographic legacy of so many actors, particularly older stars and silent-era performers. Roddy is also a hugely vocal ambassador for the MPTF, always emphasizing the importance of caring for the industry's elders and those who had fallen on hard times, especially behind-the-scenes workers who often lack financial security in retirement.

When Ken Scherer comes in to head the MPTF in 1996, Edie Wasserman, wife of Universal chairman Lew Wasserman, a powerful figure in her own right within philanthropic circles and the MPTF's "saint," encourages Ken to reach out to Roddy. He can bring his own connections to help further the organization's goals in very personal ways.

For instance, Jodie Foster, someone in Roddy's orbit since her transition from her career as a child actor, makes a major gift to create a swimming pool for the residents. Jodie's mother has arthritis, and swimming helps her a great deal. Ken Scherer wants to honor Jodie, and so he reaches out to Roddy to make a speech. "What he wrote brought tears to my eyes," Ken Scherer says. "I didn't yet know Roddy that well, and I didn't really know Jodie either, but it was so incredibly beautiful. So that was where we began. And then we just, we just developed a relationship. And I think, frankly, he knew that I was someone who was interested in keeping his own legacy alive as well."

Roddy approaches his charitable activities with focus and passion, but he wants his legacy to be his work. Everyone is connected in real ways, making moments like this count, with emotional investments that resonate. In turn, that inspires others to become involved. Roddy becomes one of Ken's go-to sources for connecting those in need with those who want to help, and even more important, with those who may not yet know they want to help. He is a tirelessly devoted advocate.

For a keen cadre of horror fans, Roddy's legacy rests on *Fright Night*, a classic from 1985, playing a character whose name, Peter Vincent, is an homage to two horror icons, Peter Cushing and Roddy's close friend Vincent Price. It's a charmed experience from beginning to end—going on to great critical and box-office success, and a sequel. William Ragsdale plays a young horror film aficionado who finds himself and his single mother in mortal danger from his new next-door neighbor, vampire Chris Sarandon. Roddy is a washed-up actor, once famous for his own horror films, now hosting a local TV horror film showcase. William Ragsdale turns to Roddy for help, with not a moment to lose—the sexy Chris Sarandon is making moves on William's mother. Roddy doesn't believe in vampires and only agrees to help when William's girlfriend, Amanda Bearse, and best bud, Stephen Geoffreys, bribe him with the badly needed cash he needs to pay his back rent. Roddy becomes a believer when things turn perilous. He rises to the occasion, delivering the final blow that saves the day.

"I was thrilled to get this part," Roddy is quoted in an unidentified article clip from his archives. "To play a bad actor is a great challenge because all you do is really make the wrong choices. You act in a way that you would be arrested, but it had to be done with enormous conviction and with integrity and good taste. It's wonderful to make absolutely dreadful choices! Peter Vincent is essentially the Cowardly Lion, a wonderful character."

Chris Sarandon isn't initially overjoyed when he gets the script for the project. "At the time I had a sort of skewed view of my place in the pantheon of the film world," he says. "I saw the title *Fright Night*, and I thought, I can't do a movie called *Fright Night*. I'm a great classical actor, and an Academy Award nominee! But I've always felt that if somebody offers you something, you owe them the courtesy to read it. And I sat down and started reading it. Within ten pages I thought, this is really pretty good.

And by the time I finished the script, I jumped at it. And I'm so glad I did."

Joanna Gleason, Roddy's costar on the *Charley's Aunt* tour, is Chris Sarandon's wife. She tells him what a lovely person Roddy is, but Chris is surprised by Roddy's collegiality and his level of cooperation and collaboration. "There was never a sense that the job was somehow beneath him. He treated the film as if it were every bit as important as *How Green Was My Valley*. We all felt that we were all part of the same kind of jolly band of players, if you will. He was always running around taking videos of everything, but also checking in on all of us, finding out if we were doing okay. It was spectacular, the feeling of inclusion and warmth he created."

William Ragsdale is delighted but surprised when he learns that Roddy is cast as Peter Vincent. William is a huge fan from *Night Gallery* and *The Legend of Hell House*, as well as the *Planet of the Apes* movies, but he thinks of Roddy as relatively young. "I was imagining someone like Vincent Price or Christopher Lee," he says. "Of course, there's a lot of physical stuff with killing Chris and his minions and all that, so maybe that was a consideration. I guess Vincent Price might have been a little too old for all of that."

Director Tom Holland is a respected screenwriter, but this is his first time helming a movie. He has a theater background and convinces the studio to allow for two weeks of rehearsal before shooting. The sets are marked out with tape on the soundstage floor and at Tom's request the cast writes character bios. Roddy's is six pages long. His process is meticulous, not different from creating Octavian or Ariel. "He had such a strong sense of who the guy was," says William Ragsdale. "There's a couple of scenes in the movie where he's reminiscing about his character and it's quite moving, you know? Kind of devastating really. His own history and this encyclopedic knowledge of Hollywood runs all through it."

Chris, along with Joanna Gleason and William, become regulars at Roddy's dinners. "We were there one night with Roddy, and I think Stefanie Powers, R.J. Wagner, and Jill St. John, and the producer David Chasman, who was sitting on the ledge by Roddy's fireplace. Unbeknownst to any of us, his sweater caught fire. We're all sitting there trying to figure out what this ungodly smell is—wool, or wool and polyester, I guess. Suddenly Chasman gets up, and people are throwing water on him and drinks. And then everyone goes right on telling stories and making each other laugh. I have a great picture of Joanna and I with Roddy, Tim Curry, David Hockney, Liza Minnelli, and Doris Roberts. We would get ready to go to Roddy's saying, 'I wonder if he's serving cat again.' Because the food was not very good. It was abominable, actually. But every time we were there, it was extraordinary. Not just because of people being famous or whatever. Roddy created an atmosphere of love and appreciation. You always felt good-looking and smart and funny—like you were your best self—but somehow without effort."

"I was there most often during the two *Fright Night* movies," says William Ragsdale. "But he always kept up with little notes on your birthday, or you were opening in something. He was just so thoughtful, and he really enjoyed the presence of other people and knowing what was going on in their lives. Oh my God, imagine if he'd had Facebook! But you know, I will remember his dinners for the rest of my life. I felt like I was invited into a special world. Old Hollywood to an extent, I mean I sat next to Lauren Bacall at one dinner and Nancy Walker at another, but he didn't think of himself or his friends as museum pieces at all. He was always interested in new things and new people. He also became friends with Illeana Douglas, and Laura Dern, and Billy Bob Thornton. You know, it's funny. I've heard people talking over the years about the food not being good, but I was young and hungry all the time, so to me, as long as there was a whole lot of it, I was fine."

"Every cook, whoever worked for Roddy, did the same appalling job with his standard menu," writes Doris Roberts. "Pounded fried chicken in a flour base, gluey mashed potatoes, and cold, overworked vegetables. Always terrible guacamole before and dessert was usually a terrible store-bought pie."

But no one is ever there for the food anyway. Nurturing friendships is what matters to Roddy, and he isn't above a little nudging. He isn't averse to arranging subtle networking opportunities. A writer or a director might find the right star for their project sitting across from them at dinner. Someone new in the business might get a chance to meet a mentor. Someone down on their luck might meet someone who can help them revive a fading career. "I was always excited, like a little kid, the day I got an invitation," writes Doris. "You might find some of the people intimidating in other circumstances, but at Roddy's they came as his friends and behaved that way. For people in Hollywood, he created a real fantasy island. Everything was magical. Everything was magical except the pie."

"I don't remember the food at all, because by the time we got to the table, we'd all have had four of five glasses of wine," says Illeana Douglas, who becomes very close with Roddy in the 1990s, so close he walks her down the aisle when she marries George and Joan Axelrod's son Jonathan. Roddy takes candid photos of Illeana the first time they meet, at lunch at Hugo's, a West Hollywood institution. "He was just so *interested* in me. Like immediately, he seemed to care about what I thought and who I was." She confides in Roddy about her anxieties over her audition for *To Die For* just before they meet. Roddy commiserates, and she's shocked to discover that Roddy often still has to audition. She thinks of him as Hollywood royalty. Why should he have to audition for *anything*? Roddy doesn't look at it that way at all. As much as he still hates the audition process itself, he doesn't begrudge anyone for asking him to read or test for a part. (At a recent audition for Fran Drescher's new project, *The*

Nanny, everyone loves him, but reportedly Fran nixes the idea, believing he's too iconic to play second banana as the butler.)

At the time Roddy and Illeana meet, she's in a relationship with director Martin Scorsese, a passionate advocate for film preservation and restoration, who proves very helpful to the restoration and remastering of *Tam Lin*. "But once Marty and I broke up, Roddy made it clear to me that I was his friend, and nothing would change about that. I don't think he ever saw Marty again, which says something about how remarkable he was about who he chose to stay friends with. I have to say, for people in my life who felt like they needed to choose once Marty and I were no longer together, Roddy was one of the only ones who chose me."

Neil Zevnik is Elizabeth Taylor's private chef for a number of years, and he remembers a slightly different side of Roddy. "I loved that we could have really erudite, complex conversations where he didn't perceive you to be pretentious because you have a good vocabulary and discuss abstract ideas." Neil is delighted to find someone who can knowledgeably and passionately talk about seemingly anything—philosophy, art, and social issues and behavior, show business, whatever. "Obviously we often talked about Elizabeth, but no baring of secrets or personal history. More like funny little stories. He loved telling about meeting her on *Lassie Come Home* and giggling at how beautiful she was, with her double row of lashes the cameraman thought were fake. I just remember never being bored, and I'm bored easily. He was interesting and verbal and perceptive."

While Roddy is shooting an episode of a short-lived Showtime anthology series called *Nightmare Classics,* starring opposite Meg Tilly, as an inspector who suspects she's a vampire, he gets the terrible news that Laurence Olivier has died. It's not unexpected, but it's a blow, nonetheless. As Roddy carves out his adult career in the 1950s, he's almost always the youngest member of his circle of friends and colleagues. Now the age difference means he's rapidly becoming the last man standing. The fact that he's always working at least means he can usually avoid the public spectacle of the funerals. He wants to honor his friends, but he loathes the public aspect of photographers ghoulishly trying to get shots of crying celebrities—profiting off the private grief of public figures.

Another miniseries comes up—*Around the World in 80 Days* with Pierce Brosnan as Phileas Fogg. Roddy is one of the Bank of England representatives accusing Pierce of theft, joining a list of actors doing cameos that includes Henry Gibson, John Hillerman, Eric Idle, Jack Klugman, Christopher Lee, Patrick Macnee, Darren McGavin, John Mills, Peter Ustinov, Robert Wagner, and Simon Ward. Also on hand is Roddy's costar in many projects starting from *You Will Remember* in 1940, Robert Morley, as his boss at the Bank of England.

Roddy also shows up in the 1991 miniseries as a gossip columnist named Cyril Rathbone (that name!) in *An Inconvenient Woman*, an adaptation of his friend Dominick Dunne's roman à clef about the murder of Alfred Bloomingdale's mistress. And in the 1992 miniseries *Sidney Sheldon's The Sands of Time*, Roddy is a private detective looking for a nun being pursued by an evil army colonel in Spain, on the lam with two other nuns and a band of revolutionaries. It could happen.

In the 1990s, Roddy's acting career increasingly becomes focused on animation. His first job on an animated production is all the way back in 1967 on a sequence for *The Danny Thomas Hour* called "Cricket on the Hearth." He voices a cricket who seeks to rescue a poor toymaker and his blind daughter from an exploitative miser. It's for the creative team of Jules Bass and Arthur Rankin Jr., already well-known for the stop-motion animated TV special *Rudolph the Red-Nosed Reindeer*, featuring Burl Ives. In the 1970s he voices all the male characters in a Rudyard Kipling adaptation for legendary animator Chuck Jones called *The White Seal* and most of the male characters and the narrator, again for Chuck Jones, in *Mowgli's Brothers*, a *Jungle Book* story about Mowgli saving his wolf parents from a tiger's malevolent influence. And in 1980, he voices Samwise Gamgee in what is still the only animated version ever created of *Return of the King*, with John Huston as Gandalf, Orson Bean as Frodo and Bilbo Baggins, Theodore Bikel as Aragorn, and Casey Kasem as Merry Brandybuck. It's also for Jules Bass and Arthur Rankin Jr., as is *The Wind in the Willows*, where he voices Ratty.

Those all rely on traditional narratives with fablelike endings. When Roddy books a job on the series *Darkwing Duck* in 1992, he's happily surprised by its modern tone. *Darkwing* is aimed at children, but it has a wry sense of humor and sophistication totally absent from the earlier, more earnest efforts Roddy is in. The character of Darkwing Duck is a bumbling and egotistical superhero who battles bizarre criminals with the help of his dimwitted pilot sidekick, Launchpad McQuack, and a rambunctious adopted daughter, Gosalyn Waddlemeyer. In Roddy's episode he plays one of Darkwing Duck's supposedly illustrious crime-fighting ancestors who travels to the present via a time machine and reveals that Darkwing Duck's predecessors are a motley bunch, with Roddy proclaiming, "We are the rust spots on the armor of crime!"

Its tongue-in-cheek tone appeals to Roddy, as does the way of working—fast, sometimes improvisational, and expansive. When he comes in with notes and ideas, he feels free to experiment. Animation directors *want* the actors to bring something surprising. From an acting standpoint, the demands of animation require clear choices and bold decisions. Sometimes actors swap roles in the middle of recording sessions; oftentimes changes are collaboratively made in how a character sounds and behaves. It feels exciting and new.

Roddy recurs as Jervis Tetch, a.k.a. the Mad Hatter, for *Batman: The Animated Series* and, later on, in *The New Batman Adventures.* Jervis starts out as a meek and socially awkward scientist experimenting with mind control equipment for Wayne Enterprises. When a romantic interest spurns him, he goes off the deep end and becomes obsessed with using his newfound power to control people, forcing them to serve his panoply of evil intentions. He takes on the identity of the Mad Hatter, ending up in Arkham Asylum, but of course escaping again and again to cause mayhem.

Animator Kevin Nowlan remembers being quite unhappy with the original designs of the character, and its adherence to the Lewis Carroll source material. "The Mad Hatter always looked very awkward to me, reminding me of the toothy, chinless John Tenniel drawings from the original book," he says. "In the end, it didn't matter because Roddy McDowall did the voice and just acted up a storm. No one noticed the character design, good or bad. They were focused on Roddy McDowall's virtuoso performance."

Another memorable performance is in a backdoor pilot for *Gargoyles* creator Greg Weisman in "The New Olympians." The setup of *Gargoyles* is a clan of heroic night creatures pledging to protect modern New York City as they did in Scotland one thousand years earlier. "The New Olympians" introduces a new milieu, the hidden city of New Olympus, where magical creatures live in isolation, mortally wary of humans and deeply prejudiced against them. Proteus is the shape-shifting supervillain of the piece. "Roddy seemed to truly enjoy making Proteus deliciously villainous," says Greg Weisman, who remembers Roddy as thoroughly prepared and flexible. The episode features an impressive collection of voice actors, including series regular Keith David, and guest artists Michael Dorn and Dorian Harewood. The backdoor pilot isn't picked up, but Roddy's character Proteus would likely have been a series regular. The show is now considered a classic by many animation aficionados, with fan events and a podcast examining each episode from the 1990s in detail still going in 2025.

During the 1990s Roddy voices for *Camp Candy*, *Red Planet*, *Secret Squirrel*, *Friends Are Forever: Tales of The Little Princess*, *2 Stupid Dogs*, *SWAT Kats: The Radical Squadron*, *The Tick*, *The Real Adventures of Jonny Quest*, *Animaniacs*, *Pinky and the Brain*, *Duckman*, *Jumanji*, *The New Superman Adventures*, and *Godzilla: The Series.* One of the best things about animation is how little time it takes. There's no sitting in his trailer waiting for camera setups, no costume fittings, no worrying about blemishes or whether your chin is sagging a little.

Roddy uses the free time to embark on new projects. He meets producers Victor Simpkins and John Dawson though his friend John Glover. They're all also part of New York circles that include Sybil Burton Christopher. Victor and John Dawson are optioning materials and developing films for features and for TV, some of them with Roddy's friend and colleague Gavin Lambert. One thing leads to another, and Roddy begins several years of working with Victor and John. He acts as a connector and consultant while also giving notes on potential properties and ongoing drafts of various scripts.

"We had this project we thought would be perfect for Anjelica Huston," says Victor Simpkins. "I said to Roddy one day, 'You have to get me to her!' And I mean, the very next week we were sitting in a meeting with Anjelica Huston. It was beautiful. Anjelica had read the project and loved it." Though the movie with Anjelica doesn't gets made, Victor and John go on to do a number of projects, including a Gavin Lambert script for TNT. Two very high-profile projects have their roots in the association between Victor, John, and Roddy, although neither one is produced under the auspices of the original company.

Victor Simpkins goes on to produce the smash indie film *Swingers*, with Jon Favreau and Vince Vaughn. Roddy executive produces and costars in *Overboard*, with Goldie Hawn and Kurt Russell. Many of the projects Roddy wants to develop at the time are remakes. Two of his favorites are *Libeled Lady* and

Love Crazy. *Libeled Lady* is the story of a socialite suing a newspaper for libel, with the editor who's responsible for the article enlisting his fiancée and a former employee to frame her and make the false story seem true. The original stars Jean Harlow, William Powell, Myrna Loy, and Spencer Tracy. *Love Crazy* is another William Powell and Myrna Loy film. When she suspects infidelity and starts divorce proceedings, he pretends to be insane in order to delay the divorce and clear up the misunderstanding. Neither gains any traction at the studios, but Roddy hits pay dirt with *Overboard*, a loose remake of the 1958 film *Houseboat*, starring Cary Grant and Sophia Loren, influenced by the Lina Wertmüller film *Swept Away*.

Overboard casts Goldie Hawn as a rich bitch who treats others appallingly, with Roddy as her long-suffering butler. When she and husband Edward Herrmann moor their yacht in Elk Cove, Oregon, she hires local carpenter Kurt Russell to build a closet addition for her shoes on the yacht. Despite Kurt doing a phenomenal job, Goldie finds fault, capriciously refusing to pay—throwing his tools overboard when he protests. Later that night after setting sail, she falls overboard herself, hits her head, and loses her memory. Edward Herrmann sees it as a fantastic opportunity to ditch her. Meanwhile when Kurt Russell sees her as a bedraggled Jane Doe on the news, he rushes in, claiming to be her husband. His plan is to basically make her his housemaid and force her to care for his four rambunctious sons until she earns out the equivalent of what she owes him. He plans on making her work for a month.

The general ick factor of intimacy is tactfully avoided, with Goldie sleeping on the couch until she gets her memory back. No one—not director Garry Marshall, screenwriter Leslie Dixon, Goldie, nor Kurt—wants to insinuate that Kurt takes advantage of her sexually under the false guise of marriage. Of course, Goldie and Kurt fall in love for real and she comes to love the children as her own. Though she feels brutally betrayed when she gets her memory back, she ultimately chooses him. Kurt expresses surprise that she's willing to walk away from all that money to be with him, but the twist is that the money is hers, not her husband's.

Roddy and Goldie have a wonderful moment once she regains her memory and returns to the yacht. She apologizes to him for all of her past behavior, expressing how grateful she is for all that he has always done for her. She's changed by her experience with Kurt and his kids and feels like she doesn't fit in anywhere anymore. Is she wrong for thinking about going back to Kurt? "Oh no, Madam, oh no," Roddy replies. "Most of us go through life with blinders on, Madam, knowing only that one little station to which we were born. But you, Madam, on the other hand, have had the rare privilege of escaping your bonds for just a spell—to see life from an entirely new perspective. How you choose to use that information, Madam, is entirely up to you." The movie is a big hit, and to his dying day, Garry Marshall thinks it's one of the funniest pictures he ever makes.

Just before *Overboard* comes out, Roddy creates the first of three sequels to his photo anthology book *Double Exposure,* utilizing his comprehensive collection of photos from earlier eras, but also adding newer stars like Johnny Depp, Whoopi Goldberg, Debra Winger, John Glover, Cher, Michelle Pfeiffer, Bette Midler, Tom Hanks, Jamie Lee Curtis, Tracey Ullman, and Tom Cruise. Proceeds from all three benefit the MPTF. The photographs are vital and surprising. The essays give rare glimpses into the ways creative artists view one another.

Joan Rivers writing about Cher isn't at all jokey. She cares deeply and regards Cher as truly inspiring. "She is the most contemporary kind of modern woman," Joan writes. "She really is free. . . . When things get too rough, I pretend I'm her. 'What would Cher do?' I ask myself. And when I have the answer, I know I'll get through." Cher, on the other hand, writes very little about Michelle Pfeiffer. "I won't diminish her by trying to explain her. That would be like putting pins in a butterfly to slow it down so people could get a better look."

Some of the juxtapositions are surprising just for their very existence. Roddy's poignant 1980 photo of silent movie temptress Pola Negri accompanies a tribute from Hayley Mills, who, it turns out, was once in a movie with Pola—a 1964 film called *The Moon-Spinners*, where eighteen-year-old Hayley is on the island of Crete, searching for a collection of priceless stolen jewels—and she can't be sure whether or not she should trust the enigmatic Pola, a wealthy and mysterious former belly dancer with an opulent yacht and a lavish lifestyle. Who knew?

Andy Garcia summons the poetry of Cuban nationalist hero José Martí (Cesar Romero's grandfather) to describe Kenneth Branagh. "I'll cultivate a white rose—in June or in January—for a sincere man—who gives me his—honest hand." Jim Bridges offers his own diary entry about meeting John Travolta, who very much wants to do *Urban Cowboy*. "But you have to promise me one thing," John tells Jim. "If I'm not good in the movie, and you're not getting what you want, promise you'll fire me."

Unlike with the first *Double Exposure,* Roddy has help with the sequels. His romantic partner at the time is Steven Jongeward, a writer, researcher, production associate, and a frequent contributor to *Cinefantastique*, a magazine covering fantasy, horror, and science-fiction cinema. They have much in com mon. When they meet, Steven is coming off a stint as a production associate and liaison between author Arthur C. Clarke and director Peter Hyams on *2010: The Year We Make Contact*, the sequel to *2001: A Space Odyssey.* Steven compiles the lengthy correspondence between the two in a book called *The Odyssey File*, and he works with Peter again on the film *Running Scared.* Though Steven doesn't remember his first meeting with Roddy, logically it might be when Steven becomes the research director of *The Late Show Starring Joan Rivers* on the fledgling Fox network. Roddy is a guest on the show several times, and of course, he and Joan are close friends. Steven and Roddy go on to develop a direct-to-video series together, *Roddy McDowall's Legends of Hollywood*, but legal and financial obstacles prevent the project from moving forward.

Steven remembers Virginia with particular affection. "She was lively and a delightfully witty, lovely lady," he says. "Every year on Virginia's birthday, Roddy would have her and her friends over to the house for her favorite meal, corned beef and cabbage." At the time, Steven is working at various jobs across film and television, and Virginia is someone who has paid her dues throughout her life, with jobs at various studios and with different directors. They always have a lot to talk about.

As Roddy is working on the *Double Exposure* sequels he also recommits to magazine work, becoming an editor-at-large for *Architectural Digest*, a contributing editor at *Interview*, and a contributing editor at *Poz*, a publication devoted to people living with and affected by HIV/AIDS. His photos are also featured in *Cosmopolitan*, *Ladies' Home Journal*, *Stern*, *Glamour*, *Saturday Review*, *Business Week*, *Photograph*, and an ad campaign for MPTF.

One of his main targets is *Premiere* magazine, a groundbreaking publication that is a hybrid of Hollywood trade press, film journal, and mainstream journalism—all beautifully printed in a glossy oversized magazine devoted exclusively to movies and moviemakers. Roddy is fascinated with the approach and wants to be involved. Whenever he's in New York, he meets with editor Howard Karren to pitch ideas. Roddy seems almost as interested in Howard's life as he is in the magazine. "I was in my thirties—this younger gay guy who has a long-term boyfriend, a professional career, and who's living a kind of responsible life," says Howard. "I think it kind of interested him, how totally public and open my life was. 'How are you and yours?' is how he would ask about my partner. He was very, the German word is *gemütlich*, just socially very charming."

Howard remembers Roddy referring obliquely to breaking up with a partner—presumably Steven—but giving few details. He still marvels at Roddy's levelheadedness, despite growing up in Hollywood. "We dealt with a lot of stars at *Premiere*, and there's a lot of really childish and indulgent behavior that goes on," says Howard. "Roddy had none of that at all. There wasn't this ego stroking that you needed to do. He was very aware of what he commanded, who he was, where he stood in the map of importance and fame. He never abused it—he just always made everything very easy." Roddy does do several pieces for the magazine, and they run some of his photographs, but as much as he's open to new people and new ideas, Roddy is more interested in pitching stories about icons who may soon pass away, people like Greer Garson, Robert Mitchum, Irene Sharaff, and Sydney Guilaroff. *Premiere* is more focused on the present than the past.

Past and present are both involved as Roddy gets ready for a very special screening. His restoration and reconstruction of *Tam Lin,* begun with the help of Martin Scorsese, but carried on under Roddy's supervision, is finally complete. For Roddy, it's a wonderful present-day moment of righting a twenty-plus-year-old wrong. People now can see *Tam Lin* as he conceived it in 1969—actually even better, since he's made some changes in the editing room. The audience response at the Pacific Design Center screening room is warm and admiring, which is to be expected—it's largely friends and family—but for Roddy it's a revelation and a catharsis. A revelation, because seeing it with others allows him an objectivity he doesn't have in the editing room. People are just as enthralled as he is with Ava Gardner's magnetic otherworldliness. And while some of the techniques may seem very much of their moment, he feels the film hangs together. Ian McShane and Stephanie Beacham are wonderful, and he feels vindicated. That vindication is part of the catharsis. It's also a bit melancholy. Why in the world didn't he ever direct again? He loved it. And he was good at it. Maybe Louise Brooks was right all those years ago. Who knows, maybe he'll start a new career as a director right now.

All these thoughts are running through his head as Michael Aspel, a man he has met before in London, comes out on stage. *Oh God, no, no, no, no . . .* "Roddy McDowall, This Is Your Life!" Suddenly it dawns on Roddy why so many of his oldest friends are at this event. "Thank you very much," he says shyly. "I don't know what to say, but I guess I have to go along!" Some of the people are expected, but others, like his old *Murder in the Family* costar from 1938, Glynis Johns, Ronald Neame from *The Poseidon Adventure*, as well as *Murder in the Family*, and Maureen O'Hara are hiding backstage during the screening itself, so they're part of the surprise.

It's overwhelming. Virginia McDowall, Anna Lee, Juliet Mills, and Maxwell Caulfield also speak. There are taped tributes from Lauren Bacall, Anjelica Huston, Carol Burnett, Lydia and Charlton Heston, Ian McShane, John Schlesinger, and Joan Plowright. The show airs on ITV in the UK the next month.

Later the same year, on one of Roddy's New York trips to pitch stories to Howard Karren at *Premiere*, he also invites Howard to a very special event. Scheduled to coincide with the publication of *Double Exposure, Take Four,* Roddy gets his very first gallery showing of his photographs. Sponsored by publisher William Morrow and Nikon, the show is at New York's House Gallery in Rockefeller Center. Howard isn't shocked by the guest list—he understands Roddy's place in the world—but he finds it incredible. "I mean, I talked to Farley Granger, and Lauren Bacall showed up, Maggie Smith, Johnny Mathis, Tony Perkins. And there's Roddy, just smiling like it's the most normal thing in the world. But he must have been so thrilled." Elizabeth Taylor can't attend because of an important AIDS fundraising gala on the same night. She is also mindful that there are times when her presence adds to the event, like giving

Roddy his American Cinema Foundation Award, and there are times when her presence might distract. This is Roddy's night about his work. She wants people at the gallery to focus on him, not on her.

Once his fourth volume of *Double Exposure* comes out and he's no longer doing any consulting or development work, Roddy gets bored. Just after Labor Day in 1995, he starts rehearsals for an extensive five-month, fourteen-city tour of *Dial M for Murder* as the wily inspector whose cat-and-mouse tactics eventually solve the crime. His costars are Nancy Allen and John James. They play Detroit; Washington, DC; New Haven; Denver; Philadelphia; Cleveland; and Minneapolis, before finishing in Chicago.

Roddy departs the Windy City for the Pearl of the Indian Ocean: Sri Lanka. Roddy has another date with some simians, as the unhinged, flamboyant King of the Bandar-Log (a chaotic tribe of monkeys) in *Rudyard Kipling's The Second Jungle Book: Mowgli and Baloo*. Roddy is exhausted by the ungovernable monkeys and sees Mowgli as the perfect person to take over—let *him* deal with the little bastards. Director Duncan McLachlan gives Roddy free rein to go as deliciously hammy as he wants, and Roddy turns in a bravura performance that's every bit as interesting, if not as widely seen, as his work in *Fright Night*—though not everyone agrees. Reviews are decidedly mixed.

Roddy is hungry for another stage experience, and an unusual opportunity comes up. Hal Linden has signed on as Scrooge for the 1997 production of *A Christmas Carol* at Madison Square Garden. It's a massive show with music by Alan Menken, lyrics by Lynn Ahrens, and choreography by Susan Stroman, with book and direction by Mike Ockrent. The production is Broadway-level quality, with elaborate sets and costumes, a huge cast, and spectacular effects, including flying ghosts, snowfall in the theater, and pyrotechnics. The theater has 5,600 seats and *A Christ-*

mas Carol plays fifteen shows per week. Starting in 1994, the show is a beloved New York tradition. Hal will be the fourth actor to play Scrooge in this version of the show, following Walter Charles, Terrence Mann, and Tony Randall. But before rehearsal starts, Hal expresses his doubts about his ability to withstand the brutal schedule of fifteen shows per week. He wants to pull out, but the producers propose an unconventional solution.

What if Hal shares the role?

They make an offer for Roddy to alternate in the role with Hal Linden, and Roddy happily accepts. He will be the fifth actor to play Scrooge. It is an incredibly brisk rehearsal process. The production team has done the show before and everything moves like efficient clockwork. Roddy is in heaven.

"Out of the blue I got a call one day from the producers of *A Christmas Carol*," says Ken Scherer. "They said they donate the proceeds from one performance every week to a charity, and when it's Roddy's turn to choose who gets the money, he chose us, the MPTF. The *Christmas Carol* producers were very honest. They said they didn't want to give it to us because they really like giving to New York charities, but Roddy just kept saying, very politely, but very firmly, that he would only choose us."

Ken agrees to go to New York to get the check and do a photo op. He decides to take his family, including his six-year-old daughter. When he takes her to meet Roddy backstage after the show, Roddy takes her by the hand and looks deeply into her eyes, asking if she wants to see the set. It's like Roddy is reading her mind. Seeing that set is all she can think about, but she couldn't summon the courage to ask. Somehow Roddy just *knows* without even asking. Roddy patiently shows her every nook and cranny of the set, explaining how everything works. "That kid is now thirty-three, working at Universal in the backlot as the head costumer for the Transformers on the Park," says Ken, "and she still remembers it as one of the most amazing experiences of her life. Roddy was the star of the show, but he wasn't focused on all the important people who were backstage to see him; all he cared about was this little girl who was fascinated by the magic of the theater."

Lawrence Van Gelder in *The New York Times* isn't a huge fan of this production, one he has seen in its prior years as well. But he writes: "Mr. McDowall's performance restores some much-needed balance to a show that all but subsumes Charles Dickens's classic Christmas tale beneath soulless spectacle. . . . [He] may not be a Pavarotti when it comes to carrying a tune or a Schwarzenegger when it comes to hoisting Tiny Tim on his shoulder, but as they say in school, he works and plays well with others and makes the most of the rare comic line."

The *Times* reviewer notices something Roddy hopes to hide, that he's having terrible pain after wrenching his back while lifting the little boy playing Tiny Tim—a small kid, not heavy at all. When Roddy is back in Los Angeles he goes to the chiropractor and to a massage therapist, but nothing helps. He goes to his regular doctor who sends him to a specialist. One test leads to another, one doctor to another. Roddy is in pain because he has metastatic lung cancer—inoperable and terminal. He will probably be dead within the year.

Roddy is shocked but not surprised, or surprised but not shocked he doesn't know which. He's a very pragmatic, logical person. After a lifetime of heavy smoking, a lung cancer diagnosis is logical if horrible. Smoking is a habit he picks up as a kid on the Fox lot. Everyone smokes back then. He finally gives it up in the late 1980s, but apparently not soon enough. Virginia still smokes. God, he can't bear to think about telling Virginia—to think about telling anyone, really. He needs time to figure out how *he* feels and what *he* wants to do.

He knows he doesn't want a spectacle. Nor does he want to be surrounded by quivering lips and tearful tributes. There's too much to do. His mind immediately starts ticking away all of the things he wants to get done. He feels relatively fine at the moment, but he knows from what his doctors tell him, that he will likely need help very soon—a lot of help. Steve Sondheim, still a close friend from his New York days, is in decent health again after a bout with prostate cancer, with a terrific carer and companion helping him through it. Roddy knows because Steve is one of the few people aware of the fact that Roddy also had a bout with prostate cancer, several years before. The treatment didn't have side effects—no hair loss or anything like that—so Roddy kept the whole thing to himself at the time. Even Elizabeth didn't know. And Roddy doesn't want her to know about his new diagnosis. At least not yet.

As luck has it, Steve's carer and companion is in Los Angeles now. This is how Dennis Osborne comes to play such a large role in the last months of Roddy's life. Dennis is the kind of person who can create trust and intimacy quickly, not unlike Roddy. For his part, Dennis comes to view his relationship with Roddy as romantic in nature if not in physicality. Carefully, Roddy begins to arrange his remaining papers and files to go to Boston, he chooses special items he wants each of his friends to have, and he decides to tell at least one friend.

"I have terminal cancer," Roddy tells Doris Roberts. "I won't make it until Christmas." As she tries to process this terrible information he goes on. "My lawyer knows. My doctor knows. And now you know." Doris panics. "What about your sister? What about all your friends, Roddy? You can't do that to them. They need to know!" He shakes his head calmly. "No, they'll know in time. I can't tell them now because they will act inappropriately."

Doris stops to think. She appreciates that Roddy knows she won't fall apart or make it difficult for him by becoming too emotional. She can give him the space to have his own emotions—or to express no emotions at all, whatever he chooses—without her making it into a drama about her. Roddy knows Doris can and will keep a secret. She keeps quiet, but it almost kills her. She's close to so many of his friends. "I wanted to lighten my burden by sharing it with them so we could all have a good cry," she says. "But to do that would be a betrayal, the greatest sin, as far as Roddy was concerned."

Dennis arranges for home nurses and, as the pain worsens, Roddy goes on an IV drip of morphine. He spends his days writing letters to all of the people in his life, finding the right thing to give them—an Hermès scarf, a silver bibelot, a trinket, a piece of art—slowly going through his memory and his address book, wanting everything he leaves behind to be meaningful and perfect. This isn't to say he spends the rest of the time he has left in 1998 resting and writing letters. He continues on the board of the MPTF, chairs the Student Academy Awards Committee, serves as president of the Academy Foundation Board of Trustees, and treasurer and chair of the finance committee of AMPAS; he's interviewed for dozens of documentaries and *Biography* episodes about old Hollywood; he completes several voice jobs in animated projects for TV and film; and he appears at several events honoring the thirtieth anniversary of *Planet of the Apes*.

His last job is a voice role in *A Bug's Life*. He's Mr. Soil, a refined, kindly ant advisor to the queen, Phyllis Diller, who helps bridge a leadership crisis between Phyllis and her daughter the princess, Julia Louis-Dreyfus.

As Roddy's seventieth birthday approaches, Army Archerd at *Variety* calls to give his best wishes. Roddy instructs Dennis to tell Army about his terminal cancer, and Army breaks the news on September 11, 1998. It's like a bomb going off. Roddy tells Elizabeth Taylor, Lauren Bacall, and Sybil Burton Christopher shortly before the news goes public. Elizabeth is immediately at his side, and Sybil and Lauren both fly in from New York.

Everyone he knows is desperate to see him or at least speak with him on the phone. The idea of a world without Roddy is too terrible to contemplate. There's an odd undercurrent, as if people are hoping for reassurance. If they can be with him, maybe he'll tell them it's not true. That there *is* hope. That he won't die.

Doris Roberts is relieved to be able to speak with others about her sadness but is careful not to divulge the fact that she knew months before most of his friends, even Elizabeth and Sybil. Actually, *especially* Elizabeth and Sybil. Roddy knows they will take it hard, and they do. Doris doesn't speak publicly about knowing earlier than everyone else until five years later when she publishes her memoirs.

Roddy determines to see as many people as he can while his strength holds out. For about three weeks, he has small gatherings, receiving people almost every day, sitting in his wheelchair, wearing a smoking jacket and an ascot, discreetly attached to his IV. He wants things to feel normal, with people telling stories and keeping him up-to-date about everything going on in their lives. He has long calls with those unable to travel to Los Angeles, like Robby Lantz, Dirk Bogarde, and Boaty Boatwright.

John Glover and Adam Kurtzman are at the house on a daily basis, helping Dennis Osborne navigate the visits, the outsized personalities, and the mounting panic and grief. They pick up Sybil from the airport when she flies in from New York. She's an emotional mess until they get to Roddy's house. She quickly pulls herself together, ready to make her time with Roddy about him. She doesn't want to make him worry about the agony she's in, but her feelings run deep, and there's only so much she can hide. Elizabeth is inconsolable.

"She just didn't see it coming at all," says Neil Zevnik. "It was like the life went out of her completely. This was her oldest friend, the one who knew where all the bodies were buried so to speak. Hell, metaphorically he helped her *bury* those bodies." Like Sybil, Elizabeth is determined to make whatever time she has with Roddy about him. She does her best, but it's impossible not to show her devastation. Roddy understands. This is why he waited so long to break the news. He's used to the idea of dying now, and he has room for other people's pain.

For her part, Lauren Bacall is the one among this trio of powerful women who's most successful at hiding her feelings and focusing on Roddy, on what needs to happen next—on what she can *do*. Lauren can be there with anyone, but Roddy and Dennis are careful not to have Sybil and Elizabeth there at the same time. The *Cleopatra* days are long ago, certainly not uppermost in either of the women's minds, but they live on separate coasts, and apart from Roddy they have few close friends in common. There is no reason for them to spend time together.

"Some days were so intense," Adam remembers. "But it could also be funny and surreal. I remember this one time, Lauren Bacall was storming around the house, upset about something, I don't remember what, and all of a sudden, she comes in very close and stares into my eyes intently, putting both hands on my face. 'Darling,' she says in that deep voice, 'Would you make me a roast beef sandwich with mustard?' Lauren fucking Bacall has her hands on my face like she's going to bite me or kiss me, or I don't know what, but all she wants is a sandwich."

Emotions run high for many of Roddy's visitors and callers. Just about everyone interviewed for this book is among his visitors. All have bittersweet memories of their final conversations with Roddy, and he makes sure everyone leaves with a special memento. For Joanna Gleason and Chris Sarandon, it's a bench Roddy once outbids a furious Ethel Merman to get that he now wants them to have. He gives John Glover most of his clothes, and John and Adam still wear some of those pieces. He gives Carol Burnett the chair by the fireplace where she used to sit listening to people like Bette Davis spin their tales of old Hollywood. He gives Doris Roberts a special lamp. He gives Neil Zevnik a pair of antique sterling silver sugar tongs. This is part of what he's been doing for months—choosing these tokens that he hopes will mean something to his friends and loved ones.

"That whole year, every time I saw him, he looked thinner and thinner. But he never let on," Illeana Douglas remembers. "I think one of the last times I saw him—which was not good, he looked terrible—Roddy asked me if he could come over. He put this beautiful sterling silver tray in my hands, saying, 'I want you to have it.' I wanted to ask him about his health, about what was happening, but I took my cue from him, you know? With Roddy, if you found yourself starting to cry, he would smile and be like, 'None of that.' You always wanted it to be like you were in a Roddy McDowall movie, with a stiff upper lip." Illeana shoots six movies in 1998 and is out of town on a job during the final weeks of friends visiting Roddy. That's exactly where Roddy wants her to be: on a movie set, working. He wishes the same for all of his beloved visitors. It's wonderful they are there with him, but he would rather they be on location somewhere, or on a studio lot, a theater stage. Those are the best places in the world.

Roddy has a talent for making people feel special, and many think of themselves as among his closest, closest friends. They may very well be dear and special to him, but he's also losing strength and in a great deal of pain. Sometimes he can't come to the phone. He can't come to dinner. In their sadness and confusion, some of Roddy's friends direct their anger at Dennis, blaming him for keeping them from seeing Roddy. "He really took the brunt of it all," says Adam. "Especially from Sybil. She just became convinced that Dennis had all of these evil designs or whatever, or that he wanted to steal things, or was dishonest.

I don't think that was true. Dennis was just overwhelmed. And Roddy was dying. He had no strength. People just didn't want to accept what was happening."

Ken Scherer gets a call from Edie Wasserman, who tells him Roddy wants to see him. He goes over to the house that day. Roddy's bed is in the living room now. He's in pajamas, attached to his morphine drip, very weak. A distraught Kirk and Anne Douglas are at his side. Roddy waves Ken in. "Dennis is going to take you out in the garden," he tells him.

Dennis leads Ken out to the garden and shows him the statue of Caesar from *Conquest of the Planet of the Apes.* It's been in Roddy's rose garden all these years. "He's giving that to you to take to the fund," Dennis tells him. Ken goes back into the house. Kirk and Anne Douglas are leaving, emotionally shaken, carrying some special salt and pepper shakers Roddy wants the two of them to have.

Roddy turns to Ken. "Dear boy, I'm giving you the statue for the home. What will you do with it?"

"Well, we're going to put it in a rose garden," Ken says.

"Where?" Roddy asks.

"I don't know. We haven't built it yet, but we'll build a rose garden and we're going to put the statue there."

Ken is getting emotional, realizing this may be the last time he sees Roddy. He turns to see Elizabeth Taylor and Sybil Burton Christopher, arriving at the same time, as if on cue. When they get over the shock of being in the same room together, Roddy looks up at the two women.

"Ken's going to put my Caesar statue in a rose garden and you're going to help him raise the money to build it," Roddy says, looking pointedly at them both.

"If you don't do it—*I will haunt you from my grave.*"

"Elizabeth and Sybil were just frozen," Ken says. "They were having to deal with each other after all those years ago on

Cleopatra. But that was Roddy. He was the only one who could broker that peace. He just had a magic touch that I've never seen in a person before or since."

Roddy slips out of consciousness later that afternoon and dies a few days later on October 3, 1998. The Academy quickly announces a memorial event, but they have to cancel their plans when they learn of Roddy's last wishes. He wants no memorial, no funeral, and no burial. His ashes are to be cremated and scattered at sea by the Neptune Society.

All he wants is the rose garden.

Elizabeth Taylor and Sybil Burton Christopher keep their promise. They issue joint fundraising letters and quickly raise the money. They consult on the design with Ken Scherer. MPTF builds a garden with a small pond. Caesar has pride of place. At Virginia's request, Adam Kurtzman creates a sculpture of Roddy.

In 2001, Elizabeth and Sybil appear together at the opening dedication of the Roddy McDowall Rose Garden. There is still a frisson of tension or excitement in the crowd at seeing the two women together. Elizabeth goes off script from her prepared remarks and does something totally unexpected. Almost forty years after the fact, Elizabeth Taylor publicly apologizes to Sybil Burton Christopher. Sybil is gobsmacked and accepts the apology graciously. They hug. Tears flow freely. They are there in solidarity. For Roddy.

There's a temptation to end Roddy's story with that apology. If there's an afterlife, he's undoubtedly thrilled to see the spirit of mutual respect and friendship that develops between these two women who mean so much to him. But bringing peace to Elizabeth Taylor and Sybil Burton Christopher isn't the apex of the story of Roderick Andrew Anthony Jude McDowall, born September 17, 1928, died October 3, 1998.

He is so much more than everyone's best friend.

This man makes magic in his lifetime, not just with his kindness and generosity, but with his *work*—with the thing that matters most to him. Roddy's work represents a lifetime of love, passion, sacrifice, guts, talent, and pain.

When Roddy is a twelve-year-old boy, 20th Century-Fox reimagines one of their most important movies of the year for him, making him the heart and soul of *How Green Was My Valley*.

MGM readjusts their entire schedule for *Lassie Come Home* so that Roddy McDowall can play the lead.

Roddy McDowall is the first man to play Ariel in a major production of *The Tempest* since the late nineteenth century.

In *Cleopatra,* among some of the most famous and talented actors on the planet, the legendary Noël Coward thinks Roddy McDowall gives the *only* performance that matters.

With *Planet of the Apes*, Roddy McDowall becomes the linchpin of one of the most successful film franchises in history.

Fright Night becomes a classic largely because Roddy McDowall approaches the character of a washed-up actor exactly the way he would approach playing Falstaff.

He makes 121 films and wins Best Acting honors from the National Board of Review.

He makes 877 appearances on TV and wins an Emmy.

He stars in 35 stage plays and wins a Tony.

He makes 44 audio recordings.

He publishes over 500 photographs in magazines, newspapers, and books, and on album covers.

He is a pioneer in the movement for film preservation and restoration.

His legacy includes the Roddy McDowall Photograph Archive at the Margaret Herrick Library of the Academy of Motion Picture Arts and Sciences, the Roddy McDowall Rose Garden at the Motion Picture and Television Fund Wasserman Campus, and the Roddy McDowall Special Collection at the Howard Gotlieb Archival Research Center at Boston University.

When *A Bug's Life* is released the month after he dies, the film is critically acclaimed from coast to coast, including raves in both the *Los Angeles Times* and *The New York Times.* And it racks up a worldwide box-office take of over $360 million.

None of that is about being somebody's best friend.

Media:
Films, Television and Radio, and Theater

As noted in the introduction, although many reference sources list *Yellow Sands*, *Sarah Siddons*, *Murder Will Out*, and *Poison Pen* among Roddy McDowall's credits, the author believes the inclusion of these titles is in error.

1938

Convict 99 (Jimmy)
Hey! Hey! U.S.A.! (Dock Urchin)
I See Ice! (Boy on Train)
John Halifax—a.k.a. *John Halifax, Gentleman* (Boy)
Murder in the Family (Peter Osborne)
Scruffy (Boy)

1939

The Outsider (Boy Patient)

1940

Dead Man's Shoes (Boy)
His Brother's Keeper (Boy)
Just William (Ginger)
Saloon Bar (Christmas Caroler)
You Will Remember (Young Bob Slater)

1941

Confirm or Deny (Albert Perkins)
How Green Was My Valley (Huw Morgan)
Man Hunt (Vaner)
This England (Hugo)

1942

On the Sunny Side (Hugh Aylesworth)
The Pied Piper (Ronnie Cavanaugh)
Son of Fury: The Story of Benjamin (Benjamin Blake as a boy)

1943

Lassie Come Home (Joe Carraclough)

My Friend Flicka (Ken McLaughlin)

1944

The White Cliffs of Dover (Sir John Ashwood as a boy)

1945

The Keys of the Kingdom (Francis Chisolm as a boy)

Molly and Me (Jimmy Graham)

Thunderhead, Son of Flicka (Ken McLaughlin)

1946

Holiday in Mexico (Stanley Owen)

1948

Kidnapped (David Balfour) (Associate Producer)

Macbeth (Malcolm)

Rocky (Chris Hammond) (Associate Producer)

1949

Black Midnight (Scott Jordan) (Associate Producer)

Tuna Clipper (Alec MacLennan) (Associate Producer)

1950

Big Timber (Jimmy) (Associate Producer)

Everybody's Dancin' (Self)

Killer Shark (Ted White) (Associate Producer)

1952

The Steel Fist (Eric Kardin) (Associate Producer)

1960

Midnight Lace (Malcolm)

The Subterraneans (Yuri Gligoric

1962

The Longest Day (Pvt. Morris)

1963

Cleopatra (Octavian, Caesar Augustus)

1964

Shock Treatment (Martin Ashley)

1965

Inside Daisy Clover (Walter Baines)

The Greatest Story Ever Told (Matthew)

The Loved One (D.J. Jr.)

That Darn Cat (Gregory Benson)

The Third Day (Oliver Parsons)

1966

The Defector (Agent Adams)

Lord Love a Duck (Alan Musgrave)

1967

The Adventures of Bullwhip Griffin (Bullwhip Griffin)

The Cool Ones (Tony Krum)

It! (Pimm)

1968

5 Card Stud (Nick Evers)

Planet of the Apes (Cornelius)

Roddy McDowall's Planet of the Apes Home Movie (Self)

1969

Angel, Angel, Down We Go (Santoro)

Hello Down There (Nate Ashbury)

Midas Run (Wister)

1970

Beneath the Planet of the Apes (Narrator)

Games and Toys (Narrator) (Director) [UK Release of *Tam Lin*]

1971

Bedknobs and Broomsticks (Mr. Jelk)

Escape from the Planet of the Apes (Cornelius)

Journey to Murder (Rollo Verdew) [Film release of an episode of the British TV show *Journey to the Unknown*]

Pretty Maids All in a Row (Proffer)

The Devil's Widow (Narrator) (Director) [USA release of *Tam Lin*]

1972

Conquest of the Planet of the Apes (Caesar)

The Life and Times of Judge Roy Bean (Gass)

The Poseidon Adventure (Acres)

1973

Battle for the Planet of the Apes (Caesar)

The Legend of Hell House (Ben Fischer)

1974

Arnold (Robert)

Dirty Mary Crazy Larry (George Stanton)

1975

Funny Lady (Bobby)

Mean Johnny Barrows (Tony Da Vince)

1976

Embryo (Frank Riley)

That's Entertainment, Part 2 (Self)

1977

Sixth and Main (Skateboard)

1978

The Cat from Outer Space (Mr. Stallwood)

Laserblast (Dr. Mellon)

Rabbit Test (Gypsy Grandmother; Dr. D&C Fishbine)

1979

The Black Hole (V.I.N. CENT., Voice)

Circle of Iron (White Robe)

Nutcracker Fantasy (Franz/Fritz, Voice)

Scavenger Hunt (Jenkins)

1981

Charlie Chan and the Curse of the Dragon Queen (Gillespie)

1982

Class of 1984 (Terry Corrigan)

Evil Under the Sun (Rex Brewster)

1985

Fright Night (Peter Vincent)

Zoo Ship (Actor, Voice)

1986

GoBots: Battle of the Rock Lords (Nuggit, Voice)

1987

Dead of Winter (Mr. Murray)

Overboard (Andrew) (Executive Producer)

1988

Doin' Time on Planet Earth (Minister)

1989

The Big Picture (Judge)

Batman (Video) (Narrator)

Cutting Class (Mr. Dante)

Fright Night: Part 2 (Peter Vincent)

Heroes Stand Alone (Actor)

1990

The Color of Evening (Henry Seaton)

Shakma (Sorenson)

1991

Going Under (Secretary Neighbor)

Timmy's Gift: A Precious Moments Christmas (Narrator)

1992

Double Trouble (Philip Chamberlain)

The Magical World of Chuck Jones (Self)

The Naked Target (Ernest Peabody)

1993

The Evil Inside Me (Pauly)

1994

Angel 4: Undercover (Geoffrey Kagen)

Mirror Mirror 2: Raven Dance (Dr. Lasky)

That's Entertainment III: Behind the Screen (Self)

1995

The Grass Harp (Amos Legrand)

Last Summer in the Hamptons (Thomas)

1996

It's My Party (Damian Knowles)

Star Hunter (Riecher)

1997

Mary Pickford: A Life on Film (Self)

Rudyard Kipling's The Second Jungle Book (King Murphy)

1998

A Bug's Life (Mr. Soil, Voice)

Louise Brooks: Looking for Lulu (Self)

Something to Believe In (Gambler)

Star Power: The Creation of United Artists (Self)

Tam Lin (Narrator) (Director) [restored version]

When It Clicks (Professor Bark)

Posthumous Appearances

1999

Keepers of the Frame (Self)

2001

Friends Are Forever: Tales of the Little Princess (Zak the Cat, Voice)

The Return of Captain Sinbad (Narrator, Voice)

Television and Radio

Many online sources list attendance at awards shows and specials as TV appearances. This list only includes appearances at such events when Roddy McDowall is a host, participant, or presenter.

1942

Lux Radio Theatre, Radio Anthology, "How Green Was My Valley" (Huw Morgan)

Lux Radio Theatre, Radio Anthology, "The Pied Piper" (Ronnie Cavanaugh)

1943

Lux Radio Theatre, Radio Anthology, "My Friend Flicka" (Ken McLaughlin)

1945

Command Performance USA, Armed Forces Radio Network Radio (Self)

Hollywood's Open House: America's Children, Radio Variety (Self)

1946

Colgate Sports Reel, Radio Sports (Self)

Academy Award Theatre, Radio Anthology, "Keys of the Kingdom" (Francis as a boy)

Lux Radio Theatre, Radio Anthology, "Thunderhead: Son of Flicka" (Ken McLaughlin)

1947

Family Theater, Radio Anthology, "The World of David Lee" (Host)

Suspense, Radio Anthology, "One Way Street"

The Voyage of the Scarlet Queen, Radio Anthology

1948

Family Theater, Radio Anthology, "The Man Who Died Twice"

The Kate Smith Hour: Keep Up with the Kids, Radio Quiz Show

Kidnapped, Radio Anthology (David Balfour)

Rocky III and the Dead Man's Chest, Radio Anthology

1949

Family Theater, Radio Anthology, "Altar of Freedom" (Host)

Family Theater, Radio Anthology, "Don Quixote" (Host)

Hallmark Playhouse, Radio Anthology, "National Velvet" (Mi Taylor)

1950

HI Talent Battle, Competition Show (Host)

Family Theater, Radio Anthology, "Hans Brinker" (Host)

Family Theater, Radio Anthology, "Lullaby of Christmas" (Host)

Family Theater, Radio Anthology, "The Prince and the Pauper" (Host)

People Are Funny, Radio Comedy

The Roddy McDowall Show, KMPC Radio Music/Talk Show (Host)

1951

Celanese Theatre, Television Anthology, "Ah, Wilderness!" (Richard)

Chance of a Lifetime, Music/Variety/Game Show (Self)

Family Theater, Radio Anthology, "In Shining Armor" (Self)

Family Theater, Radio Anthology, "The Flame and the Sword" (Host)

Family Theater, Television Anthology, "Hill Number One: A Story of Faith and Inspiration" (Pvt. Huntington)

Freddy Martin Show, Music/Variety Series (Self)

Goodrich Celebrity Time, Game Show (Self)
Lux Video Theatre, Television Anthology, "The Blues Street" (Pete)
Robert Montgomery Presents, Television Anthology, "When We Are Married" (Gerald Forbes)
The Steve Allen Show, Talk Show/Variety Series (Self)

1952

Battle of the Ages, Talent Show (Self)
Broadway Television Theatre, Television Anthology, "It Pays to Advertise" (Rodney Martin)
The Gulf Screen Guild Theater, Radio Anthology, "Lullaby of Christmas"
Hollywood Screen Test, Talent Show, "Blind Victory" (Self)
Hollywood Screen Test, Talent Show, "For the Love of Mike" (Self)
Kraft Television Theatre, Television Anthology, "Philip Goes Forth" (Philip)
Lux Video Theatre, Television Anthology, "Salad Days" (Bellamy Partridge)
U.S. Steel Hour, Radio Anthology, "The Thief"
Twenty Questions, Game Show (Self)

1954*

Angel Auditions, Documentary, "The Homeward Look" (Self)
Armstrong Circle Theater, Anthology Series, "My Client, McDuff" (Tim McDuff)
Campbell Television Soundstage, Anthology Series, "The Shy One"
The Elgin Hour, Anthology Series, "Yesterday's Magic" (Jamie)
Encounter, Anthology Series, "Bruno and Sydney" (Bruno)
Goodyear Television Playhouse, Anthology Series, "Buy Me Blue Ribbons"

*All anthology series from 1954 on are television series.

Kraft Television Theatre, Anthology Series, ("Emma" Mr. Elton)
Medallion Theatre, Anthology Series, "A Suitable Marriage"
Pond's Theater, Anthology Series, "Philip Goes Forth" (Philip)
Pond's Theater, Anthology Series, "The Shop at Sly Corner"
Robert Montgomery Presents, Anthology, "Great Expectations: The Promise Part I" (Pip)
Robert Montgomery Presents, Anthology, "Great Expectations: The Reality Part II" (Pip)

1955

The Ed Sullivan Show, Scene from "The Tempest" (Ariel)
The Ed Sullivan Show, Scene from "No Time for Sergeants" (Ben Whitledge)
Pond's Theater, Anthology Series, "The Silver Box" (John Barthwick Jr.)

1956

Goodyear Television Playhouse, Anthology Series, "In the Days of Our Youth"
General Electric Theater, Anthology Series, "O'Hoolihan and the Leprechaun" (Leprechaun)
Hallmark Hall of Fame, Anthology Series, "The Good Fairy" (Waiter)
The Kaiser Aluminum Hour, Anthology Series, "Gwyneth" (Clifford Howell)
Lux Video Theatre, Anthology Series, "Michael and Mary" (David at 22)

1957

Goodyear Television Playhouse, Anthology Series, "The Treasure Hunters"
Kraft Television Theatre, Anthology Series, "A Night of Rain"
Matinee Theater, Anthology Series, "Rain in the Morning"

Matinee Theater, Anthology Series, "Talk You of Killing?"
Matinee Theater, Anthology Series, "The Vicarious Years"
Matinee Theater, Anthology Series, "The Whiteheaded Boy"
The Alcoa Hour, Anthology Series, "He's for Me" (Max)
The Arlene Francis Show, Talk Show (Self)

1958

The American Scene, Documentary (Self)
The Arthur Murray Dance Party, Music/Variety Series (Self)
Kraft Television Theatre, Anthology Series, "The Last of the Belles" (Andy McKenna)
Matinee Theater, Anthology Series, "Washington Square" (Morris Townsend)
Playhouse 90, Anthology Series, "Heart of Darkness" (Charles Marlow)
Suspicion, Anthology Series, "The Imposter" (Derek Stratton)
Suspicion, Anthology Series, "The Woman with the Red Hair" (David)

1959

The Art Carney Show, Comedy Special, "The Best of Anything" (Self)
The Arthur Murray Dance Party, Music/Variety Series (Self)
DuPont Show of the Month, Anthology Series, "Billy Budd" (Squeak)
Oldsmobile Music Theatre, Musical Anthology Series, "Too Bad About Sheila Troy"
The Sam Levenson Show, Talk Show (Self)
The U.S. Steel Hour, Anthology Series, "Night of Betrayal" (Michel)

1960

The Arthur Murray Dance Party, Music/Variety Series (Self)
Hallmark Hall of Fame, TV Special, "The Tempest" (Self)

Person to Person, Documentary, "Nichols and May" (Self)
Sunday Showcase: Our American Heritage, Anthology Series, "Not Without Honor" (Philip Hamilton)
The Twilight Zone, Anthology Series, "People Are Alike All Over" (Sam Conrad)

1961

The Naked City, Drama Series, "The Fault in Our Stars" (Donnie Benton)
Person to Person, Documentary, "Roddy McDowall" (Self)
The Play of the Week, Anthology Series, "In a Garden" (Adrian Terry)
The Power and the Glory, TV Movie (The Mestizo)

1963

Arrest and Trial, Drama Series, "Journey into Darkness" (Paul LeDoux)
Fractured Flickers, Comedy Series (Various, Voice)
Picture This, Musical Game Show (Self)
Stump the Stars, Game Show (Self) (2 episodes)
The Tonight Show Starring Johnny Carson, Talk Show (Self)

1964

The 18th Annual Tony Awards (Presenter)
The 16th Annual Primetime Emmy Awards (Presenter)
Alfred Hitchcock Hour, Anthology Series, "See the Monkey Dance" (George)
Alfred Hitchcock Hour, Anthology Series, "The Gentleman Caller" (Gerald Musgrove)
Art Linkletter's House Party, Variety Series (Self)
Bob Hope Presents the Chrysler Theatre, Anthology Series, "Mr. Biddle's Crime Wave" (Arthur Biddle)
Bob Hope Presents the Chrysler Theatre, Anthology Series, "Wake Up, Darling" (Deerfield Prescott)

The Celebrity Game, Game Show (Self)
Combat! Drama Series, "The Long Walk" (Murfree)
The Eleventh Hour, Anthology Series "The Only Remaining Copy Is in the British Museum" (Stanton Maynard, a.k.a. Alec Harnes)
Get the Message, Game Show (Self) (13 episodes)
Kraft Suspense Theatre, Anthology Series, "The Wine-Dark Sea" (Robert "Professor" Benson)
The Match Game, Game Show (Self) (5 episodes)
The Mike Douglas Show, Talk Show (Self) (2 episodes)
Password, Game Show (Self) (10 episodes)
Password Nighttime, Game Show (Self)
The Price Is Right, Game Show (Self)
Stump the Stars, Game Show (Self)

1965

Ben Casey, Drama Series, "When I Am Grown to Man's Estate" (Dwight Franklin)
The Celebrity Game, Game Show (Self)
The Match Game, Game Show (Self) (5 episodes)
The Merv Griffin Show, Talk Show (Self) (2 episodes)
The Mike Douglas Show, Talk Show (Self)
Password Nighttime, Game Show (Self)
Password, Game Show (Self) (5 episodes)

1966

The Andy Williams Show, Music/Variety Series (Various)
Batman, Action/Comedy Series, "While Gotham City Burns/The Bookworm Turns" (The Bookworm)
Bob Hope Presents the Chrysler Theatre, Anthology Series, "The Fatal Mistake" (Harry Carlin)
The Face Is Familiar, Game Show (Self)
The Match Game, Game Show (Self)
The Merv Griffin Show, Talk Show (Self) (2 episodes)
The Mike Douglas Show, Talk Show (Self)

Password, Game Show (Self) (5 episodes)
Run for Your Life, Drama Series, "Don't Count on Tomorrow" (Gyula Bognar)
Twelve O'Clock High, Drama Series, "Angel Babe" (Sgt. Billy Willets)

1967
The Danny Thomas Hour, Animation Series, "Cricket on the Hearth" (Cricket Crocket, Voice)
The Danny Kaye Show, Music/Variety Series (Various)
Hollywood Squares, Game Show (Self) (15 episodes)
The Invaders, Drama Series, "The Experiment" (Lloyd Lindstrom)
Password, Game Show (Self) (10 episodes)
Personality, Game Show (Self) (5 episodes)
Saint Joan, TV Movie (Charles, The Dauphin)
Snap Judgment, Game Show (Self)

1968
The Felony Squad, Drama Series, "The Flip Side of Fear, Parts 1 and 2" (Ollie Otis) (2 episodes)
Hollywood Squares (Nighttime), Game Show (Self)
The Name of the Game, Drama Series, "The White Birch" (Philip Saxon)
The Woody Woodbury Show, Talk Show (Self)

1969
A Birthday Gala Tribute to Noël Coward, TV Special (Self)
The David Frost Show, Talk Show (Self)
It Takes a Thief, Drama Series, "Boom at the Top" (Roger)
Journey to the Unknown, Anthology Series, "The Killing Bottle" (Rollo Verdew)
The Legend of Robin Hood, TV Movie Musical (Prince John)
Night Gallery, Anthology Series, "The Cemetery" (Jeremy Evans)

Pay Cards! Game Show (Self) (5 episodes)
Win with the Stars, Game Show (Self) (5 episodes)

1970

Medical Center, Drama Series (Carl Marris)
The Mike Douglas Show, Talk Show (Self)
The Name of the Game, Drama Series, "Why I Blew Up Dakota" (Early McCorley)
What's My Line? Game Show (Self) (5 episodes)

1971

A Taste of Evil, TV Movie (Dr. Lomas)
Cinema, Talk Show (Self)
Ironside, Drama Series, "Murder Impromptu" (Jamie Shannon)
The Mike Douglas Show, Talk Show (Self)
The Movie Game (Self)
Terror in the Sky, TV Movie (Dr. Ralph Baird)
The Tonight Show Starring Johnny Carson, Talk Show (Self)
What's a Nice Girl Like You . . . ? TV Movie (Albert Soames)

1972

Columbo, Drama Series, "Short Fuse" (Roger Stanford)
Delphi Bureau, Drama Series, "The Man Upstairs The Man Downstairs" (Harold)
Love, American Style, Comedy Anthology Series, "Love and the Sensuous Twin" (Marvin)
McCloud, Drama Series, "The Park Avenue Rustlers" (Phil Sandler)
Mission: Impossible, Drama Series, "The Puppet" (Leo Ostrow)
Password, Game Show (Self) (10 episodes)
The Rookies, Drama Series, "Dirge for Sunday" (Fenner)

1973

AFI Life Achievement Award, Drama Special, "A Salute to John Ford" (Self)

Barnaby Jones, Drama Series, "See Some Evil . . . Do Some Evil" (Stanley Lambert)

Hollywood Squares, Game Show (Self) (5 episodes)

Love, American Style, Comedy Anthology Series, "Love and the Stutter" (Howard)

McMillan and Wife, Drama Series, "Death of a Monster . . . Birth of a Legend" (Jamie McMillan)

The Merv Griffin Show, Talk Show (Self)

Miracle on 34th Street, TV Movie (Dr. Sawyer)

Topper Returns, Comedy Series Pilot (Cosmo Topper Jr.)

1974

Bicentennial Minute, Documentary Short Series (Self) (2 segments)

The Carol Burnett Show, Comedy/Variety Series (Various)

Darryl F. Zanuck, Documentary (Self)

The Elevator, TV Movie (Marvin Ellis)

Hollywood Squares, Game Show (Self) (60 episodes)

To Lassie, With Love, Documentary (Self)

Late Night, TV Special, "That's Entertainment: 50 Years of MGM" (Self)

The Merv Griffin Show, Talk Show (Self)

Planet of the Apes, Drama Series (Galen) (14 episodes)

The Snoop Sisters, Drama Series, "A Black Day for Bluebeard" (Lionel Standish)

1975

47th Annual Academy Awards (Self)

The Carol Burnett Show, Comedy/Variety Show (Various) (2 episodes)

The Dinah Shore Show, Talk Show (Self)

Elizabeth Taylor: An Intimate Biography, Documentary (Self)

Hollywood Squares, Game Show (Self) (75 episodes)
Magnificent Marble Machine, Game Show (Self) (10 episodes)
Police Woman, Drama Series, "Pawns of Power" (Moulton)
The White Seal, Animation Special (Narrator, Voice)

1976

The Carol Burnett Show, Comedy/Variety Series (Various)
Ellery Queen, Drama Series, "The Adventure of the Black Falcon" (The Amazing Armitage)
Flood, TV Movie (Mr. Franklin)
Harry O, Drama Series, "The Mysterious Case of Lester and Dr. Fong" (Arnold Applequist)
Hollywood Squares, Game Show (Self) (60 episodes)
The Mike Douglas Show, Talk Show (Self)
Mowgli's Brothers, Animated Special (Various, Voice)
Storybrook Squares, TV Comedy Game Show (Self) (10 episodes)

1977

Hollywood Squares, Game Show (Self) (30 episodes)
The Fantastic Journey, Drama Series (Dr. Jonathan Willaway) (10 episodes)
The Feather and Father Gang, Drama Series, "The Mayan Connection" (Vincent Stoddard)
Laugh-In, Comedy Series (Self)
The New Adventures of Wonder Woman, Drama Series, "The Man Who Made Volcanoes" (Professor Arthur Chapman)
The Rhinemann Exchange, TV Miniseries (Bobby Ballard)
Sears All-Star Tribute to Elizabeth Taylor, TV Special (Self)
The Tonight Show Starring Johnny Carson, Talk Show (Self)
To Say the Least, Game Show (Self) (5 episodes)

1978

The Carol Burnett Show, Comedy/Variety Series (Various)
Hollywood Squares, Game Show (Self) (20 episodes)
The Immigrants, TV Movie (Mark Levy)
The New Adventures of Wonder Woman, Drama Series, "The Fine Art of Crime" (Henry Roberts)
The Thief of Baghdad, TV Movie (Hasan)

1979

A Man Called Sloane, Drama Series, "Night of the Wizard" (Manfred Baranoff)
Buck Rogers in the 25th Century, Drama Series, "Planet of the Slave Girls" (Governor Saroyan)
Fantasy Island, Drama Series, "Command Performance" (Richard Simmons)
Fantasy Island, Drama Series, "The Boss" (Gary Pointer)
Flying High, Comedy Series, "Eye Opener" (Joe)
Hart to Hart, Drama Series, "Pilot" (Dr. Peterson)
Hollywood Squares, Game Show (Self) (24 episodes)
Love Boat, Drama Series, "Don't Push Me" (Fred Beery)
Mork and Mindy, Comedy Series, "Dr. Morkenstein" (Chuck the Robot, Voice)
Supertrain, Drama Series, "The Green Girl" (Benjamin Warren Talcott)
Sweepstakes, Anthology Series, "Billy, Wally, Ludmilla and Theodore" (Theodore)
Trapper John, M.D., Drama Series Pilot, "Flashback" (Rev. Barnaby Bass)

1980

The British Greats: Gracie Fields, Documentary (Self)
Here's Boomer, "Boomer and Miss 21st Century" (Twins, Milo and Flournoi Acres)
Hollywood Squares, Game Show (Self) (15 episodes)
The Martian Chronicles, TV Miniseries (Father Stone)

The Memory of Eva Ryker, TV Movie (John McFarland)
Mindreaders, Game Show (Self) (5 episodes)
The New Planet of the Apes, Drama Series Reissued (Commentary)
Return of the King, Animated TV Movie (Samwise Gamgee, Voice)

1981

Fantasy Island, Drama Series, "The Devil and Mandy Breem" (Mephistopheles) (2 episodes)
The Golden Age of Television, TV Special, "No Time for Sergeants" (Host)
Judgment Day, TV Movie (Mr. Heller)
The Million Dollar Face—a.k.a. *Kiss of Gold*, Drama Series Pilot (Derek Kenyon)

1982

Circus of the Stars, TV Special (Self)
Fantasy Island, Drama Series, "Natchez Bound" (Christopher Lantree)
Hollywood's Children, Documentary (Narrator)
Mae West, TV Movie (Rene Valentine)
Natalie: A Tribute to a Very Special Lady, TV Special (Cohost)
The Making of Agatha Christie's "Evil Under the Sun," Documentary (Self)
Tales of the Gold Monkey, Adventure Series (Bon Chance Louie) (22 episodes)
The Tonight Show Starring Johnny Carson with Joan Rivers, Talk Show (Self)
Twilight Theatre, Comedy/Variety Special (Host)

1983

Faerie Tale Theatre, Children's Anthology Series, "Rapunzel" (Narrator)
Hollywood Ballyhoo, "The Greatest Story Ever Told" (Self)

The New Battlestars, Game Show (Self) (5 episodes)
Small and Frye, Comedy Series Pilot (Professor Vermeer)
This Girl for Hire, Drama Series Pilot (Manfred Hayes)
Walt Disney's Epcot Presents, Documentary Photography Shorts (Self) (5 segments)

1984

Hotel, Drama Series, "Intimate Strangers" (Anthony Spears)
London and Davis in New York, Drama Series Pilot (Paul Fisk)
The Zany Adventures of Robin Hood, Comedy Special (Prince John)

1985

The 2nd Annual American Cinema Awards (Honoree)
Alice in Wonderland / Alice Through the Looking Glass, TV Miniseries (The March Hare)
Entertainment Tonight, News (Self)
Entertainment USA, News (Self)
George Burns Comedy Week, Comedy Special, "A Christmas Carol II: The Sequel" (Bob Cratchit)
Hollywood Wives, TV Miniseries (Jason Swandle)
Murder, She Wrote, Drama Series, "School for Scandal" (Alger Kenyon)
The Tonight Show Starring Johnny Carson with Joan Rivers, Talk Show (Self)
Zoo Ship, Animated Special (Various, Voice)

1986

Just Bridges to Cross, Drama Series (Norman Parks) (6 episodes)
The Film Society of Lincoln Center Annual Gala Tribute to Elizabeth Taylor, TV Special (Self)
The Late Show Starring Joan Rivers, Talk Show (Self) (2 episodes)
Nightlife, Talk Show (Self)
This Is Your Life: Denis Quilley, Documentary Series (Self)

1987

The 4th Annual Cinema Awards (Self)
Happy 100th Birthday, Hollywood, TV Special (Self)
Matlock, Drama Series, "The Chef" (Christopher Hoyt)
MGM Greatest Moments: A Video Sampler, TV Special (Self)
Nightlife, Talk Show (Self)
Win, Lose or Draw, Game Show (Self) (5 episodes)
The Wind in the Willows, Animated TV Movie (Ratty, Voice)
The Wizard, Drama Series, "H.E.N.R.I. VIII" (H.E.N.R.I. VIII, Voice)

1988

De película, Spanish Documentary Series, "Festival de Sitges" (Self)
Film on Film, Documentary Series, "Starring Natalie Wood" (Self)
Going Hollywood: The War Years, Documentary (Self)
Lerner and Loewe: The Last of the Romantics, Documentary (Self)
Remo Williams: The Prophecy, TV Movie (Chiun)
The Kennedy Center Honors: A Celebration of the Performing Arts, TV Special (Self)
The New Hollywood Squares, Game Show (Self) (5 episodes)
The Princess Grace Foundation Special Gala Tribute to Cary Grant, TV Special (Self)

1989

The 6th Annual American Cinema Awards (Self)
America's All-Star Tribute to Elizabeth Taylor," TV Special (Self)
American Masters, Documentary, "Broadway's Dreamers: The Legacy of the Group Theatre" (Self)
American Masters, Documentary, "Harold Lloyd: The Third Genius" (Self)

Around the World in 80 Days, TV Miniseries (McBaines)
De película, Spanish Documentary Series (Self)
Encounters of The Fourth Kind, A Report on Communion, Documentary (Host)
Hollywood on Horses, Documentary (Self)
The Joan Rivers Show, Talk Show (Self)
Matlock, Drama Series, "The Starlet" (Don Mosher)
Montgomery Clift: His Place in the Sun, Documentary (Self)
Murder, She Wrote, Drama Series, "Fire Burn, Caldron Bubble" (Gordon Fairchild)
Nightmare Classics, Anthology Series, "Carmilla" (Inspector Amos)
This Is Your Life: Douglas Fairbanks Jr., Documentary Series (Self)
The Tonight Show Starring Johnny Carson, Talk Show (Self)
When We Were Young: Growing Up on the Silver Screen, Documentary (Self)

1990

Foreign Film Classics, Documentary Series (Self) (26 introductions)
The Horror Hall of Fame, Awards Show (Self)
Hotels: Geschichte und Geschichten, Documentary Series, "Chateau Marmont" (Self)
Later with Bob Costas, Talk Show (Self)
The New Lassie, Drama Series, "Guess Who's Coming to Breakfast, Lunch, and Dinner?" (Andrew Leeds) (3 episodes)
Vi: Portrait of A Silent Star, Documentary (Narrator)
Whip Valentine, Drama Series Pilot, "The Fourth Spike"

1991

An Inconvenient Woman, TV Miniseries (Cyril Rathbone)
Crazy About the Movies: Dennis Hopper, Documentary Series (Self)

Dark Water, Animated Miniseries (Niddler the Monkey-Bird, Voice)

Deadly Game, TV Movie (Dr. Aaron)

Earth Angel, TV Movie (Mr. Tatum)

The New Lassie, Drama Series, "Leeds, The Judge" (Andrew Leeds) (2 episodes)

1992

The 13th Annual Cable ACE Awards (Self)

Batman: The Animated Series (Jervis Tetch; The Mad Hatter) (2 episodes)

Camp Candy, Animated Series, "When It Rains It Snows" (Various, Voice)

Crazy About the Movies: Ava Gardner, Documentary Series (Self)

Darkwing Duck, Animated Series, "Inherit the Wimp" (Sir Quackmire Mallard, Voice)

Good Morning America, Talk Show (Self)

Legend of Prince Valiant, Animated Series, "The Battle of Greystone" (King Frederick, Voice)

MGM: When the Lion Roars, Documentary, "The Lion in Winter 1946–86" (Self)

MGM: When the Lion Roars, Documentary, "The Lion Reigns Supreme 1936–46" (Self)

Omnibus, Documentary Series, "John Ford: Part One" (Self)

Quantum Leap, Drama Series, "A Leap for Lisa: June 25, 1957" (Edward St. John V)

Sidney Sheldon's The Sands of Time, TV Miniseries (Alan Tucker)

Stars and Stripes: Hollywood and World War II, Documentary (Self)

1993

2 Stupid Dogs, Animated Series, "Chameleon" (Panoleon P. Chameleon)

AFI Life Achievement Award, TV Special, "A Salute to Elizabeth Taylor" (Self)
Batman: The Animated Series, "The Worry Men" (Jervis Tetch, The Mad Hatter)
Biography, Documentary Series, "Elizabeth Taylor" (Self)
Biography, Documentary Series, "John Ford: An American Vision" (Self)
Biography, Documentary Series, "Vincent Price: The Versatile Villain" (Self)
Dream On, Comedy Series, "Depth Be Not Proud" (Bob Jeffers)
Late Night with Conan O'Brien, Talk Show (Self)
Red Planet, Animated Series (Headmaster Marcus Howe) (3 episodes)
SWAT Kats: The Radical Squadron, Animated Series "Enter the Madkat" (Lenny Ringtail, Mudkat)
Friends Are Forever: Tales of the Little Princess, Animated Series (Zak the Cat, Voice)
This Is Your Life: Roddy McDowall, Documentary Series (Self)
Unauthorized Biographies with Peter Graves, Documentary, "Elizabeth Taylor" (Self)

1994

The 7th Annual Britannia Awards (Self)
Batman: The Animated Series (Jervis Tetch; The Mad Hatter, Voice) (5 episodes)
Biography, Documentary Series, "Bette Davis: If Looks Could Kill" (Self)
Burke's Law, Drama Series, "Who Killed Alexander the Great?" (Maurice Gillette)
Galaxy Beat, Comedy Series Pilot (Corporal Cod, Voice)
Hart to Hart: Home Is Where the Hart Is, TV Movie (Jeremy Sennet)

Heads, TV Movie (Fibris Drake)

The Kennedy Center Honors: A Celebration of the Performing Arts (Self)

Meet Me in St. Louis: The Making of an American Classic, Documentary (Self)

The Story of Lassie, Documentary (Self)

The Tick, Animated Series (Various, Voice) (6 episodes)

1995

The Alien Within—a.k.a. *Unknown Origin*, TV Movie (Dr. Henry Lazarus)

Biography, Documentary Series, "Darryl Zanuck: 20th Century Filmmaker" (Self)

The Fantasy Worlds of Irwin Allen, Documentary (Self)

Great Performances, TV Special, "Julie Andrews: Back on Broadway" (Self)

1996

Animaniacs, Animated Series, "Snowball" (Snowball) (5 episodes)

Biography, Documentary Series, "Alice Faye: The Star Next Door" (Self)

Biography, Documentary Series, "Boris Karloff: The Gentle Monster" (Self)

Biography, Documentary Series, "Carmen Miranda: The South American Way" (Self)

Biography, Documentary Series, "Katharine Hepburn: On Her Own Terms" (Self)

Biography, Documentary Series, "Shirley Temple: The Biggest Little Star" (Self)

Biography, Documentary Series, "Tyrone Power: The Last Idol" (Self)

Bullet Hearts—a.k.a. *Heart Attack and Vine*, TV Movie

Dead Man's Island, TV Movie (Trevor Dunnaway)

Duckman, Animated Series, "Apocalypse Not" (Akers)

Gargoyles, Animated Series (Proteus, Voice) (2 episodes)
Pinky and the Brain, Animated Series (Snowball, Voice) (2 episodes)
Remember WENNst, Comedy Series, "Don't Act Like That" (Giles Aldwych)
Sex, Censorship and the Silver Screen, Documentary Series (Self) (2 episodes)
TODAY, Talk Show (Self)
The Tracey Ullman Show, Comedy Series, "Tracey Takes On . . . Nostalgia" (Rex Gaydon)
Unlikely Angel (St. Peter)

1997

20/20, News Show, "Elizabeth Taylor" (Self)
20th Century Fox: The First 50 Years, Documentary (Self)
Biography, Documentary Series, "Andy Griffith: Hollywood's Homespun Hero" (Self)
Biography, Documentary Series, "Audrey Hepburn: The Fairest Lady" (Self)
Biography, Documentary Series, "Barbara Stanwyck: Straight Down the Line" (Self)
Biography, Documentary Series, "Henry Fonda: Hollywood's Quietest Hero" (Self)
Biography, Documentary Series, "Sonja Henie: Fire on Ice" (Self)
CBS This Morning, Talk Show (Self)
Jumanji, Animated Series, "Air Judy" (Fervish the Humble, Voice)
Obsessed with Vertigo, Documentary (Self)
Pinky and the Brain, Animated Series (Snowball, Voice) (2 episodes)
Travel the World, Documentary Series (Self) (9 episodes)
Turner Classic Movies' Preservation Showcase, Documentary Series (Host) (32 introductions)
Walter Matthau: Diamond in the Rough, Documentary (Self)

1998

A Tribute to John Chambers, Documentary (Self)
Behind the Planet of the Apes, Documentary (Narrator)
Beyond Titanic, Documentary (Self)
Biography, Documentary Series, "Ida Lupino: Through the Lens" (Self)
Biography, Documentary Series, "Myrna Loy: A Class by Herself" (Self)
Edith Head, Documentary (Self)
Hollywood Salutes Easter Seals, TV Special (Self)
Louise Brooks: Looking for Lulu, Documentary (Self)
The New Batman Adventures, Animated Series (Jervis Tetch; The Mad Hatter, Voice) (2 episodes)
Pinky and the Brain, Animated Series (Snowball, Voice) (2 episodes)
Planet of the Apes 30th Anniversary Marathon (Self)
This Morning, Talk Show (Self)
Twiggy's People, Talk Show (Self)

Posthumous Appearances

1998

Biography, Documentary Series, "Roddy McDowall: Hollywood's Best Friend" (Self)
Loss of Faith, TV Movie (Henry Stokes)
The New Superman Adventures, Animated Series, "Knight Time" (Jervis Tetch; The MadHatter, Voice)
Omnibus, Documentary Series, "Julie Andrews" (Self)

1999

Godzilla: The Series, Animated Series, "Deadloch" (Dr. Hugh Trevor, Voice)
Intimate Portrait, Documentary Series, "Lauren Bacall" (Self)
Keepers of the Frame, Documentary (Self)

2000

20th Century Fox: The Blockbuster Years, Documentary (Self)

Backstory, Documentary Series, "How Green Was My Valley" (Self)

Backstory, Documentary Series, "The Longest Day" (Self)

Backstory, Documentary Series, "The Poseidon Adventure" (Self)

Biography, Documentary Series, "Maureen O'Hara: Wild Irish Rose" (Self)

2001

Boom! Hollywood's Greatest Disasters, Documentary (Self)

Theater

The heading "Regional" here includes regional theaters as defined by Actors' Equity Association, but it also includes stock companies, civic light operas, and dinner theaters.

1946

Young Woodley (Roger Woodley) Tour

1947

Macbeth (Malcolm) Regional

1948

The First Mrs. Fraser (Ninian Fraser) Regional
The Hasty Heart (Lachie) Tour (1948–50)

1951

O Mistress Mine (Michael Brown) Tour
The Youngest (Richard) Tour (1951–52)

1952

Remains to Be Seen (Waldo) Regional

1953

Misalliance (Bentley Summerhays) Off-Broadway, Broadway
Charley's Aunt (Lord Fancourt Babberley) Regional
Debut (Dabney Featherstone) Regional
Escapade (Daventry) Broadway
Highlights of the Empire, The Importance of Being Earnest (Algernon) Special Performance

1954

The Homeward Look (Edgar Cosgrove) Off-Broadway
Aboard the Bandwagon (Revue) Regional

1955

Bell, Book and Candle (Nicky Holroyd) Regional
The Doctor's Dilemma (Louis Dubedat) Off-Broadway

Julius Caesar (Octavius Caesar) Regional
The Tempest (Ariel) Regional
No Time for Sergeants (Ben Whitledge) Broadway (1955–56)

1956
The Diary of a Scoundrel (Yegor Gloumov) Off-Broadway

1957
Good (Gold Benjamin Franklin) Broadway
Compulsion (Artie Straus) Broadway

1958
The Firstborn (Rameses) Pre-Broadway Tour
Handful of Fire (Pepe) Broadway

1959
Look After Lulu (Marcel Blanchard) Broadway
The Fighting Cock (Tarquin Edward Mendigales) Broadway (Tony Award)

1960
Meet Me in St. Louis (Boy Next-Door) Regional
Camelot (Mordred) Broadway (1960–61)

1967
The Astrakhan Coat (Claud) Broadway

1973
A Shakespeare Cabaret (Revue) Hollywood Bowl

1975
Charley's Aunt (Lord Fancourt Babberley) National Tour (1975–76)
Tubby the Tuba (Reading with Music Performer) Hollywood Bowl

1978
Otherwise Engaged (Simon Hench) Regional

1980

Harvey (Elwood P. Dowd) Tour

1995

Dial M for Murder (Inspector Hubbard) National Tour

1997

A Christmas Carol (Scrooge) Madison Square Garden (1997–98)

Audio Recordings

1956

Marc Blitzstein and His Theater Compositions: The Hotel Lobby from *The Cradle Will Rock*, with Alvin Epstein and Jane Connell

1960

Camelot: The Seven Deadly Virtues (Mordred)

1963

Many Voices: *Miracles*, Poems Written by Children, with Julie Harris

Roddy McDowall Reads the Horror Stories of H. P. Lovecraft: The Outsider; The Hound

1974

Ben Bagley's Alan Jay Lerner Revisited: Progress, with Nancy Walker and Chorus; *This Is My Holiday*, with Blossom Dearie; *You Haven't Changed at All*, with Nancy Walker; *Every Night at Seven*, with Chorus

1975

Crisis: The Tweed Cap

1982

Master of the Game by Sidney Sheldon (Produced by Roddy McDowall and Holly Sklar)

1986

Final Cut: Dreams and Disaster in the Making of Heaven's Gate by Steven Bach

Murder in Los Angeles: Dream House by M. R. Henderson

1987

Communion by Whitley Strieber (Produced by Roddy McDowall and John Soltys)

1988

Murder on the Aisle: Introduction by Mary Higgins Clark; *Saturday's Shadow* by William F. Nolan

Piggins and *Picnic With Piggins* by Jane Yolen

Transformation: The Breakthrough by Whitley Strieber

1989

Batman by Craig Shaw Gardner (Produced by Roddy McDowall and Kim Weeks)

Goldwyn: A Biography by A. Scott Berg

The Guest of Honor by Irving Wallace

Shoes of the Fisherman by Morris West

1990

Billy by Whitley Strieber (Produced by Roddy McDowall)

Scanners II by Professor Janus Kimball (Produced by Roddy McDowall)

1991

Battlefield Earth: A Saga of the Year 3000 by L. Ron Hubbard

Enchanted Tales: The Birthday of the Infanta by Oscar Wilde

Fear by L. Ron Hubbard

Final Blackout by L. Ron Hubbard

Murder in Hollywood: Stories from Ellery Queen's Mystery Magazine: *Hooray for Hollywood* by Robert Twohy; *CU: Mannix* by Richard Matheson; *One Big Happy Family* by Lionel Booker

Murder With a Twist: Stories from Ellery Queen's Mystery Magazine: Golden Tuesday by Celia Fremlin; *The Girl of My Dreams* by Donald E. Westlake; *The Ehrengraf Method* by Lawrence Block

Stamboul Train by Graham Greene

1992

The Grimaldis of Monaco by Anne Edwards

Murder in a Distant Land: The Woman in the Shadows by Stephanie Kay Bendel

Ole Doc Methuselah by L. Ron Hubbard
The Stars Shine Down by Sidney Sheldon
Twilight Zone #3: Odyssey of Flight 33 by Rod Serling

1993
I, Strahd: The Memoirs of a Vampire by P. N. Elrod
Marlene Dietrich: Life and Legend by Steven Bach
The Plot to Overthrow Christmas (Sotto Voce)
The Wolfen by Whitley Strieber

1994
Alice in Wonderland (Lewis Carroll, The March Hare)

1995
Murder in America: Vaudeville by Whitley Strieber

1996
Joy to the World
Under the Streets of Nice by Ken Follett & René L. Maurice

1997
Peter and Wendy by James Barrie (James Barrie)

1998
Mysteries in the Air: The Seven Layered Arsenic Cake of Madame LeFarge

Posthumous Releases

1999
Maps in a Mirror: Fat Farm by Orson Scott Card
Silver Lining, Volume 2, Poetry Collection, 1999

Photography

Magazines

1959

Pageant, “Shooting Star,” Photographs, May

1960

Vogue, “People Are Talking About . . . Judy Holliday,” Photographs, October 1, 1960

1962

Paris Match, Cover, Elizabeth Taylor, *Cleopatra*, April 14, 1962

1963

Playboy, Photographs, Elizabeth Taylor, January 1963

Harper's Bazaar, “Bright Young Lights,” Photographs, Jane Fonda, Peter Mann, Jill Haworth, Tony Perkins, Sal Mineo, Susan Strasberg, John Valva, June 1963

1964

McCall's, “There'll Always Be an Encore” Photographs, Judy Garland January, February 1964

TV Radio Mirror, Covers, Judy Garland, Dick Chamberlain, Donna Reed, Red Skelton, Danny Kaye, and Shirley Booth, 1964

Life, “A Dwarf's Full-Size Success,” Photographs, Michael Dunn, February 14, 1964

TV Radio Mirror, “Judy Garland: Who Am I?” Photographs, March 1964

This Week, Photos, Natalie Wood, March 19, 1964

Life, “Shakespeare at 400-Part II: The Great Sir Laurence,” Photos, Laurence Olivier, May 1, 1964

TV Radio Mirror, “Shirley Booth: Who Am I?” June 1964

Life, “Elizabeth Taylor Speaks Out,” Photographs, December 18, 1964

1965

Ladies' Home Journal, "Elizabeth Taylor . . . Elizabeth Taylor," November 1965

Playboy, Photographs, Elizabeth Taylor, filming of *Cleopatra*, December 1965

1966

Harper's Bazaar, Contributing Editor, 1966

Photography Annual, Photographs, Jonathan Winters, 1966

McCall's, Photographs *Double Exposure*, October 1966

Harper's Bazaar, "Shaffer's Black Comedy" (Peter Shaffer, Maggie Smith), August 1966

Harper's Bazaar, Photographs, Henry Fonda, November 1966

1967

Harper's Bazaar, Contributing Editor, 1967

Life, "Chaplin's Anatomy of Comedy" Photographs Charlie Chaplin, March 10, 1967

Look, "Katharine Hepburn & Spencer Tracy: A Last Visit With Two Undimmed Stars," Photographs, July 11, 1967

Harper's Bazaar, "Double Exposure," Photographs, Dirk Bogarde, Charlie Chaplin, July 1967

Harper's Bazaar, "Keep the Uglies in the Attic," Photographs, Phyllis Diller, August 1967

Harper's Bazaar, "Actors as Citizens," Photographs, Danny Kaye, Robert Ryan, September 1967

1968

Harper's Bazaar, Photographs, Tommy Steele, October 1968

1969

Life, "Mae West," Photographs, April 18, 1969

Pageant, Cover, Judy Garland, November 1969

1978

McCall's, "Carol Burnett's Own Story," Photographs, February 1978

1988

Architectural Digest, Editor-at-Large, 1988

Architectural Digest, "Architectural Digest Visits: Barbara Walters and Merv Adelson," Photographs, October 1988

1989

Architectural Digest, Editor-at-Large, 1989

Architectural Digest, "Architectural Digest Visits: Joan Rivers," Photographs, February 1989

Interview, Contributing Editor, 1989

Good Housekeeping, "Double Exposure" (Take II), Photographs, November 1989

1990

Interview, Contributing Editor, 1990

Cosmopolitan, *Ladies' Home Journal*, *Stern*, *Glamour*, *Saturday Review*, *Business Week*, Photograph, Ad Campaign, MPTF

Interview, "Tim Burton and Vincent Price," December 1990

1991

Interview, "Lynn and Vanessa Redgrave," Photographs and interview, February 1991

Premiere, "Sitting Pretty: After a Twenty Year Absence, Actress Maureen O'Hara Returns to the Silver Screen," Photographs and interview, July 1991

1992

Premiere, "Time Stands Still," Photographs, Elizabeth Taylor, March 1992

People Weekly, Cover, Elizabeth Taylor, May 4, 1992

Good Housekeeping, "Double Exposure, Take Three," Photographs, November 1992

1993

Good Housekeeping, "Double Exposure, Take Four," November 1993

1997

Poz, Contributing Editor, 1997

Poz, "Elizabeth Taylor Tells the Truth," Photographs, November 1997

1998

People Weekly, "Gallery: Brush With Fame," Photographs and commentary, various celebrities posing against murals of movie legends camouflaging construction at the Warner Bros. studio in Burbank, California, February 9, 1998

Posthumous Publications

2001

Architectural Digest, Photograph, Danny Kaye, November 2001

Cosmopolitan, *Ladies' Home Journal*, *Stern*, *Glamour*, *Saturday Review*, *Business Week*, Ad Campaign, MPTF

Books

1959

The American Shakespeare Festival: The Birth of a Theatre by John Houseman and Jack Landau

1963

The Prison Life of Harris Filmore by Jack Richardson

1964

Elizabeth Taylor: An Informal Memoir by Elizabeth Taylor

U.S. Camera Annual 1964, Portfolio and essay: "On the Set of *Cleopatra*," edited by Tom Maloney

1966

Double Exposure, Compiled and Photographed by Roddy McDowall

Othello: The National Theatre Production, with Lord Snowdon and Angus McBean

1968

The Boys in the Band by Mart Crowley

The Unimportance of Being Oscar by Oscar Levant

1969

Come Back If It Doesn't Get Better by Penelope Gilliatt

1971

Life Library of Photography: The Studio by Time-Life Books

1976

Broadway and Hollywood: Costumes Designed by Irene Sharaff by Irene Sharaff

1983

Mortal Matters by Penelope Gilliatt

1984

Twinkle, Twinkle, Little Star (But Don't Have Sex or Take the Car) by Dick Moore

1987

Elizabeth Takes Off: On Weight Gain, Weight Loss, Self-Image, and Self-Esteem by Elizabeth Taylor

1988

Scary Kisses by Brad Gooch

1989

Double Exposure, Take Two, Compiled and Photographed by Roddy McDowall

Olivier at Work, Compiled by the Royal National Theatre, with Richard Olivier and Joan Plowright

1990

Calman at the Movies by Mel Calman

Deadly Illusions: Jean Harlow and the Murder of Paul Bern by Samuel Marx and Joyce Vanderveen

Lettice and Lovage: *A Comedy* by Peter Shaffer
Life Wish and *Life Lines* by Jill Ireland

1991
How Green Was My Valley: The Screenplay for the John Ford Directed Film by Philip Dunne

1992
Double Exposure, Take Three, Compiled and Photographed by Roddy McDowall
Showman: The Life of David O. Selznick by David Thomson

1993
Double Exposure, Take Four, Compiled and Photographed by Roddy McDowall

1997
Naked: Flowers Exposed by Walter Hubert

1998
Double Exposure by Stephen Collins

Posthumous Publications

1999
Vincent Price: A Daughter's Biography by Victoria Price, 1999

2004
'Tis Herself: A Memoir by Maureen O'Hara, with John Nicoletti, 2004

Albums and CDs

1963
Cleopatra, Original Soundtrack

1964
Judy Garland Sings Lionel Bart's Maggie May, Judy Garland
Laurence Olivier in Othello, National Theatre of Great Britain
The Third Album, Barbra Streisand
Without You, Robert Goulet

1965
The Sweetheart Tree, Johnny Mathis

1966
Jordan Christopher Has the Knack, Jordan Christopher

1989
The M.G.M. Album, Michael Feinstein

1991
Just for the Record, Barbra Streisand

1993
Different Stages, Sam Harris

Film and Television

1969
Generation, Photographs featured on screen

1983
To Catch a Thief, Unit Photographer

1988
Starring Natalie Wood, Photographs, Natalie Wood

1992
Quantum Leap, "M. I. A.," Photograph, Dean Stockwell

1994
The Lassie Dog Training System, Cover and Photographs

1998
Louise Brooks: Looking for Lulu, Photographs, Louise Brooks

Posthumous Releases

1999

CNN People Profiles: Elizabeth Taylor, Photographs, Elizabeth Taylor

2004

The Dick Van Dyke Show, Season 4 Box Set, Photographs

Awards and Nominations

1941

National Board of Review, Best Acting, *How Green Was My Valley*

1942

Parents Magazine Award, Most Talented Juvenile Actor

Photoplay Awards, Best Performances of the Month, *How Green Was My Valley*

1946

Photoplay Awards, Best Performances of the Month, *Holiday in Mexico*

1960

Star on the Hollywood Walk of Fame (TV)

Tony Award, Best Performance by a Featured Actor in a Play, *The Fighting Cock*

1961

Primetime Emmy Awards, Outstanding Performance in a Supporting Role by an Actor or Actress in a Single Program, *Sunday Showcase*, "Our American Heritage: Not Without Honor"

1964

Golden Globes, Best Supporting Actor, *Cleopatra* (nominee)

Primetime Emmy Awards, Outstanding Single Performance by an Actor in a Leading Role, for *Arrest and Trial*, "Journey into Darkness" (nominee)

1965

Celebrity Hall of Fame Award from the National Association for Mental Health City of Hope Heart of the World Award

1968

Photoplay Awards, Gold Medal, Most Popular Male Star (nominee)

1971

The Count Dracula Society, Mrs. Ann Radcliffe Special Award

1983

Academy of Science Fiction, Fantasy and Horror Films, Saturn Award, Best Supporting Actor, *Class of 1984* (nominee)

1985

American Cinema Foundation Career Achievement Award

1986

Academy of Science Fiction, Fantasy and Horror Films, Saturn Award, Best Supporting Actor, *Fright Night*

1991

Motion Picture and Television Fund, Silver Medallion Award

1992

The New School Award for Photography and Motion Picture Contribution

1993

Caldwell Theatre Guild's Spotlight Award

1995

Honorary Doctorate Degree of Performing Arts, Bowling Green State University, Ohio

1997

Audrey Hepburn Hollywood for Children Fund Hall of Fame Award

Posthumous Awards

2002

The Charles W. Hemingway Audio Hall of Fame

Charity and Philanthropy

A Minor Consideration (Support group for child actors)

Academy Foundation (Chairman, Student Academy Awards Committee 1997–98)

*Academy Foundation (President, 1998–99)**

Academy Foundation (Treasurer, 1995–98)

Academy Foundation Board of Trustees (Board Member, 1994–99)

Academy of Motion Picture Arts and Sciences (AMPAS) Board of Governors (1992–2001)

AMPAS (Chairman of Actors Branch Executive Committee, 1992–97)

*AMPAS (Chairman of Finance Committee, 1998–99)**

AMPAS (Secretary, 1995–98)

*AMPAS (Treasurer, 1998–99)**

American Parkinson's Disease Association

Audrey Hepburn Children's Fund (Board Member)

Bette Davis Foundation (Board Member)

Board of the Motion Picture & Television Fund (1997–98)

Debbie Reynolds Hollywood Movie Museum

Humane Society of the United States Hollywood Office

Kennedy Center Honors (Board of Selectors)

Motion Picture & Television Fund Foundation (Board Member, 1997–98)

*When Roddy passes away in 1998 the position is left vacant in his memory for the remainder of the term.

National Multiple Sclerosis Society

Santa Fe Cares (A community AIDS foundation)

Save the Children Foundation

U.S. Marine Corps Reserve, Toys for Tots Program

UCLA Film and Television Archive (Archive Council Founder)

Vietnam Moratorium Committee

Special Thanks

This book wouldn't exist without the help of my husband, Ronald Shore; my agent, Lee Sobel, who believes Roddy is long overdue for a bio; my research assistants in Boston, Deidre Flanagan and Daniel Kammer; Kensington editor John Scognamiglio; the late Howard Gotlieb, who brought Roddy McDowall's archives to Boston University; and Roddy McDowall himself, for preserving so much of his own history as well as that of early Hollywood. The work of the Musgrave Foundation in researching his life and career is invaluable. I'm also incredibly grateful for the people whose interviews provide insight into Roddy's incredible impact on them, personally and professionally. My deepest thanks as well to the institutions and individuals whose generous support and input is evident throughout, and to those who share their historical detective work.

I would also like to thank the following organizations and individuals:

American Film Institute

Billy Rose Theatre Division of the New York Public Library

British Film Institute

Hollywood Museum

Houghton Library Archive, Harvard University

Howard Gotlieb Archival Research Center, Boston University Libraries

Margaret Herrick Library at the Academy of Motion Picture Arts and Sciences

Motion Picture & Television Fund

Musgrave Foundation

Cathy Ace
Nancy Babb
Don Bachardy
Kate Burton
Jennifer Clymer
Kathleen Kickson
Illeana Douglas
Vaughan Edwards
Leslie Gilbert Elman
Joanna Gleason
John Glover
Brad Gooch
Lee Grant
James Grissom
Robert Hofler
Dana Holland
Steven Jongeward
Howard Karren
Adam Kurtzman
Jason Lahman
Sally Mierop
Roxanne L. Mills
Jane Parr
José Pedras
Jeff Peters
Ann Pryor
William Ragsdale
Daniel Renfroe
Imelda Santos
Chris Sarandon
Ken Scherer
Matt Severson
Victor Simpkins
Steve Tollervey
Greg Weisman
Neil Zevnik

Bibliography

Books and Selected Articles

Aylesworth, Thomas G. *Hollywood Kids*. New York: E.P. Dutton, 1987.

Bacall, Lauren. *By Myself and Then Some.* London: Headline Book Publishing, 2005.

Basinger, Jeanine, and Sam Wasson. *Hollywood: The Oral History.* New York: Harper, 2022.

Bieber, Irving. *Homosexuality: A Psychoanalytic Study of Male Homosexuals.* New York: Society of Medical Psychoanalysts, 1962.

Bingen, Steven. *The MGM Effect: How a Hollywood Studio Changed the World.* Guilford, CT: Lyons Press, 2022.

Bowers, Scotty, with Lionel Friedberg. *Full Service: My Adventures in Hollywood and the Secret Sex Lives of the Stars.* New York: Grove Press, 2012.

Brooks, Tim, and Earle F. Marsh. *The Complete Directory to Prime Time Network and Cable Television Shows, 1946–Present*. New York: Ballantine, 2009.

Buckley, Michael. "Roddy McDowall," *Films in Review* (August, September, October, 1988).

Casillo, Charles. *Elizabeth and Monty: The Untold Story of Their Intimate Friendship.* New York: Kensington, 2021.

Chibnall, Steve. *Quota Quickies*. London: British Film Institute, 2007.

Dunne, Dominick. "The Company He Kept," *Vanity Fair* (December 1998).

Egan, Sean. *Planet of the Apes: The Complete History.* Guilford, CT: Applause Theatre & Cinema Books, 2020.

Fragias, Leonidas. *Annual U.S. Top Film Rentals 1912–1979; 1980–2000.* Seattle: Kindle Direct Publishing, 2017.

———. *US Weekly Box Office Top 10 Charts of the 1940s–1990s*. Seattle: Kindle Direct Publishing, 2017.

Freedland, Michael. *Jack Lemmon.* New York: St. Martin's Press, 1985.

Gam, Rita. *Actors: A Celebration*. New York: St. Martin's Press, 1988.

Gardner, Ava. *Ava: My Story.* New York: Bantam Books, 1990.

Granger, Farley, with Robert Calhoun. *Include Me Out: My Life from Goldwyn to Broadway.* New York: St. Martin's Press, 2007.

Hadleigh, Boze. *Broadway Babylon.* New York: Backstage Books, 2007.

———. *Conversations with My Elders.* New York: St. Martin's Press, 1986.

———. *Scandals, Secrets, and Swan Songs: How Hollywood Stars Lived, Worked, and Died*. Guilford, CT: Lyons Press, 2021.

Halliwell, Leslie. *Halliwell's Film Guide.* New York: Macmillan, 1977.

Hunter, Tab. *Tab Hunter Confidential.* New York: Algonquin, 2005.

Kael, Pauline. *5001 Nights at the Movies.* New York: Picador, 1982, 1984, 1991.

Katz, Ephraim. *The Film Encyclopedia, 7th Edition.* New York: Harper Collins, 2012.

Lawrence, Michael. "Bombed into Stardom! Roddy McDowall, British Evacuee Star in Hollywood." *Journal of British Cinema and Television*, 2015.

Lerner, Alan Jay. *The Street Where I Live*. New York: W.W. Norton, 1978.

Lowe, Skip. *Hollywood Gomorrah.* Seattle: Kindle Direct Publishing, 2014.

Mander, Joe, and Raymond Mitchenson. *Theatrical Companion to Coward*. New York: Macmillan, 1957.

Mayo, Mike. *The Horror Show Guide: The Ultimate Frightfest of Movies*. Detroit: Visible Ink Press, 2013.

Moore, Dick. *Twinkle, Twinkle, Little Star (But Don't Have Sex or Take the Car)*. New York: Harper & Row, 1984.

Nathan, Debbie. *Sybil Exposed*. New York: Free Press, 2011.

O'Hara, Maureen, and John Nicoletti. *'Tis Herself.* New York: Simon & Schuster, 2004.

Okuda, Ted. *The Monogram Checklist: The Films of Monogram Pictures Corporation, 1931–1952*. Jefferson, NC: McFarland, 1987.

Parish, James Robert. *Great Child Stars*. New York: Ace, 1976.

Payn, Graham. *The Noël Coward Diaries.* Foreword by Stephen Fry. London: Weidenfeld & Nicolson, 2022.

Roberts, Doris, with Danelle Morton. *Are You Hungry, Dear?* New York: St. Martin's Griffin, 2003.

Rountree, Emma Eileen. *A Nation of Hero-Worshippers: Queen Marie of Romania, the United States of America, and the Rise of the Royal Celebrity*. Guilford College (Guilford, UK), Doctorate Paper, 2016.

Royle, Alan. *Hollywood The Skeletons Are Out!* Melbourne, Australia: Royle, 2016.

Russo, Vito. *The Celluloid Closet: Homosexuality in the Movies.* New York: Harper & Row, 1981, 1987.

Stapleton, Maureen, and Jane Scovell. *A Hell of a Life.* New York: Simon & Schuster, 1995.

Stine, Whitney. *"I'd Love to Kiss You . . ." Conversations with Bette Davis.* New York: Pocket Books, 1990.

Wanger, Walter, and Joe Hyams. *My Life with Cleopatra: The Making of a Hollywood Classic.* Garden City, NY: Doubleday, 1963.

Zambrana, M. L. *Nature Boy: The Unauthorized Biography of Dean Stockwell.* Bloomington, IN: Writers Club Press, 2002.

Newspapers and Magazines

Associated Press
Atlanta Constitution
Atlanta Journal
Atlanta Journal-Constitution
Beverly Hills [213]
Boston Globe
Box Office
California Magazine
Chicago Sun-Times
Chicago Tribune
Cinefantastique
Citizen Newspapers
Cleveland Plain Dealer
Cue
Daily Variety
Detroit Free Press
East Stroudsburg Daily Record (PA)
Entertainment Weekly
Film Daily
Filmfacts
FilmInk
Films in Review
Hello!
Hollywood Citizen-News
Hollywood Evening News
Hollywood Reporter
Hollywood Studio
Illustrated London News
Independent
Journal of British Cinema and Television
LA Weekly
Los Angeles City News
Los Angeles Daily Mirror
Los Angeles Daily News
Los Angeles Evening and Sunday Herald Examiner
Los Angeles Evening Herald and Express
Los Angeles Evening News
Los Angeles Examiner
Los Angeles Herald Express
Los Angeles Herald Examiner
Los Angeles Magazine

Los Angeles Mirror

Los Angeles Times

Minneapolis Star Tribune

Modern Screen

Motion Picture Herald Product Digest

Movie Album

The New Republic

(New York) Daily News

New York Evening Journal

New York Herald Tribune

New York Observer

New York Post

New York Times

New York World-Telegram

New York World-Telegram and The Sun

The New Yorker

Newsweek

North-Eastern Gazette

The Observer

Omaha World-Herald

People Weekly

Photoplay

Photoplay Film Monthly

Pittsburgh Sun-Telegraph

Register

Reuters

Rocky Mountain News

Rolling Stone

Sacramento Bee

Salt Lake Tribune

San Francisco Chronicle

The Saturday Evening Post

Screenland

Screenplay

St. Louis Globe-Democrat

Stage and Cinema

Time

Times (of London)

Tulane Drama Review

UCLA Daily Bruin

US Magazine

Variety

Village Voice

Websites

2010odysseyarchive.blogspot.com

66batman.com

airmail.news

awardsandwinners.com

bandsaboutmovies.com

batman.fandom.com

batmantheanimatedseries.fandom.com

bigredbook.info

blog.jameshereth.com

broadwayworld.com

countyhistorian.com

ctva.biz

dramadeskaward.com

dramatists.com

drunktv.net

duckman.fandom.com

encyclopedia-titanica.org

finboroughtheatre.co.uk

frockflicks.com

frontrowfeatures.com

glitternight.com

goldmonkey.com

greatdetectives.net

ibdb.com

j4hi.com

joebobbriggs.com

jumanji.fandom.com

junglebook.fandom.com

letterboxd.com

made-for-tv-movie.fandom.com

mardecortesbaja.com

markvoger.com

mash.fandom.com

matlock.fandom.com

mikestakeonthemovies.com

mondobizarrocinema.blogspot.com

musingsofamiddleagedgeek.blog

myrarefilms.co.uk

mysteryfile.com

nbc.fandom.com

ok.ru

oldtimeradiodownloads.com

paleycenter.org

playbill.com

popmatters.com

primevideo.com

pro.imdb.com

richard-e-grant.com

rivetsontheposterblog.wordpress.com

rottentomatoes.com

royalnavyresearcharchive.org.uk

serializd.com

silverscreenoasis.com

spiritualityandpractice.com

stageagent.com

swatkats.fandom.com

talkfilmsociety.com

theatreworldawards.org

thelastdrivein.com

themagnificent60s.com

themovieblog.com

themoviedb.org

thesoundofvincentprice.com

tonyawards.com

townandcountrymag.com

trakt.tv

transcripts.foreverdreaming.org

tvguide.com

tvmaze.com

ultimate70s.com

unobtainium13.com

video.peteduel.info

wikipedia.com

wthrockmorton.com

xmoppet.org

xtramagazine.com

Podcasts and Videos

A&E Biography, "Roddy McDowall: Hollywood's Best Friend"

LGBTQ+ Elders Project Podcast, "Don Bachardy"

Not Just Yesterday: The Roddy McDowall Podcast

Outwords, "Don Bachardy: An Identity of My Own"

This Is Your Life, "Roddy McDowall"

Tread Perilously

Index